open door to SPANISH

A conversation course for beginners

Margarita Madrigal

Prentice Hall Regents
Englewood Cliffs, N.J.

Books by MARGARITA MADRIGAL

OPEN DOOR TO SPANISH 1
OPEN DOOR TO SPANISH 2
SEE IT AND SAY IT IN SPANISH
FIRST STEPS IN SPANISH
SEE IT AND SAY IT IN FRENCH
(with Colette Dulac)
OPEN DOOR TO FRENCH
(with Colette Dulac)
FIRST STEPS IN FRENCH
(with Colette Dulac)
SEE IT AND SAY IT IN GERMAN
(with Inge Halpert)
SEE IT AND SAY IT IN ITALIAN
(with Giuseppina Salvadori)
INVITACIÓN AL INGLÉS
(with Ursula Meyer)

Illustrations by Anna Veltfort
Page design by Suzanne Bennett
Cover design by Kiffi Diamond

A set of cassettes accompanying this book is available.

Published by
Prentice-Hall, Inc.
Englewood Cliffs, NJ 07632

Printed in the United States of America

ISBN 0-13-637703-3

10 9 8 7 6

INTRODUCTION

Do you recognize these Spanish words?
capital, color, presidente, economista, cereal
There are thousands of words which are alike in Spanish and English. In this book the students are taught a large number of these cognates. The Madrigal Method teaches students the following:

- how to convert groups of English words into Spanish words
- how to identify an enormous number of Spanish words
- a large, basic vocabulary which will help students to speak, understand, read, and write in Spanish
- formulas which teach students how to change every regular verb they may encounter into all of the tenses they will need for everyday Spanish conversation
- formulas for learning irregular verbs
- confidence, which is the most important factor in learning Spanish

With the Madrigal Method students learn vocabulary easily, at a very fast pace, and have extraordinary RETENTION of the material which they have learned. This is but one of the many factors in this book which create CONFIDENCE.

The Madrigal Method encourages students to think for themselves, to feel the power of their own minds, and sense the acuteness of their own perceptions. The students are taught how to "create" their own words, sentences, and conversations. This, in turn, helps the teachers to generate a feeling of optimism and success in the classroom.

The Madrigal Method also teaches irregular verbs by simple formulas.

A large number of EXERCISES in this book clarify the material for the student. Aside from all the numbered Exercise sections in the book, there are exercises in every lesson which direct the students to close their books and repeat what they have just learned. Other exercises are suggested in the Teacher's Guide.

The Madrigal Method is famous for its fine-tuned GRADUATION. It passes gently and logically from one subject to another, without jolting the student's mind.

It took years of research in different countries for the author to discover which words are most frequently used in everyday, spoken Spanish. The author has drawn on this research to select the BASIC VOCABULARY for Spanish conversation and sample dialogues from which students can move on to improvising their own conversations.

The Madrigal Method gives the "living" words of the Spanish language. The dialogues in *Open Door to Spanish* are actually what people say in the streets, on the phone, in restaurants, or at home with friends.

After over ten years of research on the SUBJUNCTIVE, the author has developed a method which involves the sequence of lessons which lead to the subjunctive, and formulas which help the students to "create" their own subjunctives.

Now Margarita Madrigal brings you the revision of *Open Door to Spanish*, pedagogically geared for classroom use or self-instruction. After you have gone through this book, you will be able to conduct simple conversations with your Spanish-speaking friends. You will be able to understand many Spanish advertisements and articles. You will be a two-language person, a more sophisticated citizen. You will feel successful, accomplished, and more intelligent. There are many practical benefits to knowing Spanish, too. For example, knowing Spanish may help you to get a job. Applicants who know Spanish often get preference for jobs in the fields of medicine, social work, tourism, government, aviation, business, etc.

One good way to change your life is to learn a new language. Now you have an opportunity to learn Spanish. Take it eagerly. It may change your life in ways you cannot imagine now.

EXAMPLES

1. For examples of "creating" words see Word Builder 1.8, page 7.
2. For examples of "creating" regular verb tenses, see Lesson 3, page 21.
3. For examples of irregular verb formulas, see Lesson 19, page 177.
4. For examples of subjunctive formulas, see Lesson 20, pages 147 and 185.
5. For an example of a Conversation which uses the material the students have learned, see Lesson 7, page 71.
6. For an example of how students are encouraged to use their own minds and improvise, see the "class" instructions for the conversation in Lesson 7, page 71.
7. For examples of "creating" sentences, see Lesson 9, page 87.

TABLE OF CONTENTS

BASIC PRONUNCIATION

A	is pronounced "ah", as in *art*.
E	is pronounced "e", as in *desk*.
I	is pronounced "ee", as in *meet*.
O	is pronounced "o", as in *obey*.
U	is pronounced "oo", as in *too*.

B	is generally pronounced "b", as in *boat*. But when the letter "b" appears between vowels, pronounce it very softly, with your lips touching lightly. Pronounce "saber" with a very soft "b".
C	Pronounce a hard "c" before the letters "a", "o", "u", as in *can, core, cute*. Before "e" or "i" the "c" is pronounced as in *center*.
CC	is pronounced "cc" as in *accent*.
G	Pronounce a hard "g" before the letters "a", "o", "u", as in *gone*. Before "e" or "i" the "g" is pronounced "h", as in *hot*.
H	Never pronounce the letter "h". It is always silent in Spanish.
J	is pronounced "h", as in *hill*.
LL	is pronounced "y", as in *yet*.
Ñ	is pronounced "ny", as in *canyon*.
R	is trilled
RR	is strongly trilled.
Y	is pronounced as the "y" in *toy*. In Spanish, "y" means "and". In this case "y" is pronounced "ee" as in *seen*.

GUE	Pronounce as the "gue" in *guess*.
GUI	Pronounce as the "gee" in *geese*.
QUE	Pronounce as the "ke" in *kettle*.
QUI	Pronounce as the English word *key*.

LESSON 1

*The Imperfect Tense of **AR** Verbs in the Singular*

1. The Imperfect is a tense which expresses continuous or repeated action in the past. It is also used for descriptions in the past.
2. Learn the singular ending of the Imperfect Tense for AR verbs: ABA.
   Examples: progresaba, *he progressed, used to progress*
   exportaba, *he exported, used to export*
3. ABA is the ending for the I, YOU, HE, SHE, and IT forms of the verb.
   Example: CANTABA: *I sang, used to sing*
   you sang, used to sing
   he sang, used to sing
   she sang, used to sing
   it sang, used to sing

1.1 *Remember These Words*

CLASS: Your teacher will read the following Spanish words aloud. Repeat each word, in unison, after the teacher says it. Read the word in the book as you pronounce it. Look at the English meaning of each word, but do not say any English word aloud.

¿qué? *what?*
tiempo, *time*
todo el tiempo, *all the time*
el jardín, *the garden*
zapatos de tenis, *tennis shoes*
lámparas, *lamps*
en un programa de radio, *on a radio program*
¿dónde? *where?*
un suéter azul, *a blue sweater*

gris, *gray (singular)*
grises, *gray (plural)*
mucho, *much, a lot*
rosas, *roses*
el ranchero, *the rancher*
pantalones grises, *gray trousers*
en casa, *at home*
en la clase, *in the class*
cantaba, *used to sing*
progresaba, *used to progress*
importaba, *used to import*
exportaba, *used to export*
plantaba, *used to plant*
estudiaba, *used to study*

Example: ¿Qué exportaba Bárbara? *What did Barbara export?*

REMEMBER that in Spanish LL is pronounced Y as in YET.

1. When you are telling a story and wish to describe a person or a thing in the past, use the Imperfect Tense.
2. Use LLEVABA for telling what people were wearing.

zapatos de tenis

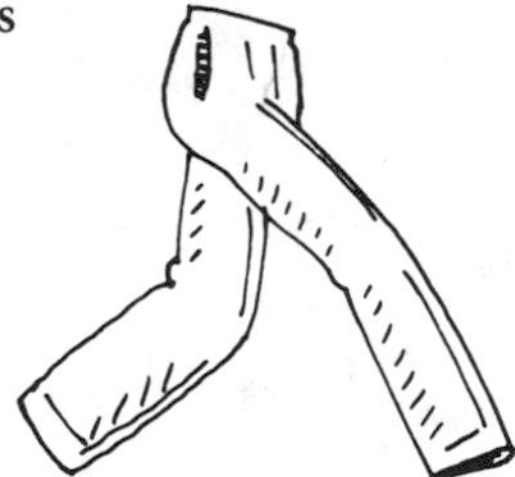

pantalones

1.2 *Hearing Exercise*

CLASS: Repeat each sentence, in unison, after your teacher says it in Spanish.

Example: El canario cantaba todo el tiempo. *The canary used to sing all the time.*

1. María cantaba mucho.
2. Roberto cantaba en un programa de radio.
3. Bárbara progresaba mucho en la clase.
4. Bernardo importaba lámparas.
5. David exportaba radios.
6. El doctor plantaba rosas en el jardín.
7. Luis llevaba zapatos de tenis. *Louis was wearing tennis shoes.*
8. Bárbara llevaba un suéter azul.
9. Luis llevaba pantalones grises.
10. Roberto llevaba un suéter azul.
11. Marta estudiaba mucho.

1.3 *Speaking Exercise*

CLASS: Your teacher will read these questions to you, and point out individual students for an answer. Read the answers in the book.

1. ¿Cantaba mucho María? Sí, María cantaba mucho.
2. ¿Qué importaba Bernardo? Bernardo importaba lámparas.
3. ¿Qué exportaba Bárbara? Bárbara exportaba radios.
4. ¿Qué llevaba Roberto? Roberto llevaba pantalones grises.
5. ¿Qué llevaba María? María llevaba un suéter azul.
6. ¿Estudiaba mucho Roberto? Sí, Roberto estudiaba mucho.
7. ¿Progresaba mucho? Sí, progresaba mucho.

CLASS: Could you answer the questions above with books closed?

1.4 *Creating Sentences*

CLASS: Repeat each word in the three columns below after your teacher says it in Spanish. Then, your teacher will point out individual students who will form a complete sentence with words from each of the columns. Create your own sentences. Not all the words in the third column correspond to the words in the first column. Don't make silly sentences.

MARÍA ROBERTO LUIS BÁRBARA EL DOCTOR LA DOCTORA *the woman doctor* EL POLICÍA *the policeman* EL CHOFER *the driver, chauffeur* EL LADRÓN *the thief* *LA ENFERMERA* *the nurse* EL RANCHERO *the rancher*	LLEVABA *was wearing*	un suéter azul *a blue sweater* pantalones grises *gray trousers* zapatos de tenis *tennis shoes* un sombrero grande *a big hat* zapatos blancos *white shoes* un vestido blanco *a white dress* un uniforme azul *a blue uniform* una chaqueta de cuero *a leather jacket* un traje gris *a gray suit* guantes *gloves*

un traje

un vestido

1.5 *Exercise*

CLASS: Your teacher will point out individual students who will give the proper verb form of the Imperfect Tense in a sentence below (Remove the AR from the Infinitive and add ABA). Read the complete sentence.

Example: Bárbara (plantar) plantaba rosas.
Barbara used to plant roses.

1. Bernardo (importar) ________ lámparas.
2. Bárbara (exportar) ________ radios.
3. El canario (cantar) ________ todo el día.
4. El doctor (plantar) ________ rosas en el jardín.
5. Roberto (cantar) ________ en un programa de radio.
6. Luis (progresar) ________ mucho en la clase.
7. Susana (estudiar) ________ mucho en casa.
8. El ranchero (llevar) ________ un suéter.
9. María (llevar) ________ un suéter azul.
10. Luis (llevar) ________ zapatos de tenis.
11. Luis (llevar) ________ pantalones grises.
12. El ranchero (llevar) ________ un sombrero grande.

THE IMPERFECT TENSE of ESTAR

When you say where a thing or person was, the verb WAS is generally ESTABA.

ESTAR (*to be*) IS FOR LOCATION.

CLASS: Repeat each of these sentences after your teacher says it in Spanish.

¿Dónde estaba el coche? *Where was the car?*
El coche estaba en el garaje. *The car was in the garage.*
El tren estaba en la estación. *The train was in the station.*
El dinero estaba en el banco. *The money was in the bank.*
El café estaba en la mesa. *The coffee was on the table.*
El astronauta estaba en la luna. *The astronaut was on the moon.*
Allí estaba. *There she was. There he was. There it was.*

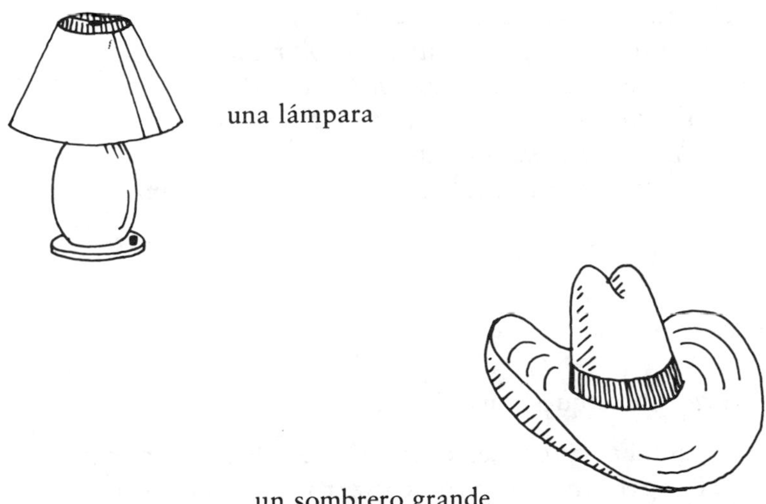

una lámpara

un sombrero grande

Review These Words

CLASS: Repeat each word, in unison, after your teacher says it in Spanish.

1. el tren, *the train* 2. el dinero, *the money* 3. el banco, *the bank* 4. el coche, *the car* 5. (el) café, *coffee* 6. el garaje, *the garage* 7. la mesa, *the table* 8. la fruta, *the fruit* 9. la crema, *the cream* 10. la estación, *the station* 11. en, *in, on, at* 12. en la clase, *in the class* 13. en casa, *at home* 14. el astronauta, *the astronaut* 15. la luna, *the moon* 16. Allí estaba. *There he was. There she was. There it was.*

1.6 *Exercise*

CLASS: Your teacher will point out individual students who will complete the following sentences.

Examples: Bernardo estaba en casa. *Bernard was at home.*
Allí estaba María. *There was Mary.*

1. El tren ________ *(was in the station).*
2. El dinero ________ *(was in the bank).*
3. El coche ________ *(was in the garage).*
4. El café ________ *(was on the table).*
5. El chocolate ________ *(was on the table).*
6. Susana ________ *(was at the station).*
7. María ________ *(was at home).*
8. La fruta ________ *(was on the table).*
9. Susana ________ *(was in the class).*
10. La crema ________ *(was on the table).*
11. Allí ________ *(he was).*
12. El astronauta ________ *(was on the moon).*

1.7 *Exercise*

Answer these questions:

1. ¿Cantaba mucho el canario? 2. ¿Estudiaba mucho Roberto? 3. ¿Progresaba mucho Roberto? 4. ¿Importaba lámparas Bernardo? 5. ¿Exportaba radios Bárbara? 6. ¿Plantaba rosas el doctor? 7. ¿Dónde estaba el dinero? 8. ¿Dónde estaba la fruta? 9. ¿Dónde estaba el tren? 10. ¿Qué llevaba Roberto? 11. ¿LLevaba un uniforme azul el policía? 12. ¿Qué llevaba Luis? 13. ¿Dónde estaba el café? 14. ¿Dónde estaba la crema? 15. ¿Dónde estaba el coche?

For the familiar form, add the letter S to the singular.
Examples: tú comprabas, *you used to buy (familiar)*
tú cantabas, *you used to sing (familiar)*

El astronauta estaba *(was)* en la luna.

1.8 *Word Builder*

How to change words that end in TION into Spanish words.

STUDENT: There are thousands of words in Spanish that are identical or similar to their corresponding English words. These are important because you already know them. If you know how the groups of words differ from their English equivalents, you can, in effect, "invent" your own words, which is very satisfying.

CLASS: The teacher will read the following GUIDELINES aloud for you. Sight-read in the book as the teacher reads aloud.

1. Most English words which end in ION are similar to their corresponding Spanish words. These ION words are wonderful, because you don't have to learn them, you already know them. Only practice their Spanish pronunciation. Be sure to stress the final ÓN, like this: la complexiÓN (*the complexion*), la tensiÓN (*the tension*).
2. English words which end in TION, end in CIÓN in Spanish. Example: la emoción (*the emotion*).
3. In Spanish we do not have double T, double F, double S. Examples: pasión (*passion*), diferente (*different*), atacar (*to attack*).
4. CC is pronounced KS as in the English word "accept."
   Examples: acción (*action*) is pronounced ak-seeON.
   tracción (*traction*) is pronounced trak-seeON.
   atracción (*attraction*) is pronounced atrak-seeON.

1.9 *List of **IÓN** Words*

CLASS: Repeat each word, in unison, after the teacher says it in Spanish. Read the words as you repeat them. Notice that they are feminine.

ION = IÓN
TION = CIÓN

la pasión	la ambición	la composición
la acción	la aviación	la condición
la tracción	la profesión	la creación
la atracción	la información	la expresión
la invitación	la liberación	la impresión
la nación	la construcción	la emoción

1.10 *Mini-Test*

STUDENT: Translate the following English words into Spanish. Write the Spanish words in your notebook. Change the TION to CIÓN.

Example: *the direction,* la dirección.

1. the action 2. the traction 3. the intention 4. the reaction 5. the transaction 6. the construction 7. the production 8. the protection 9. the publication 10. the satisfaction.

After the test, one student will write the words on the blackboard in Spanish, as the teacher dictates them in English. The students in the class will offer to correct any mistakes on the blackboard by raising their hands. Now, check your Mini-Test words to see if they are correct. Always study (at home) any words you wrote incorrectly in any Exercise or Mini-Test.

1.11 *Additional **IÓN** Words*

STUDENT: These words are included so you see that there are many, many IÓN words in Spanish. In fact, there are many more than these. Read a FEW words for practice.

la confusión, la depresión, la elección, la explosión, la ilusión, la investigación, la admiración, la conclusión, la constitución, la discusión, la exportación, la invasión, la posición, la revolución, la tensión, la compasión, la decoración, la excepción, la invención, la ocasión, la opinión, la reservación, la visión.

STUDENT: Repeat a few IÓN words from time to time. If you are familiar with these words, you will be able to recognize and write a great number of Spanish words correctly.

1.12 *Hearing Exercise*

CLASS: Repeat each Spanish sentence, in unison, after your teacher says it. Do not read the English sentence aloud. ONLY sight-read it.

1. ¿Dónde estaba Roberto? *Where was Robert?*
2. ¿Dónde estaba María? *Where was Mary?*
3. ¿Dónde estaba Susana? *Where was Susan?*
4. ¿Dónde estaba Bárbara? *Where was Barbara?*
5. ¿Dónde estaba Carlos? *Where was Carl?*
6. ¿Dónde estaba Alberto? *Where was Albert?*
7. ¿Dónde estaba Julia? *Where was Julia?*
8. ¿Dónde estaba Ricardo? *Where was Richard?*
9. ¿Dónde estaba papá? *Where was dad?*

Repeat: en el parque, *in the park*
en el cine, *at the movies*
en el teatro, *at the theater*
en el banco, *at the bank*
en el hotel, *at the hotel*
en el restaurante, *at the restaurant*
en la fiesta, *at the party*
en casa, *at home*

en el cine

1.13 *Conversation*

CLASS: Your teacher will select students, two by two, who will go to the front of the class and conduct a conversation. Take your book with you, and begin by reading the questions and answers in the block. Then, close your books, and have a conversation of your own. Speak in natural tones. Use your acting skill.

ASKING AND TELLING WHERE YOUR FRIENDS WERE

First student —¿Dónde estaba Roberto?
Second student—En el hotel.
First student —¿Dónde estaba María?
Second student—En el restaurante.
First student —¿Dónde estaba Julia?
Second student—En el parque.
First student —¿Dónde estaba Alberto?
Second student—En el banco.
First student —Bárbara estaba en la fiesta.
Second student—¿Dónde estaba Ricardo?
First student —En el teatro.
Second student—¿Dónde estaba Susana?
First student —En el cine.
Second student—¿Dónde estaba papá?
First student —En casa.

NOTE ON SPEED READING:

Speed reading opens up a lively competition among pupils. Every student should have an opportunity to practice speed as soon as possible and as often as time permits. Since this type of exercise is very fast, it does not consume much time in the class. In the end, it actually saves time because pupils get used to working fast in Spanish and learn to cover twice as much material in any given time. Speed reading also improves diction, since it is impossible for a student to drawl out a word when he is repeating it quickly. Some pupils may resist this exercise at first, but they will love it after a few lessons.

There is nothing which keeps a class on its toes more effectively than speed reading.

1.14 *Speed Exercise*

Read these sentences very fast. Don't pause between sentences.

1. María cantaba mucho.
2. Roberto galopaba en el rancho.
3. Luis estudiaba mucho.
4. Bárbara exportaba radios.
5. El doctor plantaba rosas.

1.15 *Vocabulary*

For the Story below

CLASS: Repeat each word or phrase, in unison, after your teacher says it in Spanish.

1. el rancho de Pancho, *Pancho's ranch* 2. un rancho fantástico, *a fantastic ranch* 3. durante mis vacaciones, *during my vacations* 4. visitaba, *I used to visit* 5. en su rancho, *on his ranch* 6. tenía, *had* 7. una casa grande, *a big house* 8. y, *and* 9. un río, *a river* 10. con agua, *with water* 11. fresca, *fresh (fem.)* 12. pura, *pure (fem.)* 13. llevaba, *used to wear* 14. azules, *blue (pl.)* 15. pantalones azules, *blue pants* 16. una chaqueta de cuero, *a leather jacket* 17. botas, *boots* 18. un sombrero grande, *a big hat* 19. el caballo, *the horse* 20. montaba a caballo, *he rode (mounted) horseback* 21. muy bien, *very well* 22. siempre, *always* 23. siempre tenía, *he always had* 24. caballos excelentes, *excellent horses* 25. el caballo favorito de Pancho, *Pancho's favorite horse* 26. era, *was (imperfect of ES)* 27. galopaba, *used to gallop* 28. como el viento, *like the wind* 29. todos los días, *every day* 30. me invitaba, *he used to invite me* 31. a montar a caballo, *to ride horseback* 32. yo galopaba, *I galloped* 33. al río, *to the river* 34. estaba feliz, *I was very happy.*

1.16 *Story*

CLASS: Your teacher will read the story. Sight-read in the book. Listen carefully.

EL RANCHO DE PANCHO

Pancho tenía un rancho fantástico en México. Durante mis vacaciones, visitaba a Pancho en su rancho. El rancho tenía una casa grande, y un río con agua fresca y pura.

Pancho llevaba pantalones azules, botas, una chaqueta de cuero, y un sombrero grande. Montaba a caballo muy bien. Siempre tenía caballos excelentes. El caballo favorito de Pancho era blanco, y galopaba como el viento.

Todos los días Pancho me invitaba a montar a caballo. Yo galopaba al río con Pancho. Siempre estaba feliz en el rancho de Pancho.

LESSON 2

The Imperfect Tense of singular ***ER*** *and* ***IR*** *verbs*

1. Learn this singular ending of the Imperfect Tense for ER and IR verbs: ÍA
   Examples: vendía, *he sold, used to sell*
   escribía, *he wrote, used to write*
2. ÍA is the ending for the I, YOU, HE, SHE, and IT forms of the verb.
   Example: TENÍA: *I had, used to have*
   you had, used to have
   he had, used to have
   she had, used to have
   it had, used to have

2.1 *Remember These Words*

CLASS: Your teacher will read the following Spanish words aloud. Repeat each word, in unison, after your teacher says it. Read the word in the book as you pronounce it. Look at the English meaning of each word, but do not say any English word aloud.

todas, *every, all (fem. pl.)*
todas las mañanas, *every morning*
composiciones, *compositions*
una bicicleta, *a bicycle*
una motocicleta, *a motorcycle*
el elevador, *the elevator*
una silla, *a chair*
su jefe, *your boss*
muy bien, *very well*
la Casa Blanca, *the White House*
artículos, *articles*
en el periódico, *in the newspaper*
el carpintero, *the carpenter*
en una fábrica, *in a factory*
un escritorio, *a desk*
un diseño, *a design*

Carlos, *Charles*
Margarita, *Margaret*
en el segundo piso, *on the second floor*
la cerradura, *the lock*

veinte años, *twenty years*
dieciséis años, *sixteen years*
un acumulador solar, *a solar car battery*
un coche, *a car*

yo corría, *I ran, I used to run*
escribía, *wrote, used to write*
vivía, *lived, used to live*
hacía, *made, used to make, did he make? did she make?*
vendía, *sold, used to sell*
romper, *to break, to tear*
subir, *to go up*
tenía, *had, used to have, did he have? did she have?*
tenía veinte años, *he was twenty years old (he had twenty years)*
tenía dieciséis años, *she was sixteen years old (she had sixteen years)*
a la clase, *to the class*

2.2 *Hearing Exercise*

CLASS: Repeat each sentence, in unison, after your teacher says it in Spanish.

Examples: Susana vivía en una casa.
Susan lived in a house (continuously).
Alberto vendía periódicos.
Albert used to sell newspapers (repeatedly).

1. Bárbara tenía una motocicleta *(continuously)*.
2. Alberto vivía en el segundo piso *(continuously)*.
3. El carpintero hacía muchos diseños *(repeatedly)*.
4. Luis vendía coches *(repeatedly)*.
5. Margarita hacía ensaladas deliciosas *(repeatedly)*.
6. Corría todas las mañanas *(repeatedly)*.
7. Yo tenía una bicicleta *(continuously)*.
8. Yo vivía en San Francisco *(continuously)*.
9. Mi jefe hacía muchos diseños *(repeatedly)*.
10. Luis corría a la clase *(repeatedly)*.
11. Luis no corría a la clase *(repeatedly)*.
12. Bárbara hacía acumuladores solares en una fábrica.

2.3 *Speaking Exercise*

CLASS: Your teacher will read these questions to you, and point out individual students for an answer. Read the answers in the book.

1. ¿Tenía un coche Bárbara?
   Sí, Bárbara tenía un coche.
2. ¿Dónde vivía Alberto?
   Alberto vivía en San Francisco *(or in any other city or place you wish to name).*
3. ¿Escribía Susana?
   Sí, Susana escribía composiciones en la clase.
4. ¿Corría en el parque Carlos?
   A. Sí, Carlos corría en el parque.
   B. No. Carlos no corría en el parque.
5. ¿Qué hacía el carpintero? *(What did the carpenter make?)*
   El carpintero hacía sillas.
6. ¿Hacía escritorios el carpintero?
   Sí, el carpintero hacía escritorios.
7. ¿Cuántos años tenía Roberto? *How old was Robert? (How many years did Robert have?)*
   Roberto tenía veinte años.
8. ¿Cuántos años tenía María?
   María tenía dieciséis años.
9. ¿Qué hacía Susana? *What did Susan do (make)?*
   Susana hacía acumuladores solares en una fábrica.
10. ¿Qué hacía Luis?
    Luis hacía escritorios.

CLASS: Could you answer the questions above with books closed?

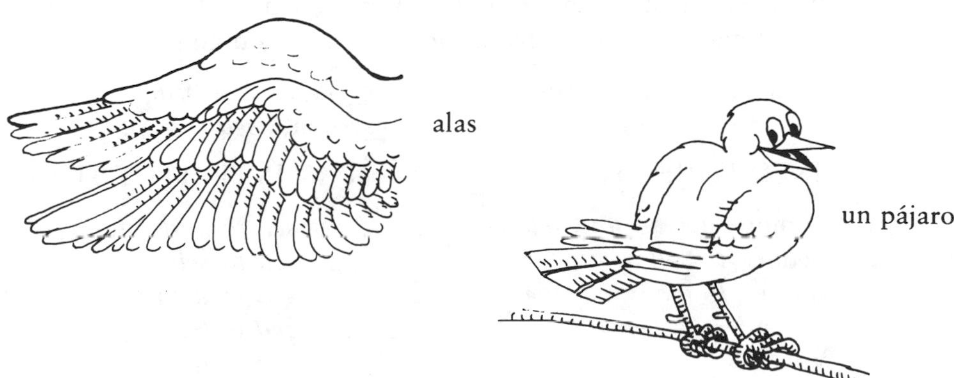

2.4 *Creating Sentences*

CLASS: Repeat each word in the three columns below, in unison, after your teacher says it in Spanish. Then, your teacher will point out individual students who will form a complete sentence with words from each of the columns. Create your own sentences by combining the words as you wish.

Bárbara		un piano
El policía		un uniforme
Carlos		un escritorio *(desk)*
El carpintero		dieciséis años
María		pantalones grises
El actor	TENÍA	veinte años
Roberto	*(had)*	muchos pacientes
La doctora		un acumulador *(a battery)*
El conductor	NO TENÍA	un traje gris *(a gray suit)*
El presidente	*(didn't have)*	un sombrero grande
El autor *(the author)*		una casa grande
La enfermera *(the nurse)*		un rancho
El capitán *(the captain)*		un paraguas negro *(a black umbrella)*
Mi jefe *(my boss)*		muchos discos *(many records)*
El avión *(the airplane)*		alas *(wings)*
El pájaro *(the bird)*		

2.5 *Exercises*

A. Give the singular of the Imperfect Tense of the following Infinitives. Remove ER or IR from the Infinitive, and add ÍA.

Examples: correr, *to run* — corría, *used to run*
escribir, *to write* — escribía, *used to write*

	INFINITIVE	SINGULAR IMPERFECT TENSE
1.	comprender, *to understand*	________ *used to understand*
2.	vender, *to sell*	________ *used to sell*
3.	querer, *to want, to love*	________ *used to want, love*
4.	aprender, *to learn*	________ *used to learn*
5.	vivir, *to live*	________ *used to live*
6.	recibir, *to receive*	________ *used to receive*

7. salir, *to go out, to leave* ________ *used to go out, leave*
8. dormir, *to sleep* ________ *used to sleep*
9. hacer, *to make, to do* ________ *used to make, do*
10. tener, *to have* ________ *used to have*
11. abrir, *to open* ________ *used to open*
12. romper, *to break, to tear* ________ *used to break, tear*

B. CLASS: Your teacher will point out individual students who will give the proper verb form of the Imperfect Tense in a sentence below. Remove the ER or IR from the Infinitive, and add ÍA. Read the complete sentence.

Example: Carlos (comer) comía en un restaurante.
Charles used to eat in a restaurant.

1. Carlos (tener) ________ muchos discos.
2. El doctor (vivir) ________ en San Francisco.
3. Luis (salir) ________ mucho.
4. Margarita (subir) ________ en el elevador.
5. Bernardo (querer) ________ una bicicleta.
6. El carpintero (hacer) ________ escritorios.
7. Carlos (dormir) ________ muy bien.
8. Susana (escribir) ________ muchas cartas.
9. El policía (salir) ________ mucho.
10. El conductor (recibir) ________ los boletos *(tickets)*.
11. María (hacer) ________ ensaladas deliciosas.
12. El avión (tener) ________ alas grandes.

el paraguas

una silla

2.6 *Exercise*

Answer these questions:

1. ¿Qué vendía Luis? 2. ¿Qué hacía el carpintero? 3. ¿Hacía escritorios el carpintero? 4. ¿Tenía un coche Bárbara? 5. ¿Escribía Susana? 6. ¿Corría en el parque Carlos? 7. ¿Cuántos años tenía Roberto? 8. ¿Cuántos años tenía María? 9. ¿Hacía ensaladas Margarita? 10. ¿Vendía coches Luis? 11. ¿Llevaba un uniforme azul el policía?

Carlos corría en el parque.

Charles used to run in the park.

2.7 *Hearing Exercise*

CLASS: Repeat each Spanish sentence, in unison, after your teacher says it. Do not read the English sentence aloud. ONLY sight-read it.

IR, *to go*
QUERÍA, *I wanted, you wanted, he wanted, she wanted*
QUERÍA IR, *I wanted to go, you wanted to go, he wanted to go, she wanted to go*
¿QUÉ QUERÍA? *What did you want? What did he want? What did she want?*
¿QUÉ QUERÍA SUSANA? *What did Susan want?*
CONMIGO, *with me (with my ego)*

2.8 *Conversation*

CLASS: Your teacher will select students, two by two, who will go to the front of the class and conduct a conversation. Take your books with you, and begin by reading the questions and answers in the block. Then, close your books, and have a conversation of your own. Speak in natural tones. Use your acting skills.

WHAT WE WANTED TO DO

First student —¿Qué quería Susana?
Second student—Quería ir al cine.
First student —¿Qué quería Roberto?
Second student—Quería ir al teatro.
First student —¿Qué quería María?
Second student—Quería ir al restaurante conmigo.
First student —¿Qué quería Alberto?
Second student—Quería ir a la fiesta conmigo.
First student —Bárbara quería ir al parque.
Second student—¿Qué quería Ricardo?
First student —Quería ir al banco.
Second student—¿Qué quería papá?
First student —Quería comprar una motocicleta.
Second student—¿Qué quería Julia?
First student —Quería una bicicleta.
Second student—¿Qué quería usted?
First student —*(Say two things you wanted.)*

2.9 *Speed Exercise*

Read these sentences very fast. Don't pause between sentences.

1. Luis vendía coches.
2. El carpintero hacía escritorios.
3. Roberto corría en el parque.
4. Carlos tenía un coche.
5. Pancho tenía un rancho.

Now, read the exercise above twice as fast as you read it the last time. Can you read all five sentences in one breath?

SUBJECT PRONOUNS

yo, *I*	nosotros, *we (masc.)* nosotras, *we (fem.)*
usted, *you*	ustedes, *you (pl.)*
él, *he*	ellos, *they (masc.)*
ella, *she*	ellas, *they (fem.)*

NOTICE that él, *he,* has a written accent. The word EL, *the (masc.)* does NOT have a written accent.

REMEMBER: IBA, *I was going, you were going*
he was going, she was going, it was going

IBA is the singular Imperfect form of IR.

EL, *the (masc.)* el parque, *the park*
A, *to*
AL, *to the (masc.)*
A + EL = AL, *to the*

Examples: Yo iba al parque. *I was going to the park.*
Ella iba al cine con él. *She was going to the movies with him.*
Ella iba al restaurante. *She was going to the restaurant.*
¿Iba usted a Madrid? *Were you going to Madrid?*
El tren iba a Madrid. *The train was going to Madrid.*
Iba a Madrid. *It was going to Madrid.*

DO NOT use the word IT before IBA.

IBA is used with Infinitives.
Example: Ella iba a cantar. *She was going to sing.*
Iba a llover. *It was going to rain.*

2.10 *Exercise*

Translate these sentences into Spanish.

1. I was going to the restaurant. 2. She was going to the movies. 3. It was going to San Francisco. 4. He was going to the ranch. 5. Were you going to the White House?

REMEMBER: Subject pronouns are frequently dropped in Spanish.

LESSON 3

How to form the Imperfect Tense of regular verbs

To form the Imperfect Tense of every regular AR verb in the Spanish language: Remove the AR from the Infinitive, and add the endings below.

I	ABA	ÁBAMOS	*we*
you, he, she, it	ABA	ABAN	*you (pl.), they*

CLASS: Repeat the following verbs, in unison, after your teacher says them in Spanish. Stress the accented A firmly.

IMPERFECT TENSE
CANTAR, *to sing*

CANTABA *I used to sing*	CANTÁBAMOS *we used to sing*
CANTABA *you used to sing* *he used to sing* *she used to sing* *it used to sing*	CANTABAN *you (pl.) used to sing* *they used to sing*

Familiar form: To make the familiar form, add a letter S to the singular Imperfect ending: tú cantabas, *you used to sing* (familiar).

EXPRESSIONS WHICH ARE USED WITH THE IMPERFECT

The following words and phrases denote repetition. They are used with the Imperfect Tense.

1. todos los días, *every day*
2. todas las mañanas, *every morning*
3. todas las tardes, *every afternoon*
4. todas las noches, *every night*
5. todas las semanas, *every week*
6. todos los meses, *every month*
7. todos los años, *every year*
8. con frecuencia, *frequently (with frequence)*
9. generalmente, *generally*
10. siempre, *always*
11. nunca, *never*

STUDENT: Copy the expressions above in your notebook, and learn them well.

3.1 *Remember These Words*

CLASS: Repeat each word or phrase, in unison, after your teacher says it in Spanish.

con frecuencia, *frequently*
mi tío, *my uncle*
sus experiencias, *his experiences*
todo, *everything, all*
todos, *everybody, all of us*
el café, *the coffee*
nos, *us*
la cena, *dinner*
los, *you (pl.)*

¿quién? *who?*
al cine, *to the movies*
con gusto, *with pleasure*
simpático, *charming*
interesante, *interesting*
en su casa, *at your house*
papas, *potatoes*
o, *or*

¿los visitaba? *did he visit you (pl.)? (repeatedly)*
¿los invitaba? *did he invite you (pl.)? (repeatedly)*
nos visitaba, *he visited us (repeatedly)*
nos invitaba, *he invited us (repeatedly)*
hablaba, *he used to talk*
hablábamos mucho, *we talked a lot (repeatedly)*
¿hablaban? *did you (pl.) talk? (repeatedly)*

cenaba, *he used to have dinner (repeatedly)*
preparaba, *you, he, she prepared (repeatedly)*
preparábamos, *we prepared (repeatedly)*
papá compraba todo, *dad used to buy everything*
aceptábamos, *we accepted (repeatedly)*
era, *was (the Imperfect of ES)*. ERA is an irregular form because it does not follow the rules.
eran, *(they) were.*

un coctel de frutas

3.2 *Hearing Exercise*

CLASS: Repeat each sentence, in unison, after your teacher says it in Spanish.

Examples: Cuando mi tío nos visitaba, comíamos rosbif o biftec, papas, una ensalada, y un coctel de frutas. *When my uncle visited us, we used to eat roast beef or beefsteak, potatoes, a salad, and a fruit cocktail.*
Hablábamos mucho. *We used to talk a lot.*

1. Mi tío Luis nos visitaba con frecuencia *(repeatedly)*.
2. Hablaba mucho *(repeatedly)*.
3. Hablaba de sus experiencias en la América Central *(repeatedly)*.
4. Todos hablábamos mucho *(repeatedly)*.
5. Hablábamos con mi tío *(repeatedly)*.
6. La conversación era interesante *(usually)*.
7. Mi tío siempre era muy simpático *(continuously)*.
8. Mi tío cenaba en mi casa *(repeatedly)*.
9. Todos preparábamos la cena *(repeatedly)*.
10. María preparaba el rosbif o el biftec *(repeatedly)*.
11. Roberto preparaba la ensalada *(repeatedly)*.

12. Mamá preparaba el coctel de frutas *(repeatedly)*.
13. Mi tío preparaba el café *(repeatedly)*.
14. Papá compraba todo *(repeatedly)*.
15. Tomábamos la cena con mucho gusto *(repeatedly)*.
16. Después de la cena, mi tío nos invitaba al cine *(usually)*.
17. Aceptábamos con mucho gusto *(repeatedly)*.

café

3.3 *Speaking Exercise*

In the exercise below, we use the Imperfect Tense because the action is either repeated or continuous.

CLASS: Your teacher will ask you the following questions, and point out individual students for an answer. Read the answer in the book.

Examples: ¿Los visitaba su tío?
Did your uncle visit (use to visit) you?
Sí, mi tío nos visitaba.
Yes, my uncle used to visit us.

1. ¿Hablaba mucho su tío? Sí, mi tío hablaba mucho.
2. ¿Hablaba de sus experiencias? Sí, hablaba de sus experiencias en la América Central.
3. ¿Los visitaba con frecuencia? Sí, nos visitaba con frecuencia.
4. ¿Hablaban todos? Sí, todos hablábamos.
5. ¿Era simpático su tío? Sí, mi tío era simpático.
6. ¿Era interesante la conversación? Sí, la conversación era interesante.
7. ¿Tomaba la cena en su casa? Sí, mi tío tomaba la cena en mi casa.
8. ¿Quién preparaba el rosbif o el biftec? María preparaba el rosbif o el biftec.

9. ¿Quién preparaba el café? Mi tío preparaba el café.
10. ¿Quién preparaba la ensalada? Roberto preparaba la ensalada.
11. ¿Quién compraba todo? Papá compraba todo.
12. ¿Los invitaba al cine su tío? Sí, mi tío nos invitaba al cine.
13. ¿Aceptaban la invitación? Sí, aceptábamos la invitación.
14. ¿Aceptaban con gusto? Sí, aceptábamos con mucho gusto.

CLASS: Could you answer the questions above with books closed?

1. ERA *(was)* is the Imperfect of ES. It is an irregular form. Use it for descriptions in the past.
   Examples:
   era alto, *he was tall*
   era guapo, *he was handsome*
   era delgado, *he was slender, thin*
   era simpática, *she was charming*
   era bonita, *she was pretty*
   Susana era muy inteligente, *Susan was very intelligent*
   la casa era bonita, *the house was pretty*
2. ESTABA *(was)* is used for expressing LOCATION in the past.
   Examples:
   estaba en casa, *you, she, it, he was at home*
   estábamos en casa, *we were at home*
   estaban en casa, *they were at home*
   ¿dónde estaba? *where were you? where was he, she, it?*
   estaba en el despacho, *I was at the office.*

un hombre alto

IMPERFECT TENSE

ESTAR, *to be (in a place)*

I was	ESTABA	ESTÁBAMOS	*we were*
you were *he was* *she was* *it was*	ESTABA	ESTABAN	*you (pl.) were* *they were*

3.4 *Exercise*

CLASS: your teacher will point out individual students who will complete a sentence below. Choose the correct verb form. Read the complete sentence.

1. *(We were)* en casa.
2. *(They were)* en la clase.
3. *(He was)* en el hotel.
4. *(It was)* en el garaje.
5. *(We were)* en el parque.
6. *(They were)* en el hospital.
7. *(She was)* en el despacho.
8. *(We were)* en el jardín.

To form the Imperfect Tense of every regular ER or IR verb in the Spanish language, remove the ER or the IR from the Infinitive, and add the following endings:

I	ÍA	ÍAMOS	*we*
you, he, she, it	ÍA	ÍAN	*you (pl.), they*

CLASS: Repeat the following verbs, in unison, after your teacher says them in Spanish. Stress the accented Í firmly.

VENDER, *to sell*

I sold	VENDÍA	VENDÍAMOS	*we sold*
you sold *he sold* *she sold*	VENDÍA	VENDÍAN	*you (pl.) sold* *they sold*

Familiar form: tú vendías, *you sold*

ESCRIBIR, *to write*

I wrote	ESCRIBÍA	ESCRIBÍAMOS	*we wrote*
you wrote *he wrote* *she wrote*	ESCRIBÍA	ESCRIBÍAN	*you (pl.) wrote* *they wrote*

Familiar form: tú escribías, *you used to write (familiar)*

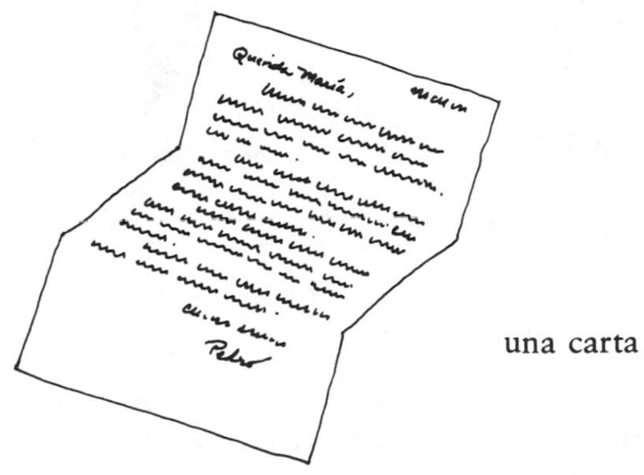

una carta

3.5 *Remember These Words*

CLASS: Repeat each word or phrase, in unison, after your teacher says it in Spanish.

todos los meses, *every month*
cartas, *letters*
su tío, *your uncle*
de, *about, of, from*
un regalo, *a present*
regalos, *presents*
mi tío, *my uncle*
nos, *us, to us*
de sus experiencias, *about his experiences*
la América Central, *Central America*

nos escribía, *he used to write to us*
vivía, *he used to live (continuously)*
tenía una casa, *he had a house (continuously)*

¿recibían cartas? *did you (pl.) receive letters?*
recibíamos, *we used to receive*
¿leían las cartas? *did you (pl.) read the letters?*
leíamos las cartas, *we read the letters*
leer, *to read*

un coche

un regalo

3.6 *Speaking Exercise*

CLASS: Your teacher will read these questions to you, and point to individual students for an answer. Read the answer in the book.

Examples: Mi tío nos escribía todos los meses.
My uncle wrote to us every month (repeatedly).
¿Recibían cartas?
Did you (pl.) receive letters?

1. ¿Escribía cartas su tío? Sí, mi tío nos escribía todos los meses.
2. ¿Recibían las cartas? Sí, recibíamos las cartas.
3. ¿Escribía su tío de sus experiencias? Sí, mi tío escribía de sus experiencias.
4. ¿Escribía de sus experiencias en la América Central? Sí, escribía de sus experiencias en la América Central.
5. ¿Leían las cartas? Sí, leíamos las cartas.
6. ¿Recibían regalos de su tío? Sí, recibíamos regalos.
7. ¿Dónde vivía su tío? Mi tío vivía en la América Central, en Costa Rica.
8. ¿Tenía una casa en Costa Rica? Sí, mi tío tenía una casa en Costa Rica.

CLASS: Could you answer the questions above with books closed?

3.7 *Vocabulary*

For the Conversation below.

CLASS: Review the following list of words which will help you to conduct the conversation at the end of this lesson.

¿Qué tenía Bárbara? *What did Barbara have?*
Tenía un radio. *She, he, had a radio.*
fantástico, *fantastic, "terrific"*
muy bonito, *very pretty (masc.)*
influenza, *the flu*
pobre Juan, *poor John*
¡Caramba! *Gee whiz!, Gosh!*

3.8 *Conversation*

CLASS: Your teacher will select students, two by two, who will go to the front of the class and conduct a conversation. Take your book with you, and begin by reading the questions and answers in the block. Then, close your books, and have a conversation of your own. Speak in natural tones. Use your acting skills.

WHAT MY FRIENDS HAD

First student —¿Qué tenía Bárbara?
Second student—Tenía un radio.
First student —¿Qué tenía Alberto?
Second student—Tenía una guitarra muy bonita.
First student —¿Qué tenía Bernardo?
Second student—Tenía un violín.
First student —¿Qué tenía Julia?
Second student—Tenía muchos discos.
First student —Tenía muchos libros también.
Second student—¿Qué tenía María?
First student —Tenía una bicicleta muy bonita.
Second student—¿Qué tenía Roberto?
First student —Tenía un coche muy bonito.
Second student—¿Qué tenía Susana?
First student —Tenía una motocicleta.
Second student—¡Caramba! ¿Una motocicleta grande?
First student —Sí, muy grande.
Second student—¿Qué tenía Juan?
First student —Tenía influenza. Pobre Juan.

3.9 *Exercise*

Answer these questions:

1. Tenía un coche Roberto? 2. ¿Tenía un radio Bárbara? 3. ¿Tenía una guitarra Alberto? 4. ¿Tenía una casa su tío? 5. ¿Escribía cartas su tío? 6. ¿Recibía usted las cartas? 7. ¿Cantaba el canario? 8. ¿Era simpático su tío? 9. ¿Quién compraba todo? 10. ¿Era interesante la conversación? 11. ¿Quién preparaba el rosbif? 12. ¿Quién preparaba el cafe? 13. ¿Era inteligente Susana? 14. ¿Dónde estaba el doctor? 15. ¿Cuantos años tenía María?

3.10 *Speed Reading Exercise*

CLASS: The teacher will guide you in reading sentences from the Hearing Exercise in LESSON ONE (1.2) as a Speed Reading Exercise. Read aloud, as quickly as you can.

una máquina de escribir

LESSON 4

Uses of the Preterite and the Imperfect
Review of the Preterite Tense

> THE DIFFERENCE BETWEEN THE PRETERITE
> AND THE IMPERFECT
>
> The Preterite Tense expresses a COMPLETED action. The Imperfect Tense expresses an often-REPEATED or CONTINUOUS action. "He had an accident." This is a completed action, indeed. "He used to visit us." This is a repeated action. "He lived in Puerto Rico." This is a continuous action. He lived there all the time (continuously).

Examples:
Me invitaba al cine. *He used to invite me to the movies.*
Me visitaba con frecuencia. *He used to visit me frequently.*
Me invitó al cine ayer. *He invited me to the movies yesterday (once).*
Me visitó anoche. *He visited me last night (once).*
Recibí una carta. *I received a letter (once).*
Mi tío escribía con frecuencia. *My uncle wrote frequently.*

> PRETERITE ENDINGS

AR verbs		ER and IR verbs	
É	AMOS	Í	IMOS
Ó	ARON	IÓ	IERON

Familiar form: ASTE   Familiar form: ISTE

> To form the Preterite Tense (past), remove the infinitive ending AR, ER, or IR, and add the above endings.

COPY the charts below in your notebook:

COMPRAR, *to buy*

COMPRÉ *I bought*	COMPRAMOS *we bought*
COMPRÓ *you bought* *he, she bought*	COMPRARON *you (pl.) bought* *they bought*

SALIR, *to leave, to go out*

SALÍ *I left*	SALIMOS *we left*
SALIÓ *you left* *he, she left*	SALIERON *you (pl.) left)* *they left*

4.1 *Exercises*

A. CLASS: Give the correct verb form in the following sentences. Remove the AR from the Infinitive, and add É (for me), Ó (for others). Remember that when you speak of yourself, you add the letter É. When you speak of anyone else (singular), you add the letter Ó. Read a complete sentence.

Examples: Yo preparé una ensalada de atún.
I prepared a tuna fish salad.
Roberto compró leche.
Robert bought milk.

1. Yo (tomar) café.
2. Susana (comprar) un suéter.
3. Yo (votar) en la elección.
4. Margarita (tomar) chocolate.
5. Yo (entrar) en la casa.
6. Marta (preparar) la lección.
7. Carlos (visitar) a María.
8. Yo (invitar) a Bernardo.
9. Yo (comprar) un radio.
10. Yo (tomar) leche.

B. CLASS: Give the correct verb form in the following sentences. Remove ER or IR from the Infinitive, and add Í (for me), IÓ (for others). Read a complete sentence.

Examples: Yo abrí los ojos.
I opened my eyes (the eyes).
Carlos salió del despacho.
Charles left the office.

la ventana

la puerta

1. Yo (abrir) la ventana.
2. Marta (escribir) una composición.
3. Yo (recibir) un regalo.
4. Yo (insistir).
5. Marta (salir, *to go out, to leave)* del despacho.
6. El hombre (salir) del garaje.
7. El Presidente (salir) de la Casa Blanca.
8. El policía (escribir) la descripción.
9. La doctora (recibir) un telegrama.
10. Yo (comprender) la conversación en la clase.

C. CLASS: Practice these. Read across the line.

PRETERITE (completed action)	IMPERFECT (continuous or repeated action)
canté	cantaba
I sang	*I used to sing*
compré	compraba
I bought	*I used to buy*
mi tío compró	mi tío compraba
my uncle bought	*my uncle used to buy*
escribí	escribía
I wrote	*I used to write*
mi tío escribió	mi tío escribía
my uncle wrote	*my uncle used to write*
Corrió del garaje.	Corría todos los días.
He ran from the garage.	*He ran every day.*

4.2 *Exercise (optional)*

CLASS: Your teacher will point out individual students who will read one of the sentences below. Choose the correct verb. Remember that if a person did a thing once, it is a completed action: use the Preterite. For repeated or continuous action, use the Imperfect.

Examples: María escribió una carta *(once).*
Mary wrote a letter (one action).
Alberto corría todos los días. *(repeatedly)*
Albert ran every day (repeatedly).

1. Alberto (escribió, escribía) una composición *(once).*
2. María (escribió, escribía) todas las mañanas *(repeatedly).*
3. Alberto (vivió, vivía) en Puerto Rico *(continuously).*
4. Carlos (salió, salía) todas las noches.
5. Luis (vendió, vendía) la casa ayer.
6. David (vendió, vendía) casas con frecuencia.
7. Susana (recibió, recibía) un telegrama anoche.
8. Carlos (recibió, recibía) una bicicleta.
9. Bernardo (recibió, recibía) telegramas todos los días.
10. Alberto (compró, compraba) café ayer.
11. Alberto (compró, compraba) café todos los días.

EXPRESSIONS WHICH ARE USED WITH THE PRETERITE

The following words denote a single, completed action.

ayer, *yesterday*
anoche, *last night*
el año pasado, *last year*
la semana pasada, *last week*

4.3 *Speaking Exercise*

1. ¿Tomó usted café? Sí. Tomé café.
2. ¿Compró usted un disco? Sí. Compré un disco.
3. ¿Visitó used a Pancho? Sí. Visité a Pancho.
4. ¿Invitó usted a Carmen? Sí, Invité a Carmen.
5. ¿Progresó usted mucho? Sí. Progresé mucho.
6. ¿Abrió usted la ventana? Sí. Abrí la ventana.
7. ¿Recibió usted el telegrama? Sí. Recibí el telegrama.
8. ¿Salió usted anoche? Sí. Salí anoche.
9. ¿Comprendió usted la lección? Sí. Comprendí la lección.

ERA, TENÍA

1. To express POSSESSION in the past, use TENÍA, *I had, you had, he had, she had, it had.*

   Examples:
   Alberto tenía una guitarra. *Albert had a guitar.*
   Mi tío tenía muchas corbatas. *My uncle had many neckties.*
   El policía tenía guantes blancos. *The policeman had white gloves.*
   Susana tenía una chaqueta bonita. *Susan had a pretty jacket.*
   María tenía una máquina de escribir. *Mary had a typewriter.*

2. For descriptions in the past, use ERA, *I was, you were, he was, she was, it was.*

   Examples:
   María era inteligente. *Mary was intelligent.*
   Mi tío era guapo. *My uncle was handsome.*
   El ladrón era bajo de estatura. *The thief was short in stature.*
   Luis era doctor. *Louis was a doctor.*
   Carlos era mecánico. *Charles was a mechanic.*
   Marta era doctora. *Martha was a doctor.*
   Mi tía era enfermera. *My aunt was a nurse.*

Mi tío era guapo.
My uncle was handsome.

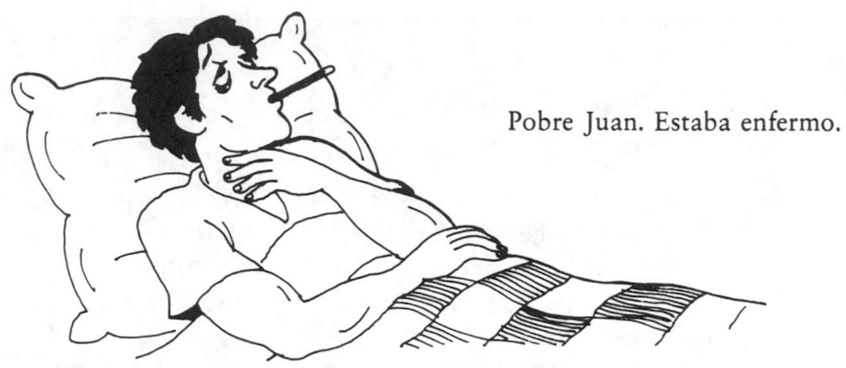

Pobre Juan. Estaba enfermo.

4.4 *Creating Sentences*

CLASS: Repeat the words in the three columns below after your teacher says them in Spanish. Then, combine the words in the three columns to form a complete sentence. Create your own sentences.

yo, *I*		simpático, *charming (masc.)*
usted, *you (sing.)*		simpática, *charming (fem.)*
él, *he*		alto, *tall (masc.)*
ella, *she*		gordo, *fat (masc.)*
Alberto		mecánico, *a mechanic*
Susana	ERA *was*	bajo, *short (masc.)*
mi tía, *my aunt*		artista, *an artist*
mi abuelo, *my grandfather*		doctora, *a doctor (fem.)*
mi abuela, *my grandmother*		rubio, *blond (masc.)*
mi hermano, *my brother*		rubia, *blond (fem.)*
mi hermana, *my sister*		bueno, *good (masc.)*

ESTABA *(was)*—LOCATION

REMEMBER that we generally use ESTABA to express LOCATION in the past.

Examples:
Estaba en la playa. *I was on the beach.*
David estaba en la cabaña. *David was in the cabin.*
Roberto estaba en el segundo piso. *Robert was on the second floor.*
Papá estaba en la cocina. *Dad was in the kitchen.*

la cocina

4.5 *Creating Sentences*

CLASS: Repeat the words in the three columns below after your teacher says them in Spanish. Then, combine the words in the three columns to form a complete sentence. Create your own sentences.

yo, *I*		en la playa, *on the beach*
usted, *you (sing.)*		en casa, *at home*
él, *he*		en el cine, *at the movies*
ella, *she*		en el parque, *in the park*
el mecánico		en la mesa, *on the table*
Roberto		en el banco, *at the bank*
María	ESTABA	en la escuela, *in school*
mi tío	*was*	en el hospital, *in the hospital*
mi tía		en la montaña, *on the mountain*
la llave, *the key*		en el lago, *at the lake*
el sándwich		en la lancha de motor, *on the motorboat*
la fruta		en el río, *on the river*

ESTABA *(was)*—TEMPORARY CONDITION

REMEMBER: Use ESTABA to express a temporary condition.

Examples: Roberto estaba cansado (masc.). *Robert was tired.*
Luisa estaba cansada (fem.). *Louise was tired.*
Bernardo estaba enfermo (masc.). *Bernard was sick.*
Susana estaba enferma (fem.). *Susan was sick.*
El presidente estaba ocupado. *The president was busy.*
La doctora estaba ocupada. *The woman doctor was busy.*

4.6 *Creating Sentences*

CLASS: Repeat the words in the three columns after your teacher says them. Combine the words to create your own sentences.

el doctor
la enfermera
Carlos, *Charles*
Elena, *Ellen, Helen*
el piloto
Margarita, *Margaret*
el profesor
Bárbara
el ladrón, *the thief*
Bernardo
Susana
el teatro
la tienda, *the store*
los estudiantes
los pantalones, *the trousers*
la ropa, *the clothes*
el vestido, *the dress*

ESTABA
was
ESTABAN
were
NO ESTABA
was not
NO ESTABAN
were not

cansado (masc.), *tired*
cansada (fem.), *tired*
enfermo (masc.), *sick*
enferma (fem.), *sick*
ocupado (masc.), *busy*
ocupada (fem.), *busy*
contento (masc.), *happy*
contenta (fem.), *happy*
triste (masc. and fem.), *sad*
encantado (masc.), *delighted*
encantada (fem.), *delighted*
cerrado (masc.), *closed*
cerrada (fem.), *closed*
contentos (masc., pl.)
sucios (masc., pl.), *dirty*
limpio (masc.), *clean*
limpia (fem.), *clean*

4.7 *Speaking Exercise*

1. ¿Estaba cansado el doctor?
   Sí, el doctor estaba cansado.
2. ¿Estaba ocupada la enfermera?
   Sí, la enfermera estaba ocupada.
3. ¿Estaba contenta Bárbara?
   Sí, Bárbara estaba contenta.
4. ¿Estaba enfermo Carlos?
   No. Carlos no estaba enfermo.
5. ¿Estaba ocupado el piloto?
   Sí, el piloto estaba ocupado.
6. ¿Estaba triste el ladrón?
   Sí, el ladrón estaba triste.
7. ¿Estaba cerrada la tienda?
   Sí, la tienda estaba cerrada.

8. ¿Estaba cerrado el libro?
   No. El libro no estaba cerrado.
9. ¿Estaba limpio el garaje?
   Sí, el garaje estaba limpio.

SUMMATION OF THE USES OF THE IMPERFECT

The Imperfect Tense is used to express:

1. POSSESSION in the past (TENÍA, *had*).
2. LOCATION in the past (ESTABA, *was*).
3. TEMPORARY CONDITION in the past (ESTABA, *was*).
4. DESCRIPTION in the past (ERA, *was*).
5. AGE in the past (TENÍA).
6. REPEATED or CONTINUOUS action in the past.
7. The Imperfect is used with expressions that denote repeated action: todos los días, *every day;* todas las semanas, *every week, etc.*

REMEMBER that you express age in the past with TENÍA. Roberto tenía veinte años. *Robert was twenty years old. (Roberto had twenty years.)*

4.8 *Creating Sentences*

CLASS: Repeat the words in the three columns below after your teacher says them in Spanish. Then, combine the words in the three columns to form a complete sentence. Create your own sentences.

Roberto		veinte (20) años
David		cincuenta (50) años
El presidente		sesenta (60) años
María	TENÍA	dieciséis (16) años
Susana	*had*	quince (15) años)
Marta	NO TENÍA	catorce (14) años
El muchacho, *the boy*	*didn't have*	diecisiete (17) años
La muchacha, *the girl*		dieciocho (18) años
Bernardo		diecinueve (19) años
La señora, *the lady*		cien (100) años
El señor, *the gentleman*		noventa (90) años
El señor López, *Mr. López*		cuarenta (40) años
La señora López, *Mrs. López*		treinta (30) años

In Spanish we do not claim parts of the body, as a rule.

Examples: los ojos, *my eyes, your eyes, his eyes, her eyes, the eyes*
la mano, *my hand, your hand, his hand, her hand, the hand*

Exception: In love talk, we say "your eyes," but we use the intimate form: "tus ojos." Tus ojos son lindos. *Your eyes are beautiful, lovely.*

4.9 *Vocabulary*

For the Conversation below.

CLASS: Review the following list of words which will help you to conduct the conversation at the end of this lesson.

IBA *(irregular verb), I, he, she, it used to go, was going, you were going*
VENIR, *to come*
VENÍA, *I, he, she, it used to come, was coming, you were coming*
DIJO QUE IBA, *he, she said that I, he, she, it was going, you were going*
DIJO QUE VENÍA, *he, she said that I, he, she, it was coming, you were coming*
¿QUÉ DIJO ROBERTO? *What did Robert say?*
Dijo que iba al restaurante. *He said that he was going to the restaurant.*
Dijo que venía a la clase. *He said that he was coming to the class.*
mi hermana dijo, *my sister said*

REMEMBER: AL is a contraction of A EL, *to the*

Example: al retaurante, *to the restaurant.*

4.10 *Conversation*

CLASS: Your teacher will select students, two by two, who will go to the front of the class and conduct a conversation. Take your book with you, and begin by reading the questions and answers in the block. Then, close your book, and have a conversation of your own. Speak in natural tones. Use your acting skills.

WHERE MY FRIENDS WERE GOING

First student —¿Qué dijo Roberto?
Second student—Dijo que iba al restaurante.
First student —¿Qué dijo Bárbara?
Second student—Dijo que iba al restaurante con Roberto.
First student —¿Qué dijo Susana?
Second student—Dijo que iba al parque.
First student —¿Qué dijo Bernardo?
Second student—Dijo que iba al parque con Susana.

First student —¿Qué dijo Carlos?
Second student—Dijo que venía a la clase.
First student —¿Qué dijo Carmen?
Second student—Dijo que venía a mi casa esta tarde.
First student —¿Qué dijo su tío?
Second student—Dijo que venía a la fiesta.
First student —¿Qué dijo su hermano?
Second student—Dijo que no venía. Dijo que no tenía tiempo.
First student —¿Qué dijo su hermana?
Second student—Dijo que venía a la estación con Ricardo.

Salió de la casa con unos papeles en la mano.
He left the house with some papers in his hand.

4.11 *Vocabulary*

For the Detective Story below.

STUDENT: The following vocabulary will help you to read and understand the Detective Story. You will not be expected to learn this vocabulary, but only to recognize it. It is a good idea to read material which is a little beyond your knowledge. It trains you in guessing the meaning of articles and stories.

1. Era sábado. *It was Saturday.* 2. Abrió los ojos. *He opened his eyes.* 3. de pronto, *suddenly* 4. cuando oyó un coche salir del garaje de su casa, *when he heard a car leave the garage of his house* 5. a todo motor, *at full speed (all motor)* 6. corrió al garaje en su pijama, *he ran to the garage in his pajamas* 7. Allí estaba su hermana María. *There was his sister Mary.* 8. ¿Qué pasó? *What happened?* 9. dijo Roberto, *said Robert.* 10. ¿Quién salió en el coche? *Who left in the car?* 11. No sé. *I don't know.* 12. dijo María, *said Mary* 13. un hombre se lo robó, *a man stole it* 14. salió de la casa, *he left the house* 15. con unos papeles en la mano, *with some papers in his hand* 16. corrió al garaje, *he ran to the garage* 17. y en un instante, *and in an instant* 18. salió en el coche a toda velocidad, *he left in the car at full speed* 19. ¿Lo viste? *Did you see him? (familiar)* 20. preguntó Roberto, *asked Robert* 21. Sí, lo vi bien. *Yes, I saw him well.* 22. era un hombre delgado, *he was a thin man* 23. bajo de estatura, *short in stature* 24. de pelo negro, *(of) with black hair* 25. ojos negros, intensos, *intense black eyes* 26. tipo nervioso, *a nervous type* 27. llevaba un suéter azul, *he was wearing a blue sweater* 28. pantalones grises, y zapatos de tenis, *gray trousers, and tennis shoes* 29. Roberto corrió al teléfono, *Robert ran to the phone* 30. a llamar a la policía, *to call the police (department)* 31. después, *after that, afterwards* 32. se vistió rápidamente, *he dressed quickly (rapidly)* 33. fue a la cocina, *he went to the kitchen* 34. donde tomó leche con galletas, *where he had milk with crackers (cookies)* 35. Un policía llegó en cinco minutos. *A policeman arrived in five minutes.* 36. la interrogación, *the questioning (interrogation)* 37. fue larga y complicada, *was long and complicated* 38. preguntó, *he asked.*

4.12 *Detective Story (Part 1)*

STUDENT: See how much of the story below you recognize when your teacher reads it aloud.

CLASS: Your teacher will read the Detective Story below for you. Sight-read in the book. Listen carefully.

ROBERTO Y MARÍA, DETECTIVES

5 A.M. (las cinco de la mañana)

Era sábado. Roberto abrió los ojos de pronto, cuando oyó un coche salir del garaje de su casa a todo motor. Corrió al garaje en su pijama. Allí estaba su hermana María. Roberto le preguntó:

—¿Qué pasó? ¿Quién salió en el coche?

—No sé—dijo María—un hombre se lo robó. Salió de la casa con unos papeles en la mano, corrió al garaje, y en un instante salió en el coche a toda velocidad.

—¿Lo viste?

—Sí, lo vi bien. Era un hombre delgado, bajo de estatura, de pelo negro, ojos negros, intensos. Tipo nervioso. Llevaba un suéter azul, pantalones grises, y zapatos de tenis.

Roberto corrió al teléfono a llamar a la policía. Después, se vistió rápidamente. Fue a la cocina donde tomó leche con galletas. Un policía llegó en cinco minutos. La interrogación fue larga y complicada. *(To be continued)*

4.13 *Reading Exercise*

CLASS: Your teacher will point out individual students who will read a sentence aloud in the Detective Story above. Read it as smoothly as you can, in a loud, clear voice.

4.14 *Translating Exercise (optional)*

CLASS: Your teacher will point out individual students who will read one sentence in the Detective Story above, and translate it into English.

ADJECTIVES WHICH ARE MASCULINE AND FEMININE

As a rule, adjectives which do not end in O or A are both masculine and feminine.

Examples: grande, *big (masc. & fem.)*
verde, *green (masc. & fem.)*
interesante, *interesting (masc. & fem.)*
inteligente, *intelligent (masc. & fem.)*

María es inteligente. *Mary is intelligent.*
Carlos es inteligente. *Carlos is intelligent.*

PLURALS WHICH DO NOT END IN A VOWEL

To form the plural of words which do not end in a vowel, add ES.

Examples: capital capitales
flor flores

4.15 *Exercise*

Give the plural of the following words (add ES).

1. color 2. cereal 3. capital 4. canal 5. tren 6. árbol *(tree)* 7. actor 8. animal 9. autor *(author)* 10. profesor 11. papel *(paper)*

LESSON 5

The Present Progressive Tense

THE PRESENT PROGRESSIVE TENSE

AR verbs

CANTAR, *to sing*

ESTOY CANTANDO *I am singing*	ESTAMOS CANTANDO *we are singing*
ESTÁ CANTANDO *you are singing* *he, she is singing* *it is singing*	ESTÁN CANTANDO *you (pl.) are singing* *they are singing*

Familiar form: tú estás cantando, *you are singing (familiar)*

CLASS: It is agreeable to say this little sing song: ING is ANDO. Then, repeat: singing is cantando, dancing is bailando, playing is jugando, etc.

Está nevando
It's snowing

5.1 *Remember These Words*

CLASS: Repeat each word or phrase, in unison, after your teacher says it in Spanish. No English, please.

la terraza, *the terrace*
los niños, *the children*
mi tía, *my aunt*
¿Quién? *Who?*
el secretario, *the secretary (masc.)*
la secretaria, *the secretary (fem.)*
está muy ocupada, *she is very busy*
el piloto, *the pilot*
su pipa, *his pipe*
en este momento, *at this moment*
divertido, *amusing (masc.)*
divertida, *amusing (fem.)*
en la fiesta, *at the party*
la novela, *the novel*
el espacio, *space*
está volando, *he, she is flying*
están preguntando, *they are asking (questions)*
está cantando, *he, she is singing*
los niños están jugando, *the children are playing*
está jugando bridge, *he, she is playing bridge*
están preparando la cena, *they are preparing dinner*
están trabajando, *they are working*
están limpiando, *they are cleaning*
estamos hablando, *we are talking*
mi tío está fumando, *my uncle is smoking*
¿qué está haciendo? *what are you doing? what is he, she doing?*
¿qué están haciendo? *what are they doing?*
están estudiando, *they are studying*
está tocando la guitarra, *he is playing the guitar*
están jugando, *they are playing (games)*
está dando, *he, she is giving*
está dictando, *he, she is dictating*
está contestando, *he, she is answering*
está nevando, *it is snowing*
está bailando, *he, she is dancing*

El piloto está volando

NOTE: JUGAR means to play a game.
TOCAR means to plan an instrument.

PRESENT PARTICIPLE

To form the Present Participle of AR Verbs, remove the AR from the Infinitive, and add ANDO.

IMPORTANT: The words ¿Qué está haciendo? are run together in Spanish. Pronounce them like this: kestasiendo. Repeat several times.

Está volando
en el espacio

5.2 *Speaking Exercise*

CLASS: Your teacher will point out individual students who will answer these questions. Read the answers in the book.

Examples: ¿Qué está haciendo su tío? *What is your uncle doing?*
Está trabajando. *He is working.*

1. ¿Qué está haciendo María?
   Está cantando en la terraza.
2. ¿Qué está haciendo su tío?
   Está fumando su pipa en el jardín.
3. ¿Qué están haciendo los niños?
   Están jugando en el jardín.
4. ¿Qué está haciendo papá?
   Está trabajando.
5. ¿Qué está haciendo el canario?
   El canario está cantando.
6. ¿Qué estamos haciendo en este momento?
   Estamos hablando español en este momento. Es muy divertido.
7. ¿Qué están haciendo Carlos y Bernardo?
   Están jugando béisbol.

8. ¿Está ocupada la profesora?
   Sí, la profesora está muy ocupada. Está dando una clase.
9. ¿Qué está haciendo su jefe (*boss*)?
   Está dictando una carta.
10. ¿Qué está haciendo la secretaria?
    Está contestando el teléfono.
11. ¿Está nevando? *Is it snowing?*
    No, no está nevando.
12. ¿Qué está haciendo Marta?
    Está bailando en la fiesta.
13. ¿Qué está haciendo Bernardo?
    Está tocando la guitarra.
14. ¿Qué está haciendo el piloto?
    Está volando en el espacio.

CLASS: Could you do the exercise above with books closed? Answer anything you wish, and make your answers as long as you can.

THE PRESENT PROGRESSIVE TENSE

ER, IR verbs

COMER, *to eat*

ESTOY COMIENDO *I am eating*	ESTAMOS COMIENDO *we are eating*
ESTÁ COMIENDO *you are eating* *he, she is eating*	ESTÁN COMIENDO *you (pl.) are eating* *they are eating*

Familiar form: tú estás comiendo, *you are eating (familiar)*

SUFRIR, *to suffer*

ESTOY SUFRIENDO *I am suffering*	ESTAMOS SUFRIENDO *we are suffering*
ESTÁ SUFRIENDO *you are suffering* *he, she is suffering* *it is suffering*	ESTÁN SUFRIENDO *you (pl.) are suffering* *they are suffering*

Familiar form: tú estás sufriendo, *you are suffering (familiar)*

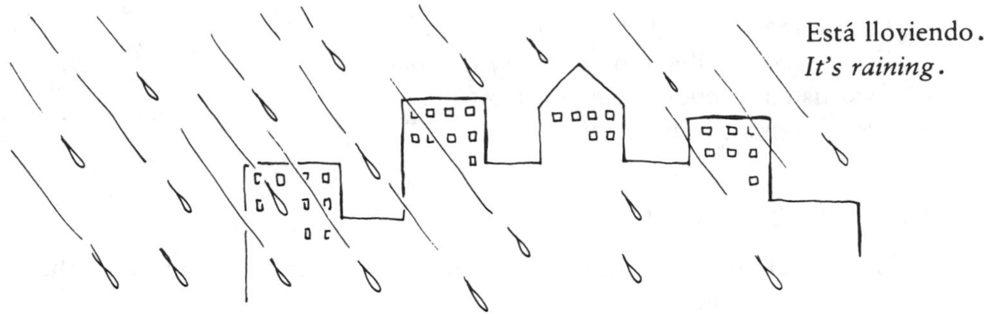

Está lloviendo.
It's raining.

5.3 *Exercise*

CLASS: Give the "I" form of the Present Progressive Tense of the following verbs, as indicated below.

Example: escribir, *to write.* Yo estoy escribiendo, *I am writing.*

1. correr, *to run*	4. aprender, *to learn*	7. recibir, *to receive*
2. comer, *to eat*	5. ver, *to see*	8. escribir, *to write*
3. ofrecer, *to offer*	6. vender, *to sell*	9. sufrir, *to suffer*

NOTE: LEYENDO *(reading)* is irregular.
Estoy leyendo. *I am reading.*

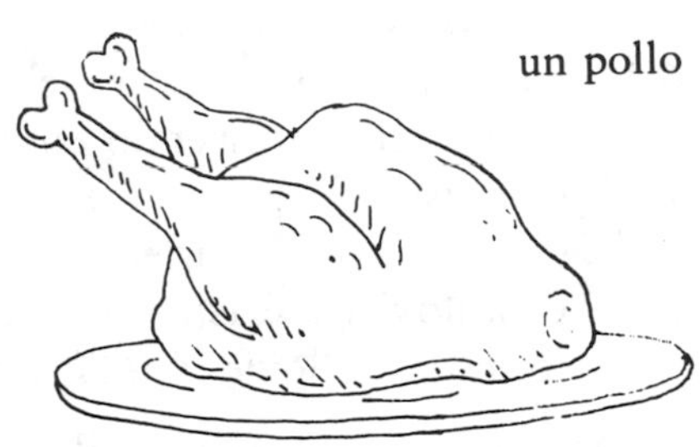

un pollo

5.4 *Remember These Words*

CLASS: Repeat each word or phrase, in unison, after your teacher says it in Spanish.

usted, *you (singular)*
ustedes, *you (plural)*
una silla, *a chair*
libro de español, *Spanish book*
sopa de pollo, *chicken soup*
una ensalada, *a salad*
para la cena, *for dinner*
una carta, *a letter*
¿Qué está haciendo? *What are you doing?*
Estoy haciendo una ensalada. *I am making a salad.*
haciendo, *doing, making*

¿Está usted corriendo? *Are you running?*
¿Está usted escribiendo? *Are you writing?*
¿Está usted leyendo? *Are you reading?*
Estoy leyendo. *I am reading.*

5.5 *Speaking Exercise*

STUDENT: Answer a question as your teacher calls on you. Read the answer in the book.

Examples: ¿Qué está haciendo? *What are you doing.*
Estoy haciendo una ensalada. *I am making a salad.*

1. ¿Qué está haciendo?
   Estoy haciendo café.
2. ¿Qué está haciendo?
   Estoy haciendo rosbif para la cena.
3. ¿Qué está haciendo Bárbara?
   Está haciendo sopa de pollo para la cena.
4. ¿Qué está haciendo el carpintero?
   El carpintero está haciendo una silla.
5. ¿Está usted escribiendo una carta?
   No, no estoy escribiendo una carta.
6. ¿Está usted corriendo en el parque?
   No, no estoy corriendo en el parque. Estoy en la clase.
7. ¿Está usted leyendo la lección?
   Sí, estoy leyendo la lección en el libro de español.
8. ¿Está lloviendo? *Is it raining?*
   No, no está lloviendo. Sí, está lloviendo.

CLASS: Could you answer the questions above with books closed?

5.6 *Vocabulary*

For the Detective Story below.

STUDENT: The following vocabulary will help you to understand the Detective Story.

1. La interrogación fue larga y complicada. *The questioning (interrogation) was long and complicated.* 2. El policía escribió. *The policeman wrote.* 3. María López, de dieciséis años de edad. *Mary López, (of) sixteen years of age.* 4. de veinte años de edad, *(of) twenty years*

of age 5. hermano, *brother* 6. declaran, *declare* 7. que un hombre entró en su casa, *that a man came into (entered) their house* 8. antes de las cinco de la mañana del doce de junio, *before five o'clock in the morning on the (of the) twelfth of June* 9. entró por la ventana de la cocina, *he came in (entered) through the kitchen window* 10. Fue a la sala. *He went to the living room.* 11. Rompió la cerradura de un escritorio. *He broke the lock of a desk.* 12. Se robó cinco hojas de papel. *He stole five sheets of paper.* 13. que tenían los diseños de un acumulador solar, *that had the designs of a solar battery* 14. que había inventado Roberto López, *that Robert López had invented* 15. para la fábrica donde trabaja, *for the factory where he works* 16. La Companía Metropolitana de Energía Solar, S.A. *The Metropolitan Company of Solar Energy, Inc.* 17. S.A. (Sociedad Anónima), *Incorporated (anonymous society)* 18. El policía escribió la descripción del coche. *The policeman wrote the description of the car.* 19. el número de la licencia, *the license number* 20. la descripción de los diseños, *the description of the designs* 21. y también del hombre que se los robó, *and also of the man who stole them* 22. El policía preguntó: "¿Dónde están sus padres?" *The policeman asked: "Where are your parents (fathers)?"* 23. María respondió: "En San Francisco" *Mary answered: "In San Francisco"* 24. "Ay, caramba," dijo el policía, *"Oh, gosh (gee-whiz)" said the policeman.* 25. durante la interrogación Roberto estaba muy impaciente, *during the questioning Robert was very impatient* 26. porque pasaba el tiempo y el ladrón se escapaba, *because time passed and the thief was escaping* 27. Por fin terminó la interrogación, *finally the questioning ended* 28. en el momento que el policía salió de la casa, *at the moment that the policeman left the house.* 29. María dijo, *Mary said* 30. ¿Qué crees?, what do you think? 31. ¿Quién se robó los diseños? *Who stole the designs?*

Note: In some countries the translation for license plate is "chapa," and in others it is "placa."

una hoja

una hoja de papel
a sheet (leaf) of paper

5.7 *Detective Story (Part 2)*

CLASS: Your teacher will read the Detective Story below for you. Sight-read in the book. Listen carefully.

ROBERTO Y MARÍA, DETECTIVES

La interrogación fue larga y complicada. El policía escribió: "María López, de dieciséis años de edad, y Roberto López, de veinte años de edad, hermano de María, declaran que un hombre entró en su casa antes de las cinco de la mañana del doce de junio. Entró por la ventana de la cocina. Fue a la sala. Rompió la cerradura de un escritorio. Se robó cinco hojas de papel que tenían los diseños de un acumulador solar que había inventado Roberto López para la fábrica donde trabaja, la Compañía Metropolitana de Energía Solar, S.A."

El policía escribió la descripción del coche, el número de la licencia, la descripción de los diseños y también del hombre que se los robó. El policía preguntó:

—¿Dónde están sus padres?

—En San Francisco.

—Ay, caramba—dijo el policía.

Durante la interrogación Roberto estaba muy impaciente porque pasaba el tiempo y el ladrón se escapaba. Por fin terminó la interrogación. En el momento que el policá salió de la casa, María dijo:

—¿Qué crees? ¿Quién se robó los diseños? *(To be continued)*

5.8 *Reading Exercise*

CLASS: Your teacher will point out individual students who will read a sentence aloud in the Detective Story above. Read it as smoothly as you can, in a loud, clear voice.

5.9 *Vocabulary*

For the Conversation below.

CLASS: Repeat each word or phrase, in unison, after your teacher says it in Spanish.

Some verbs in the Present Tense are followed by the Present Progressive Tense.

Examples:
CREO QUE, *I think (believe) that*
DICE QUE, *he, she says that*
Roberto dice que está trabajando. *Robert says that he is working.*
María dice que está nadando. *Mary says that he is swimming.*
Creo que está trabajando demasiado. *I think that you are working too much.*
¿Qué dice Roberto? *What does Robert say?*
¿Dónde está Ricardo? *Where is Richard?*
Mi tía, *my aunt*

El ladrón entró por la ventana de la cocina.

5.10 *Conversation*

CLASS: Your teacher will select students, two by two, who will go to the front of the class and conduct a conversation. Take your book with you, and begin by reading the questions and answers in the block. Then, close your book, and have a conversation of your own. Speak in natural tones. Use your acting skills.

WHAT MY FRIENDS ARE DOING

First student —¿Qué dice Roberto?
Second student—Dice que está trabajando.
First student —¿Qué dice María?
Second student—Dice que está estudiando.
First student —¿Dónde está Ricardo?
Second student—Creo que está nadando.
First student —¿Qué dice Bárbara?
Second student—Dice que está comiendo.
First student —Creo que David está comiendo también.

Second student—¿Qué dice Juan?
First student —Dice que está tocando la guitarra.
Second student—¿Qué dice Carmen?
First student —Dice que está preparando la lección.
Second student—¿Dónde está mi tía?
First student —Creo que está jugando tenis.

5.11 *Exercise*

Answer these questions:

1. ¿Está cantando María? 2. ¿Está trabajando su papá? 3. ¿Está estudiando Roberto? 4. ¿Está usted escribiendo? 5. ¿Está usted estudiando? 6. ¿Está usted ocupado (ocupada)? 7. ¿Está ocupada la profesora? 8. ¿Está ocupado el profesor? 9. ¿Está escribiendo la secretaria? 10. ¿Está nevando? 11. ¿Está lloviendo? 12. ¿Qué está haciendo usted?

LESSON 6

The Past Progressive Tense

THE PAST PROGRESSIVE TENSE

CANTAR, *to sing*

estaba cantando *I was singing*	estábamos cantando *we were singing*
estaba cantando *you were singing*	estaban cantando *they were singing*

Examples: estábamos cantando, *we were singing*
estaban corriendo, *they were running*
estaba volando, *I was flying*
you were flying,
he was flying,
she was flying,
it was flying

un pescado

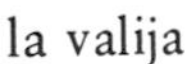

la valija

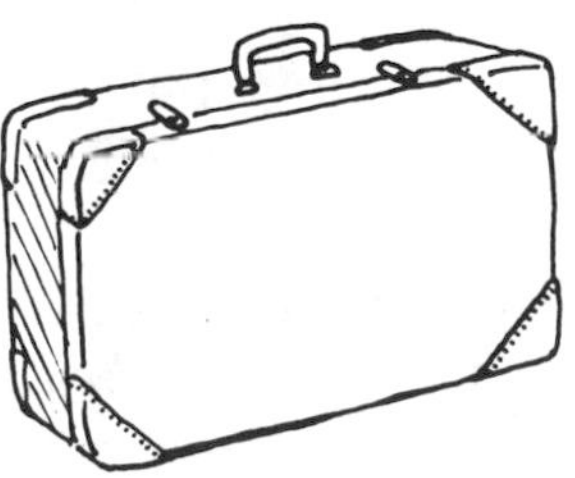

6.1 *Remember These Words*

CLASS: Repeat these words and phrases, in unison, after the teacher says them in Spanish. Do not use English. Only look at the meaning of each word.

el perro, *the dog*
la valija, *the suitcase*
la cena, *dinner*
una carta, *a letter*
un poema, *a poem*
mi primo, *my cousin (masc.)*
mi prima, *my cousin (fem.)*
comiendo, *eating*
en el río, *in the river*
discos mexicanos, *Mexican records*
dulces, *candy*
un coctel de frutas, *a fruit cocktail*
en el parque, *in the park*
un pescado, *a fish*
su tía, *your aunt*

Roberto estaba estudiando. *Robert was studying.*
Estaba haciendo una ensalada. *I was making a salad.*
Marta estaba escribiendo. *Martha was writing.*
Mi tía estaba jugando. *My aunt was playing (a game).*
Yo estaba tocando. *I was playing (an instrument).*
Papá estaba comiendo. *Dad was eating.*
coser, *to sew*
¿Quién estaba cosiendo? *Who was sewing?*
Roberto estaba pescando en el río. *Robert was fishing in the river.*
Estaba hablando por teléfono. *I, he, she was talking on the phone.*
Estaba empacando la valija. *I was packing the suitcase.*
Estaba nadando. *I was swimming.*
Estaba caminando en el parque. *I was walking in the park.*

ENTRÉ
I came in,
I went in

ENTRÓ
you, he, she came in
you, he, she went in

LLEGUÉ
I arrived
got there

LLEGÓ
you, he, she arrived,
got here, got there

VINE
I came

VINO
you, he, she, it came

cuando entré, *when I came in, when I went in*
cuando llegué, *when I arrived, got here, got there*
cuando vine, *when I came*

cuando entró, *when you came in, went in*
cuando llegó, *when you, he, she, it arrived, got here, got there*

6.2 *Hearing Exercise*

CLASS: Repeat each sentence, in unison, after the teacher says it in Spanish.

1. Roberto estaba estudiando cuando entré.
   Robert was studying when I went in.
2. Susana estaba haciendo la cena cuando llegué.
   Susan was making dinner when I arrived.
3. Luis estaba escribiendo una carta cuando vine.
   Louis was writing a letter when I came.
4. Marta estaba tocando discos mexicanos.
5. Mi tía estaba jugando con el perro cuando llegué.
6. Juan estaba haciendo café cuando entré.
7. Mi primo estaba haciendo dulces cuando llegué.
8. Mamá estaba empacando la valija cuando entré.
9. Papá estaba comiendo cuando vine.
10. Yo estaba haciendo un coctel de frutas cuando entró.
11. Estaba caminando en el parque cuando llegó.
12. Mi prima estaba leyendo un libro cuando entré.

REMEMBER that HACIENDO means both "doing" and "making."

6.3 *Speaking Exercise*

CLASS: Answer these questions when your teacher calls on you. Read the answers in the book.

Examples:
¿Qué estaba haciendo cuando llegué?
What were you doing when I arrived?
Estaba escribiendo una carta.
I was writing a letter.

1. ¿Qué estaba haciendo cuando llegué?
   Estaba preparando un pescado para la cena.
2. ¿Qué estaba haciendo cuando vine?
   Estaba estudiando la lección de español.
3. ¿Qué estaba haciendo cuando entré?
   Estaba escribiendo una carta.

4. ¿Qué estaba haciendo cuando su tío entró?
   What were you doing when your uncle came in?
   Estaba tocando el violín.
5. ¿Qué estaba haciendo cuando Roberto llegó?
   Estaba pescando en el río.
6. ¿Qué estaba haciendo cuando María llegó?
   Estaba empacando la valija.
7. ¿Qué estaba haciendo cuando Bernardo llegó?
   Estaba haciendo café.
8. ¿Qué estaba haciendo cuando Carlos entró?
   Estaba hablando por teléfono.
9. ¿Qué estaba haciendo cuando su tía llegó?
   Estaba caminando en el parque.
10. ¿Qué estaba haciendo cuando Alicia llegó?
    Estaba nadando.
11. ¿Quién estaba nadando?
    Susana estaba nadando.

6.4 *Exercise*

CLASS: Give the three forms of a verb, as shown in the example below:

Example: hablar, *to speak:*

estaba hablando	estábamos hablando	estaban hablando
I was speaking	*we were speaking*	*they were speaking*

1. volar, *to fly*
2. nadar, *to swim*
3. empacar, *to pack*
4. pescar, *to fish*
5. comer, *to eat*
6. hacer, *to do, to make*
7. tocar, *to play (an instrument)*
8. lavar, *to wash*
9. besar, *to kiss*
10. abrazar, *to hug*

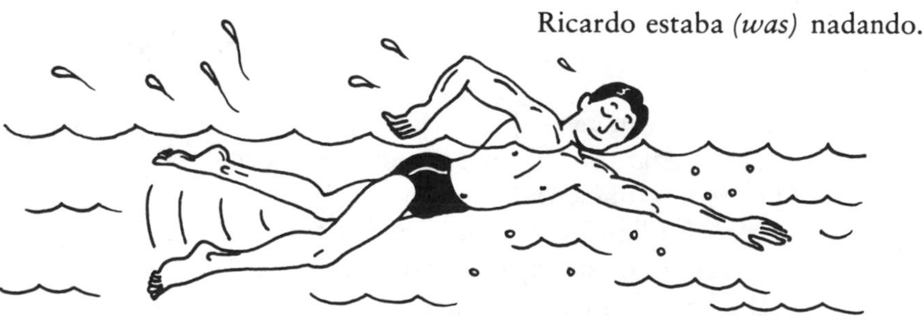

Ricardo estaba *(was)* nadando.

DIJO QUE, *he said that, she said that, you said that*
DIJO QUE is used with the Past Progressive Tense.

Examples:
Roberto dijo que estaba estudiando español.
Robert said that he was studying Spanish.
Juan dijo que estaba pescando.
John said that he was fishing.
Margarita dijo que su papá estaba comiendo.
Margaret said that your father was eating.

6.5 *Remember These Words*

CLASS: Repeat each word or phrase, in unison, after your teacher says it in Spanish.

demasiado, *too much*
comprometidos, *engaged*
en el río, *in the river*
en el parque, *in the park*

Estaban enamorados. *They were in love (enamored).*
Bernardo se enamoró de Susana. *Bernard fell in love with Susan.*
Susana se enamoró de Bernardo. *Susan fell in love with Bernard.*
Están comprometidos. *They are engaged.*
No lo sabía. *I didn't know it. (Imperfect)*
Me enamoré de la música. *I fell in love with music.*
Ricardo dijo que estaba progresando. *Richard said that he was progressing.*
Marta dijo que estaba estudiando. *Martha said that she was studying.*
dijo que estaba nadando, *he said that he was swimming*
dijo que estaba pescando, *he said that he was fishing*
Papá dijo que Luis estaba trabajando demasiado. *Dad said that Louis was working too much.*
Carmen dijo que Bernardo estaba besando a Susana. *Carmen said that Bernard was kissing Susan.*
Bernardo dijo que estaba enamorado. *Bernard said that he was in love.*

6.6 *Hearing Exercise*

CLASS: Repeat each sentence, in unison, after your teacher says it in Spanish.

1. Marta dijo que estaba estudiando español.
2. Ricardo dijo que estaba progresando mucho en la clase.
3. Juan dijo que estaba nadando en el río.
4. Ricardo dijo que estaba pescando en el río.
5. Carmen dijo que Bernardo estaba besando a Susana en el parque.
6. Están enamorados.
7. Bernardo se enamoró de Susana.
8. Susana se enamoró de Bernardo.
9. Están comprometidos.
10. No lo sabía.
11. Bernardo dijo que estaba enamorado.
12. Susana dijo que estaba enamorada.

REMEMBER:
ESTABA means: *I was, you were, he was, she was, it was*
Estaba estudiando, *I was studying, you were studying, he was studying, she was studying*

6.7 *Creating Sentences*

CLASS: Repeat the words in the two columns below after your teacher says them in Spanish. Then, each student will combine words from the two columns to form a complete sentence. Create your own sentences.

DIJO QUE, *you said that, he said that, she said that* DIJE QUE *I said that*	estaba estudiando estaba cantando estaba pescando estaba comiendo estaba escribiendo estaba progresando tú estabas nadando (familiar) estaba leyendo estaba trabajando estaba jugando estaba corriendo *(was, were running)* estaba volando *(was, were flying)* estaba empacando *(was, were packing)* estaba ocupado *(he was busy)* estaba ocupada *(she was busy)*

6.8 *Vocabulary*

For the Conversation below.

CLASS: Repeat each word or phrase, in unison, after your teacher says it in Spanish.

1. ¿Qué dijo? *What did you say? What did he say? What did she say?*
2. Dijo que estaba ocupado. *You said that you were busy, he said that he was busy.*
3. Dijo que estaba enamorado. *He said that he was in love.*
4. Hablando por teléfono, *talking on the phone.*
5. Caminando en el parque, *walking in the park.*

REMEMBER: Use masculine adjectives when you are speaking of a man or a boy (end the adjectives in the letter O). Use feminine adjectives when you are speaking of a woman or a girl (end the adjectives in the letter A).

Examples: Roberto dijo que estaba ocupado. *Robert said that he was busy.*
María dijo que estaba ocupada. *Mary said that she was busy.*

Roberto estaba pescando.

6.9 *Conversation*

CLASS: The teacher will select students, two by two, who will conduct a conversation. The blocks below will serve you as a guide. Use your acting skills.

ASKING AND TELLING WHAT PEOPLE SAID

First student —¿Qué dijo Ricardo?
Second student—Dijo que estaba estudiando.
First student —¿Qué dijo Bárbara?
Second student—Dijo que estaba jugando tenis.
First student —Carlos dijo que estaba ocupado.
Second student—¿Qué dijo su tío?
First student —Dijo que estaba trabajando.
Second student—¿Qué dijo Susana?
First student —Dijo que estaba empacando.
Second student—¿Qué dijo Juan?
First student —Dijo que estaba haciendo café.
Second student—¿Qué dijo Bernardo?
First student —Dijo que estaba enamorado.
Second student—¿Qué dijo Carmen?
First student —Dijo que Bernardo estaba besando a Susana en el parque.

CLASS: Continue the Conversations, asking and telling what people said.

Examples:
¿Qué dijo Roberto? *What did Robert say?*
¿Qué dijo . . . ? *(use any name you wish)*
Dijo que estaba . . . , *He said that he was, she said that she was. . . .*

6.10 *Answer these questions*

1. ¿Estaba estudiando María? 2. ¿Estaba haciendo la cena Susana? 3. ¿Estaba tocando el violín María? 4. ¿Estaba pescando en el río Roberto? 5. ¿Estaba haciendo café su tío? 6. ¿Estaba usted estudiando? 7. ¿Estaba usted empacando la valija? 8. ¿Estaba usted escribiendo una carta? 9. ¿Estaba usted hablando por teléfono? 10. ¿Estaba nadando Susana?

Translate these sentences into Spanish:

11. He said that he was studying. 12. She said that she was progressing. 13. I said that I was working. 14. She said that she was making sandwiches.

Elena estaba caminando.

6.11 *Vocabulary*

For the Detective Story below.

CLASS: The following Vocabulary will help you to understand the Detective Story.

1. ¿Quién se robó los diseños? *Who stole the designs?* 2. Roberto contestó, *Roberto answered* 3. ahora que lo pienso, *now that I think of it* 4. creo que he visto al ladrón antes, *I think that I have seen the thief before* 5. hace un mes, *a month ago* 6. yo estaba en el despacho de la fábrica en el segundo piso, *I was in the office at the factory on the second floor* 7. dictando una carta, *dictating a letter* 8. cuando entró mi jefe, *when my boss came in* 9. y dijo, *and said* 10. No quiero interrumpir. *I don't want to interrupt.* 11. Yo continué dictando. *I continued dictating.* 12. mi jefe fue a la ventana, *my boss went to the window* 13. y después de un momento, dijo, *and, after a moment, he said* 14. ¿Quién es ese hombre que está tomando notas? *Who is that man who is taking notes?* 15. fui a la ventana, *I went to the window* 16. y vi a un hombre pasando de tractor a tractor, *and saw a man passing from tractor to tractor* 17. escribiendo notas en una libreta, *writing notes in a little notebook* 18. mi jefe dijo, *my boss said* 19. yo no conozco a ese hombre. *I don't know that man.* 20. ¿Usted lo conoce? *Do you know him?* 21. dije que no, *I said that I didn't (I said "no")* 22. mi jefe habló por teléfono al guardia, *my boss called up the guard* 23. de la entrada de la fábrica,

at the entrance of the factory 24. ¿Quién es ese hombre que está pasando de tractor a tractor tomando notas? *Who is that man who is passing from tractor to tractor taking notes?* 25. el guardia dijo, *the guard said* 26. Voy a ver, señor, *I'll see, sir (I'm going to see, sir)* 27. de la ventana del segundo piso, *from the window of the second floor* 28. vimos al guardia correr hacia el hombre, *we saw the guard run toward the man* 29. el guardia gritó, "¡Ven acá!"; *the guard shouted, "come here!"* 30. En un instante, el ladrón entró en un coche. *In an instant, the thief got in (went into) a car.* 31. y salió por la entrada de la fábrica, *and left (went out) through the entrance of the factory* 32. a todo motor, *full speed ahead (all motor)* 33. le, *to you, to him, to her* 34. le dijo, *told him, told her, said to him, said to her*

6.12 *Detective Story (Part 3)*

CLASS: Your teacher will read the Detective Story below for you. Sight-read in the book. Listen carefully.

ROBERTO Y MARÍA, DETECTIVES

—¿Quién se robó los diseños?

—Ahora que lo pienso—contestó Roberto—creo que he visto al ladrón antes. Hace un mes, yo estaba en el despacho de la fábrica, en el segundo piso, dictando una carta, cuando entró mi jefe y dijo: "No quiero interrumpir." Yo continué dictando. Mi jefe fue a la ventana y, después de un momento, dijo: "¿Quién es ese hombre que está tomando notas?"

Fui a la ventana y vi a un hombre pasando de tractor a tractor, escribiendo notas en una libreta. "Yo no conozco a ese hombre," dijo mi jefe, "¿usted lo conoce?"

Dije que no. Y mi jefe habló por teléfono al guardia de la entrada de la fábrica y le dijo: "¿Quién es ese hombre que está pasando de tractor a tractor y tomando notas?" El guardia dijo: "Voy a ver, señor."

6.13 *Reading Exercise*

CLASS: Your teacher will point out individual students who will read one sentence in the story above. Read in a loud, clear voice. Read as smoothly as you can.

6.14 *Translating Exercise (Optional)*

CLASS: Your teacher will point out individual students who will read one sentence in the story above, and translate it into English, or translate an English phrase from the vocabulary into Spanish.

CREÍ, *I thought* (preterite)
CREÍ QUE, *I thought that*

1. CREÍ QUE is used with the Imperfect Tense.
   Example: Creí que tenía un piano. *I thought you had a piano.*
2. CREÍ QUE is used with the Past Progressive Tense.
   Example: Creí que estaba nadando. *I thought you were swimming.*

6.15 *Creating Sentences*

CLASS: Repeat the words in the columns below after your teacher reads them in Spanish. Then, each student will combine words from each column to form complete sentences. Create your own sentences.

CREÍ QUE
I thought that

IMPERFECT TENSE

tenía
you, he, she had
estaba
you were; he, she was
hablaba
you, he, she spoke
vivía
you, he, she lived
escribía
you, he, she wrote

PAST PROGRESSIVE TENSE

estaba trabajando
you were working; she, he was working
estaba comiendo
you were eating; she, he was eating
estaba nadando
estaba lavando
estaba empacando

en Colombia
una guitarra
en casa, *at home*
con su hermano, *with his brother*
inglés
tiempo, *time*
muchas cartas, *many letters*
los platos, *the dishes*
un coctel de frutas
cartas, *letters*
la valija, *the suitcase*
un artículo
en el río, *in the river*
en el parque
sopa
en casa

CLASS: Please close your books. See how many of the sentences above you can repeat by heart, or how many sentences using CREÍ QUE you can invent.

6.16 *Speed Reading Exercise*

CLASS: The teacher will guide you in reading sentences from the Speaking Exercise in LESSON 4 (4.3) as a Speed Reading Exercise. Read aloud, as quickly as you can.

LESSON 7

Stresses and Accents

1. You stress a letter with your voice.
2. Accents are written. When you see a written accent, stress the accented letter with your voice. Example: café
3. The Spanish words for WHAT, WHEN, HOW, WHERE, WHICH, and WHO take a written accent in questions and exclamations. It is difficult to remember to write accents on all of these. For that reason, students call them "the little stinkers."

LEARN these words by heart:

1. ¿Qué? *What?*
2. ¿Cuándo? *When?*
3. ¿Cómo? *How?*
4. ¿Dónde? *Where?*
5. ¿Quién? *Who?*
6. ¿Cuál? *Which? (which one?)*

ALWAYS write accents on the above words when they are used in questions or exclamations.

CLASS: Your teacher will call on individual students to repeat the six words above and give the meaning by heart.

7.1 *Everyday Expressions*

CLASS: Repeat these expressions after your teacher says them in Spanish. Copy these expressions in your notebook. Learn them.

¿Qué pasó? *What happened?*
¿Cuándo pasó? *When did it happen?*

¿Cómo pasó? *How did it happen?*
¿Dónde pasó? *Where did it happen?*
¿Quién sabe? *Who knows?*
¿Cuál es? *Which is it?*
¿Cómo se llama usted? *What is your name? (What are you called?)*
¿Qué pasó? *What happened?*
¿Cuánto? *How much? How much does it cost?*
¿Dónde está el teatro? *Where is the theater?*

¡Qué terrible! *How terrible!*
¡Qué raro! *How strange! (How rare!)*
¡Qué lindo! *How beautiful!*
¡Qué bueno! *How good! What a good thing!*
¡Qué feo! *How ugly!*
¡Qué día! *What a day!*
¡Qué sol! *How sunny it is! (What a sun!)*
¡Qué miedo! *How scary! (What fear!)*
¡Cómo nada! *How she (he) swims!*
¡Cómo duele! *How it hurts!*

STRESSES AND ACCENTS

1. In general, the stress is as follows: When a Spanish word ends in A, E, I, O, U, stress the next to the last syllable. Examples: CA-sa, tra-BA-jo, JE-fe, RO-sa.
2. When a word ends in N or S, stress the next to the last syllable. Examples: CA-sas, res-tau-RAN-tes, tra-BA-jan.
3. When a word ends in any letter except A, E, I, O, U or the letters N or S, stress the last syllable. Examples: ca-NAL, pa-PEL, fa-VOR, a-ves-TRUZ *(ostrich)*.

   Therefore, all infinitives are stressed on the last syllable. Examples: a-bra-ZAR *(to hug)*, be-SAR *(to kiss)*.
4. Any word which does not follow the above rules has a written accent. Examples: azúcar, limón, atracción, teléfono, café.
5. Words which receive the stress BEFORE the next to the last syllable have a written accent. Examples: espárragos, Atlántico, ridículo, muchísimo, música.

Hola Luis. Ven acá.
Hi, Louis. Come here.

7.2 *Exercises*

A. Translate into Spanish:

1. What happened in the park? 2. Who knows? 3. Where did it happen? 4. Where is the telephone? 5. It's ridiculous. 6. Which is it? 7. How he swims!

IMPORTANT: Did you remember the accent marks?

B. Form logical sentences with the words below:

1. El presidente llevaba	un vestido blanco
2. El ladrón llevaba	una blusa linda
3. El policía llevaba	zapatos de tenis
4. La enfermera llevaba	un traje gris
5. El ranchero montaba	un sombrero con rosas
6. La señorita llevaba	a caballo
7. María llevaba	un uniforme azul

7.3 *Vocabulary*

For the Conversation below.

This Vocabulary illustrates how written accents are used on the word QUÉ in questions and exclamations.

CLASS: Repeat each sentence, in unison, after your teacher says it in Spanish.

1. ¡Qué linda está la playa! *How lovely the beach is!* 2. Sí, hoy está fantástica. *Yes, today it is fantastic.* 3. ¿Estás contento? *Are you happy? (masc.)* 4. ¿Estás contenta? *Are you happy? (fem.)* 5. ¿Y tú? *And you? (familiar)* 6. Yo también. *I too. (me too)* 7. Estoy encantado. *I'm delighted (enchanted) (masc.).* 8. Estoy encantada. *I'm delighted (fem.).* 9. Es un día lindo. ¿No? *It's a lovely day. Isn't it?* 10. precioso, *simply beautiful* 11. ¡Qué sol! *What a sun!* 12. ¿Quieres nadar? *Do you want to swim?* 13. Vamos a nadar. *Let's swim.* 14. El agua está fresca. ¿No? *The water is cool. Isn't it?* 15. El agua está fría. *The water is cold.* 16. No quiero entrar. *I don't want to go in.* 17. ¡Ven! *Come!* 18. ¡Ven pronto! *Come quickly!* 19. ¡Ay, caramba! *Oh, gee-whiz!* 20. ¡Qué frío! *How cold it is!* 21. Después de unos momentos está bien. *After a few moments it's O.K.* 22. ¡Caramba! ¡Cómo nadas! *Gee-whiz! How you swim!* 23. ¡Mira! Aquí está un pececito (diminutive) *Look! Here is a little fish.* 24. ¡Ay, qué lindo! *Oh, how beautiful!* 25. Nada muy aprisa. *It swims very fast.* 26. Mejor que yo. *Better than I (do).* 27. Claro. *Of course.* 28. Tú no eres pececito. *You are not a little fish (familiar).*

la playa

7.4 *Conversation*

CLASS: Your teacher will select students, two by two, who will go to the front of the class and conduct a conversation. The blocks below will serve you as a guide. Take your books with you, and begin by reading the block in the book. Then, close the book and try a conversation on your own. Speak with enthusiasm. This is your chance to practice acting, as if you were on the stage.

A DAY AT THE BEACH

First student —¡Qué linda está la playa!
Second student—Sí, hoy está fantástica.
First student —¿Estás contento (contenta)?
Second student—Sí, estoy muy contento (contenta). ¿Y tú?
First student —Sí, yo también. Estoy encantado (encantada).
Second student—Es un día lindo. ¿No?
First student —Sí, precioso. ¡Qué sol!
Second student—¿Quieres nadar?
First student —Sí, vamos a nadar. El agua está fresca. ¿No?
Second student—Sí, está muy fresca y transparente.

First student —Ay, el agua está fría.
Second student—Sí, muy fría. No quiero entrar.
First student —Sí, ven. ¡Ven pronto!
Second student—¡Ay, caramba! Brr. ¡Qué frío!
First student —Después de unos momentos está bien. ¡Caramba! ¡Cómo nadas!
Second student—¡Mira! Aquí está un pececito.
First student —¡Ay, qué lindo! Nada muy aprisa. Nada mejor que yo.
Second student—Claro. Tú no eres pececito.

7.5 *Vocabulary*

For the Detective Story below.

CLASS: Repeat each word or phrase below, in unison, after your teacher says it in Spanish. You will not be expected to learn all of these words.

1. en un instante el ladrón entró en un coche; *in an instant the thief got into a car* 2. salió por la entrada de la fábrica a todo motor, *he left by the entrance of the factory, full speed ahead* 3. el guardia lo persiguió, *the guard pursued him* 4. continuó, *he continued* 5. por muchas calles, *by many streets* 6. hasta que llegó al campo, *until he got to the country* 7. el guardia tras de él, *the guard after him* 8. después de unos veinte kilómetros, *after about twenty kilometers* 9. llegaron a un cerro que tenía rocas enormes, *they got to a hill that had enormous rocks* 10. árboles y arbustos, *trees and bushes* 11. el coche desapareció en una curva, *the car disappeared on a curve* 12. buscó entre los árboles, *he searched among the trees* 13. pero no encontró al hombre, *but he didn't find the man* 14. en la tarde de ese mismo día, *on the afternoon of that same day* 15. todos se esparcieron entre los árboles, *they all dispersed (spread out) among the trees* 16. pero no encontraron al hombre, *but they didn't find the man* 17. varios detectives hicieron una investigación, *several detectives made an investigation* 18. buscaron huellas, *they looked for tracks* 19. pero no encontraron nada, *but they didn't find anything* 20. nunca encontraron al hombre ni su coche, *they never found the man nor his car* 21. después del incidente, *after the incident* 22. escribieron una descripción del ladrón, *they wrote a description of the thief* 23. era un hombre delgado, *he was a thin man.* 24. pelo negro, *black hair* 25. ojos negros, *dark (black) eyes.* 26. bajo de estatura, *short in stature* 27. llevaba, *he was wearing.*

7.6 *Detective Story (Part 4)*

CLASS: Your teacher will read the Detective Story below for you. Sight-read in the book. Listen carefully.

ROBERTO Y MARÍA, DETECTIVES

En un instante el ladrón entró en un coche y salió por la entrada de la fábrica a todo motor. El guardia lo persiguió en su coche. El ladrón continuó a toda velocidad por muchas calles hasta que llegó al campo. Y el guardia tras de él.

Después de unos veinte kilómetros llegaron a un cerro que tenía rocas enormes, árboles, y arbustos. El coche desapareció en una curva. El guardia salió de su coche, buscó entre los árboles y las rocas, pero no encontró al hombre.

En la tarde de ese mismo día, unos policías y detectives regresaron al cerro. Todos se esparcieron entre los árboles y las rocas, pero no encontraron al hombre. Varios detectives hicieron una investigación. Buscaron huellas del auto o del hombre, pero no encontraron nada. Nunca encontraron al hombre ni su coche.

Después del incidente, el jefe, el guardia, y Roberto escribieron una descripción del ladrón para la policía. "Era un hombre delgado, de pelo negro, ojos negros, bajo de estatura. Llevaba un suéter azul, pantalones grises, y zapatos de tenis." (To be continued)

7.7 *Reading Exercise*

CLASS: Your teacher will point out individual students who will read one sentence at a time in the story above. Read in a loud, clear voice. Read as smoothly as you can.

7.8 *Translating Exercise (optional)*

CLASS: Repeat each word or phrase that follows, in unison, after your teacher says it in Spanish. You will not be expected to learn all of these words.

REMEMBER: Use ERA *(was)* for occupations: Era doctor, *he was a doctor.*

7.9 *Exercises*

A. Translate:

1. He was a pilot. 2. She was a carpenter. 3. Albert was a doctor. 4. Alicia was a nurse. 5. I was a student. 6. I was not an actor.

B. Answer these questions:

1. ¿Estaba linda la playa? 2. ¿Quiere usted nadar? 3. ¿Está usted volando? 4. ¿Está usted hablando? 5. ¿Está usted escribiendo frases? 6. ¿Escribía bien Shakespeare? 7. ¿Estaba escribiendo Shakespeare en su clase? 8. ¿Estaba el presidente en su clase o en la Casa Blanca? 9. ¿Estaba cantando el paciente durante la operación en el hospital? 10. ¿Estaba aplaudiendo el doctor durante la operación? 11. ¿Estaba muy ocupado el doctor? 12. ¿Estaba muy ocupada la enfermera? 13. ¿Está usted trabajando en el banco en este momento? 14. ¿Estaba fría el agua?

HOW TO FORM THE COMPARATIVE

To form the comparative in Spanish, use the word MÁS *(more)* before EVERY regular adjective.

caro, *expensive (masc.)* más caro, *more expensive*
cara, *expensive (fem.)* más cara, *more expensive*
alto, *tall (masc.)* más alto, *taller*
alta, *tall (fem.)* más alta, *taller*

7.10 *Exercise*

Give the comparative of the following adjectives (use the word MÁS before each adjective).

1. barato, *cheap* 2. bonito, *pretty* 3. alta, *tall* 4. grande, *big* 5. bonita, *pretty* 6. blanco, *white* 7. amarillo, *yellow* 8. amarilla, *yellow* 9. feo, *ugly* 10. caro, *expensive* 11. verde, *green*

USE OF THE COMPARATIVE

Learn:

más caro QUE, *more expensive than*
más barato QUE, *cheaper than*
Es más verde QUE, *It's greener than*
Mi hermano es más alto que Luis. *My brother is taller than Louis.*
María es más bonita que Pancho. *Mary is prettier than Pancho.*

Irregular comparatives are not formed with MÁS *(more)*.

Examples: bueno, *good* mejor, *better*
malo, *bad* peor, *worse*

7.11 *Exercise*

Translate these words:

1. It's better than 2. It's worse than 3. It's more expensive than (masc.) 4. It's more expensive than (fem.) 5. It's taller than (masc.) 6. It's uglier than (masc.) 7. It's cheaper than (masc.) 8. It's cheaper than (fem.) 9. It's yellower than (masc.) 10. It's prettier than (fem.)

LESSON 8

Use of the Present Tense

PRESENT TENSE
verb endings

AR

o	amos
a	an

ER

o	emos
e	en

IR

o	imos
e	en

Example:

comprar, *to buy*

I buy	compro	compramos	*we buy*
you buy	compra	compran	*they buy*

8.1 *Exercises*

A. CLASS: Make charts of the Present Tense of the following verbs:

Example: pintar, *to paint*

pinto	pintamos
pinta	pintan

1. nadar, *to swim* 2. besar, *to kiss* 3. vender, *to sell* 4. comprender, *to understand* 5. vivir, *to live* 6. escribir, *to write* 7. abrazar, *to hug*

B. CLASS: Your teacher will give you one of the seven Infinitives above. Read your chart of that verb to your teacher to see if it is correct.

8.2 *Verb Exercise*

CLASS: Give the correct Present Tense form of the verbs in the sentences below. Read the whole sentence.

1. Alberto (nadar) ________ en el club.
2. Yo (comprender) ________ la lección muy bien.
3. Mi tío Luis (vivir) ________ en la América Central.
4. Bernardo (besar) ________ a Susana.
5. El doctor (comprender) ________ la situación perfectamente.
6. ¿Dónde (vivir) ________ usted?
7. Yo (vivir) ________ en una casa.
8. Carmen (vender) ________ autos en la agencia.
9. Yo (escribir) ________ muchas composiciones para la clase.
10. Mi tío me (escribir) ________ muchas cartas.
11. Bernardo (abrazar) ________ a Susana.

REMEMBER to stress Present Tense verbs on the next to the last syllable: PIN-ta, pin-TA-mos, PIN-tan

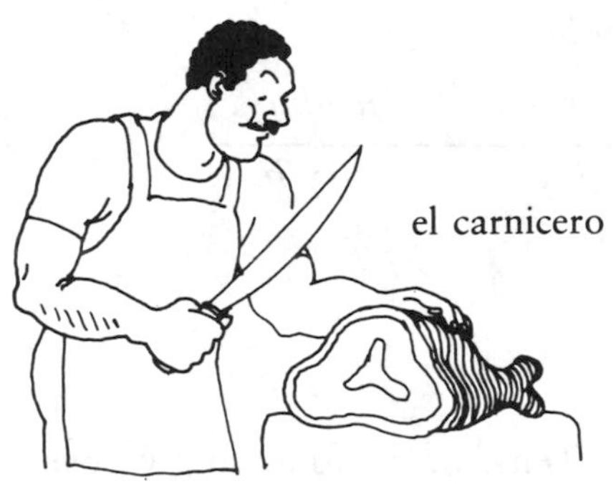

el carnicero

el zapatero

8.3 *Remember These Words*

CLASS: Repeat each word or phrase, in unison, after your teacher says it in Spanish. No English, please.

la basura, *the garbage*
el pintor, *the painter*
la pintura, *the painting*
bien, *well*
divertida, *amusing (fem.)*
la enfermera, *the nurse*
los enfermos, *sick people*

el panadero, *the baker*
la panadería, *the bakery*
la carne, *meat*
el carnicero, *the butcher*
la carnicería, *the butcher shop*
lavan la ropa, *they wash the clothes*

¿estudia usted? *do you study?*
estudio, *I study*
¿pinta usted? *do you paint?*
¿quién pinta? *who paints?*
saco, *I take out*
¿saca? *do you take out?*
¿baila usted? *do you dance?*
la clase de pintura, *the painting class*
la lavandería, *the laundry*
zapatos, *shoes*
zapatería, *shoe shop*
banquero, *banker*
voy, *I go*
¿va? *do you go?*
¿quién? *who?*
también, *also, too*

¿dónde trabaja la enfermera? *where does the nurse work?*
¿con quién trabaja? *with whom does she work?*
cortar, *to cut*
el carnicero corta la carne, *the butcher cuts the meat*
el carnicero vende, *the butcher sells*
¿Va usted a la carnicería? *Do you go to the butcher shop?*
Sí, voy a la carnicería. *Yes, I go to the butcher shop.*
¿le gusta? *do you like?*
¿le gusta la clase? *do you like the class?*

8.4 *Pronunciation Exercise*

Many of the words in Spanish for occupations are very similar to the ones in English and you already know them. Read the following out loud. Pronounce carefully.

piloto, mecánico, profesora, secretario, general, fotógrafo, carpintero, electricista, actor, profesor, inventor, pintor, naturalista, economista, artista, dentista, turista, pianista, violinista, guitarrista, florista, comediante, estudiante, veterinario.

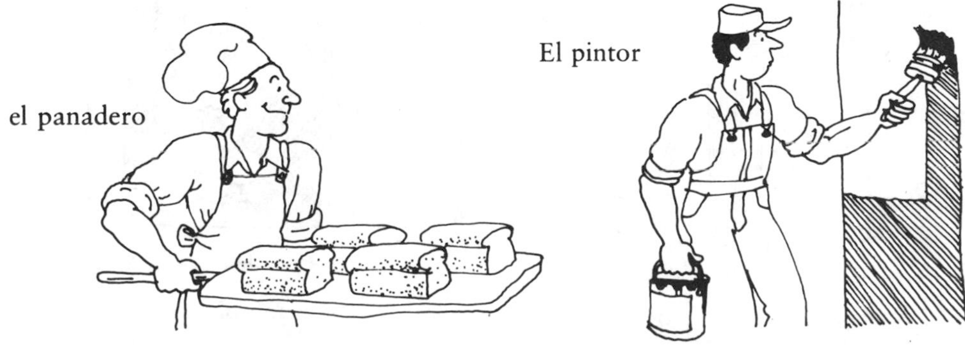

8.5 *Speaking Exercise*

CLASS: Answer these questions when your teacher calls on you. Read the answers in the book.

Examples: ¿Quién saca la basura? *Who takes out the garbage?*
Roberto saca la basura. *Robert takes out the garbage.*

1. ¿Saca usted la basura? No. No saco la basura.
2. ¿Saca la basura Roberto? Sí, Roberto saca la basura.
3. ¿Pinta usted en la clase de español? No. No pinto en la clase de español.
4. ¿Pinta usted en la clase de pintura? Sí. Pinto en la clase de pintura.
5. ¿Le gusta la clase de pintura? Sí. Me gusta mucho la clase de pintura.
6. ¿Le gusta la clase de español? Sí. Me gusta la clase de español. Es muy divertida.
7. ¿Dónde trabaja la enfermera? La enfermera trabaja en el hospital.
8. ¿Con quién trabaja la enfermera? *With whom does the nurse work?* La enfermera trabaja con los enfermos.
9. ¿Dónde trabaja el actor? El actor trabaja en el teatro.
10. ¿Dónde trabaja Carlos? Carlos trabaja en una estación de gasolina.
11. ¿Quién pinta la casa? El pintor pinta la casa.
12. ¿Dónde trabaja el panadero? El panadero trabaja en la panadería.
13. ¿Dónde trabaja el carnicero? El carnicero trabaja en la carnicería. El carnicero corta la carne. El carnicero vende carne.

la basura

una pintura

¿Le gusta la pintura? *Do you like painting?*

8.6 *Vocabulary*

For the Detective Story below.

CLASS: Repeat each word or phrase below, in unison, after your teacher says it in Spanish. You are not expected to know these words, only to recognize them.

1. el hombre que entró en la fábrica de Roberto, *the man who went into Robert's factory* 2. era un hombre delgado, de pelo negro, ojos, negros, bajo de estatura, *he was a thin man, with black hair, black eyes, short in stature* 3. llevaba un suéter azul, *he was wearing a blue sweater* 4. Roberto le dijo a María, *Robert said to Mary* 5. del hombre del incidente de la fábrica, *of the man of the incident in the factory* 6. que tú le diste al policía esta mañana, *that you gave to the policeman this morning* 7. creo que es el mismo hombre, *I think that he's the same man* 8. María pensó, *Mary thought* 9. en unos momentos le comenzaron a brillar los ojos, *in some moments her eyes began to shine* 10. es como las novelas de detectives que me gustan tanto, *it's like the detective novels that I like so much* 11. ¿Por qué no vamos tú y yo a ese lugar? *Why don't you and I go to that place?* 12. donde están las rocas y los árboles, *where the rocks and trees are* 13. Roberto dijo, "No, María, es peligroso." *Robert said, "No, Mary, it's dangerous."* 14. la policía tiene que hacer la investigación, *the police department has to make the investigation* 15. los dos hermanos tuvieron una gran discusión, y por fin María ganó, *the brother and sister (the two brothers) had a great argument, and finally Mary won* 16. Creo que ese hombre es peligroso. Déjalo. *I think that man is dangerous. Let him be.* 17. María protestó, *Mary protested* 18. Roberto decidió ir con María a buscar al hombre.

Robert decided to go with Mary to look for the man. 19. era un día lindo, *it was a beautiful day* 20. fueron a la cocina a preparar un buen almuerzo, *they went to the kitchen to prepare a good lunch* 21. hicieron sándwiches enormes de rosbif, tomates, lechuga, y mayonesa, *they made enormous sandwiches of roast beef, tomatoes, lettuce and mayonnaise* 22. Roberto empacó los sándwiches en bolsas de plástico, *Robert packed the sandwiches in plastic bags* 23. y los puso en una canasta con un termo de leche y otro termo de agua, *and he put them in a basket with a thermos of milk and another thermos of water* 24. todo el tiempo que estaba haciendo los sándwiches, Roberto pensaba en el ladrón, *all the time that he was making the sandwiches, Robert thought of the thief* 25. ¿Dónde estará? *I wonder where he is?* 26. ¿Por qué se robó los diseños? *Why did he steal the designs?* 27. ¿Para qué los quiere? *What does he want them for?* 28. la verdad es que Roberto no podía resistir la idea de perseguir al ladrón, *the truth is that Robert couldn't resist the idea of pursuing the thief* 29. María estaba muy emocionada, *Mary was very excited* 30. feliz porque su hermano estaba cooperando con ella, *overjoyed because her brother was cooperating with her* 31. en media hora, Roberto y María salieron en el coche de un amigo, *in a half hour, Robert and Mary left in a friend's car* 32. a buscar al ladrón, *to look for the thief*

8.7 *Detective Story (Part 5)*

CLASS: Your teacher will read the Detective Story below for you. Sight-read in the book. Listen carefully.

ROBERTO Y MARÍA, DETECTIVES

Descripción del hombre que entró en la fábrica de Roberto: Era un hombre delgado, de pelo negro, ojos negros, bajo de estatura. Llevaba un suéter azul, pantalones grises, y zapatos de tenis.

Roberto le dijo a María,—Esa descripción del hombre del incidente en la fábrica es exactamente la que tú le diste al policía esta mañana. Creo que es el mismo hombre.

María pensó, y en unos momentos le comenzaron a brillar los ojos.

—Es como las novelas de detectives que me gustan tanto. ¿Por qué no vamos tú y yo a ese lugar donde están las rocas y los árboles?

—No, María, es peligroso. La policía tiene que hacer la investigación. Creo que ese hombre es peligroso. Déjalo.

María protestó. Los dos hermanos tuvieron una gran discusión, y por fin María ganó. Roberto decidió ir con María a buscar al hombre.

Era un día lindo. Roberto y María fueron a la cocina a preparar un buen almuerzo. Hicieron sándwiches enormes de rosbif, tomates, lechuga y mayonesa. Roberto empacó los sándwiches en bolsas de plástico y los puso en una canasta con un termo de leche y otro termo de agua.

Todo el tiempo que estaba haciendo los sándwiches, Roberto pensaba en el ladrón. ¿Dónde estará? ¿Por qué se robó los diseños? ¿Para qué los quiere?

La verdad es que Roberto no podía resistir la idea de perseguir al ladrón. María estaba muy emocionada. Feliz porque su hermano estaba cooperando con ella.

En media hora, Roberto y María salieron en el coche de un amigo a buscar al ladrón. (To be continued)

8.8 *Reading a Sentence*

CLASS: Your teacher will point out individual students who will read a sentence or a paragraph in the story above. Read in a loud, clear voice. Read as smoothly as you can.

8.9 *Translating Exercise (optional)*

CLASS: Your teacher will point out individual students who will read one sentence in the story above, and translate it into English, or translate an English phrase from the vocabulary into Spanish.

8.10 *Vocabulary*

For the Conversation below.

CLASS: Repeat these words and sentences, in unison, after your teacher says them in Spanish.

1. ¿Por qué no estudias conmigo esta noche? *Why don't you study with me tonight?* 2. No puedo. *I can't.* 3. No tengo tiempo. *I haven't time.* 4. ¿Por qué no? *Why not?* 5. Voy a un concierto con mi papá. *I'm going to a concert with my dad.* 6. ¿Cuándo estudias? *When do you study?* 7. Por la mañana temprano. *In the morning, early.* 8. todos los días, *every day* 9. me gusta, *I like it* 10. Es divertido hablar español. *It's amusing to speak Spanish.* 11. ¿No crees?

Don't you think so? 12. estudia medicina, *he studies medicine* 13. ¡Qué bueno? *What a good thing! How good!* 14. Oye. *Listen.* 15. arquitectura, *architecture* 16. Es la liberación femenina. *It's feminine liberation.* 17. Luisa es muy inteligente. *Louise is very intelligent.* 18. Y muy simpática también. *And very charming too.* 19. ¡Mira! *Look!* 20. Bernardo está besando a Susana. *Bernard is kissing Susan.* 21. Están comprometidos. *They are engaged.* 22. La boda es en junio. *The wedding is in June.* 23. No lo sabía. *I didn't know it.* 24. ya, *already* 25. Eso ya es historia. *That's already history.* 26. ¿Dónde vive Bernardo? *Where does Bernard live?* 27. Aquí, con su familia. *Here, with his family.* 28. ¡Qué conveniente! *How convenient!* 29. ¿No es Susana enfermera? *Isn't Susan a nurse?* 30. ¿De veras? *Really?*

8.11 *Conversation*

STUDENT: Your teacher will select students, two by two, who will go to the front of the class and conduct a conversation about activities. Take your book with you. Read the blocks below first. Then close your book, and talk on your own. Practice your acting skills. Your teacher will guide you in the conversation.

TALKING ABOUT ACTIVITIES

First student —¿Por qué no estudias conmigo?
Second student—No puedo. No tengo tiempo.
First student —¿Por qué no?
Second student—Voy a un concierto con mi papá.
First student —¿Cuándo estudias?
Second student—Estudio por la mañana, temprano.
First student —¿Estudias la lección de español?
Second student—Sí. Todos los días. Me gusta mucho.
Es divertido hablar español. ¿No crees?
First student —Sí, muy divertido.
Second student—¿Dónde está Carlos?
First student —Está en la universidad. Estudia medicina.
Second student—¡Qué bueno! Oye. ¿Dónde está Luisa?
First student —Está en la universidad. Estudia arquitectura.
Second student—Ah, es la liberación femenina.

First student —Sí. Luisa es muy inteligente.
Second student—Y muy simpática también.
First student —Mira. Bernardo está besando a Susana.
Second student—Sí. Están comprometidos.
First student —¿De veras?
Second student—Sí. La boda es en junio.
First student —¡Caramba! No lo sabía.
Second student—Sí. Eso ya es historia.
First student —¿Dónde vive Bernardo?
Second student—Vive aquí, con su familia.
First student —¿Es arquitecto?
Second student—No. Es doctor.
First student —¡Qué conveniente! ¿No es enfermera Susana?
Second student—No. Susana está estudiando medicina también.

8.12 *Exercises*

A. Answer these questions:

1. ¿Dónde trabaja el ranchero?
2. ¿Dónde trabaja el banquero?
3. ¿Dónde lavan la ropa?
4. ¿Dónde trabaja el panadero?
5. ¿Dónde toma usted café?
6. ¿Dónde compra usted zapatos?
7. ¿Dónde trabaja el carnicero?

una canasta

Me gusta. *I like it.*

B. Answer these questions:

1. ¿Estudia usted la lección? 2. ¿Pinta usted en la clase de español? 3. ¿Baila usted? 4. ¿Canta usted? 5. ¿Dónde trabaja la doctora? 6. ¿Dónde trabaja la enfermera? 7. ¿Dónde trabaja el actor? 8. ¿Dónde trabaja el conductor? 9. ¿Quién pinta la casa? 10. ¿Qué vende el carnicero? 11. ¿Saca usted la basura todos los días? 12. ¿Vende usted flores? 13. ¿Va usted a clase todos los días? 14. ¿Hablamos italiano en la clase? 15. ¿Habla español el gorila?

8.13 *Speed Reading Exercise*

CLASS: The teacher will guide you in reading sentences from the Hearing Exercise in Lesson 6 (6.2) as a Speed Reading Exercise. Read aloud, as fast as you can.

La enfermera estaba ocupada.

LESSON 9

Irregularities in the Present Tense

IRREGULARITIES IN THE PRESENT TENSE

ALL regular verbs end in O in the "I" form of the Present Tense: hablo, *I speak;* corro, *I run;* abro, *I open.* Quite a few irregular verbs end in GO instead of just the letter O. Say the following verbs in Spanish:

1. tengo, *I have*
2. vengo, *I come*
3. salgo, *I go out, I leave*
4. traigo, *I bring*
5. pongo, *I put*
6. oigo, *I hear*
7. digo, *I say*
8. hago, *I do, I make*

un regalo

9.1 *Remember These Words*

CLASS: Repeat these words and phrases, in unison, after the teacher says them in Spanish. Do not use English. Only look at the meaning of each word.

muy bonitos, *very pretty*
le, *to him, to you, to her*
me trae, *he, she brings me*
muy elegante, *very elegant*
su primo, *your cousin (masc.)*
su prima, *your cousin (fem.)*
regalos, *presents*

discos, *records*
mi cuaderno, *my notebook*
¿qué más? *what else (more)?*
tarde, *late*
a tiempo, *on time*
botas, *boots*
un lápiz, *a pencil*
con mucho gusto, *with much pleasure*
notas, *notes*
solo, *alone (masc.)*
sola, *alone (fem.)*

un cinturón de cuero, *a leather belt*
un juego electrónico, *an electronic game*
todos son regalos, *they are all presents*
una chaqueta, *a jacket*
traer, *to bring*
traigo, *I bring*
¿Qué trae? *What do you bring?*
¿Qué más trae? *What else do you bring?*
¿Qué le trae su primo? *What does your cousin bring to you?*
¿Qué más? *What else? What more?*
¿Con qué escribe? *With what do you write?*
escribo, *I write*
escribo con pluma, *I write with (a) pen*
o, *or*
¿Sale tarde? *Do you leave late?*
Salgo a tiempo. *I leave on time.*
mi primo siempre me trae, *my cousin always brings me*
¿Tiene un gorila? *Have you a gorilla?*
¡Ay, caramba! *Oh, gee-whiz!*
Eso es ridículo. *That is ridiculous.*

9.2 *Speaking Exercise*

CLASS: Your teacher will point out individual students who will answer these questions. Read the answers in the book.

1. ¿Qué le trae su primo?
   Mi primo siempre me trae un cinturón de cuero. Tengo muchos cinturones, muy elegantes. Todos son regalos de mi primo.
2. ¿Qué le trae su tío?
   Mi tío me trae botas, o una chaqueta, o un juego electrónico.
3. ¿Qué le trae su tía?
   Mi tía me trae regalos muy bonitos.
4. ¿Qué trae usted a la clase?
   Traigo mi libro a la clase.
5. ¿Qué más trae?
   Traigo una pluma y un lápiz.
6. ¿Trae su cuaderno?
   Sí, traigo mi cuaderno.
7. ¿Qué escribe en su cuaderno?
   Escribo notas en mi cuaderno.
8. ¿Con qué escribe usted?
   Escribo con lápiz o con pluma.
9. ¿Trae su canario a la clase?
   No. Eso es ridículo. No traigo mi canario a la clase. Mi canario no estudia español. No estudia nada. Canta todo el día.
10. ¿Viene usted a la clase con gusto?
    Sí. Vengo a la clase con mucho gusto.
11. ¿Viene a la clase con Carolina?
    No. No vengo a la clase con Carolina. Vengo a la clase solo (sola).
12. ¿Viene a la clase tarde?
    No. No vengo tarde. Vengo a tiempo.
13. ¿Sale de la clase tarde?
    No. No salgo de la clase tarde. Salgo a tiempo.
14. ¿Tiene usted un gorila en casa?
    ¡Ay, caramba! No tengo un gorila en casa. Tengo un canario.

9.3 *Creating Sentences*

CLASS: Repeat the words of the next three columns after your teacher says them in Spanish. Combine the words in the three columns to form a complete sentence. Create your own sentences.

A.

traer	traigo	trae	traemos	traen
to bring	*I bring*	*you bring*	*we bring*	*they bring*

Mi tío
Mi tía
Mis primos
Mi prima
Mi papá
Mi mamá
Jorge *(George)*
Mi abuelo
(My grandfather)

Mi abuela
(My grandmother)

me trae
brings me

le trae
brings you,
him, her

me traen
they bring me

botas
chocolates
dulces
un suéter
una chaqueta
flores
discos
un cinturón
libros
chicle
(chewing gum)

un lápiz
una pluma
un cuaderno

B.

hacer, *to do, to make*

hago	hace	hacemos	hacen
I do, make	*you do, make*	*we do, make*	*they do, make*

Hago
I make

¿Hace usted
Do you make

Hace
He, she makes

Hacemos
We make

Hacen
They make

Mi abuela hace
My grandmother makes

ensalada
refrescos

dulces
rosbif

biftec
limonada

naranjada
orangeade

galletas
cookies, crackers

para la cena
para la fiesta

para mi familia
para los niños

para Roberto
para Susana

para el viaje
for the trip

para todos
for everybody

botas

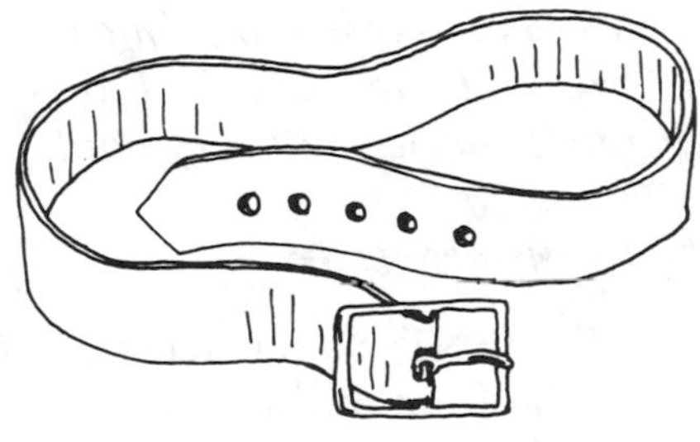

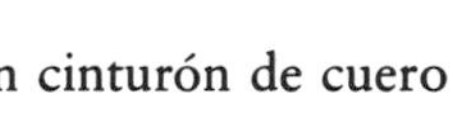

un cinturón de cuero

C.

I	II
Hago *I do*	el trabajo *the work*
Mi primo hace *My cousin (masc.) does*	muchas cosas *many things*
Mi abuelo hace *My grandfather does*	cosas interesantes *interesting things*
Carlos hace *Charles does*	cosas locas *crazy things*

9.4 *Vocabulary*

For the Conversation below

CLASS: Repeat these words and phrases, in unison, after your teacher says them in Spanish.

1. Oye. *Listen* 2. ¿Qué te trae tu primo? *What does your cousin bring you?* 3. Siempre me trae, *he always brings me* 4. un cinturón, *a*

belt 5. ¡Qué raro! *How strange!* 6. ¿Por qué? *Why?* 7. No sé. *I don't know.* 8. Es su idea. *It's his idea.* 9. ¿Qué te trae tu tío? *What does your uncle bring you?* 10. me trae, *he brings me* 11. muchas cosas diferentes, *many different things* 12. a veces, *sometimes* 13. una chaqueta de cuero, *a leather jacket* 14. un sombrero de ranchero, *a rancher's hat* 15. un juego electrónico, *an electronic game* 16. amable, *nice, kind, amiable* 17. ¡Qué amable! *How kind!* 18. una raqueta de tenis, *a tennis racket* 19. o unos casets, *or some cassettes* 20. un día me trajo, *one day he brought me* 21. Tus tíos son muy amables. *Your aunt and uncle (uncles) are very kind.* 22. te, *to you (familiar)*

9.5 *Conversation*

STUDENT: Your teacher will select students, two by two, who will go to the front of the class and conduct a conversation about presents. The blocks below will serve you as a guide. Take your book with you and read the sentences first. Then, close your book and converse on your own.

BIRTHDAY PRESENTS

First student —Oye. ¿Qué te trae tu primo?
Second student—Siempre me trae un cinturón.
First student —¡Qué raro! ¿Por qué?
Second student—No sé. Es su idea.
First student —¿Qué te trae tu tío?
Second student—Me trae muchas cosas diferentes. A veces me trae botas, a veces me trae una chaqueta de cuero, o un sombrero de ranchero, y a veces me trae un juego electrónico.
First student —¡Qué amable!
Second student—Sí. Mi tío es muy amable y muy generoso. ¿Qué te trae tu tía?
First student —Mi tía me trae libros o discos. A veces me trae dulces.
Second student—¿Qué te trae tu tío?
First student —Me trae juegos. A veces me trae una raqueta de tenis, o unos casets. Un día me trajo un radio.
Second student—Oye. Tus tíos son muy amables.

The following GO verbs are regular in the Present Tense, except for the first person ("I" form).

1. traer, *to bring*

traigo	trae	traemos	traen
I bring	*you bring*	*we bring*	*they bring*

2. poner, *to put, to set*

pongo	pone	ponemos	ponen
I put	*you put*	*we put*	*they put*

3. hacer, *to make, to do*

hago	hace	hacemos	hacen
I make	*you make*	*we make*	*they make*

4. salir, *to go out*

salgo	sale	salimos	salen
I go out	*you go out*	*we go out*	*they go out*

CLASS: Your teacher will give you one of the Infinitives above. Give the Present Tense of the verb. Close your books.

9.6 *Vocabulary*

For the Detective Story below.

CLASS: Repeat each word and sentence, in unison, after your teacher says it in Spanish.

1. salieron a buscar al ladrón, *they went out to look for the thief* 2. en el coche de un amigo, *in a friend's car* 3. pasaron por muchas calles, *they passed by many streets* 4. por fin salieron de la ciudad, *they finally left the city* 5. después de media hora, *after a half hour* 6. llegaron al lugar donde había desaparecido el ladrón, *they arrived at the place where the thief had disappeared* 7. buscaron por todas partes, *they looked all over (in all parts)* 8. entre los árboles y las rocas, *among the trees and the rocks (crags)* 9. pero no encontraron nada, *but they didn't find anything* 10. Roberto dijo, *Robert said* 11. vamos a la casa, aquí no hay nada, *let's go home (to the house), there isn't anything here* 12. pero María persistió, *but Mary persisted* 13. media hora más, *half an hour more* 13. comenzó a buscar entre unas rocas inmensas, *she began to look among some immense crags* 14. de pronto, *suddenly* 15. vio la huella de un

zapato de hombre, *she saw the footprint of a man's shoe* 16. cerca de unos arbustos, *close to some bushes* 17. el corazón le comenzó a latir muy aprisa, *her heart began to beat very fast* 18. los ojos se le pusieron como platos, *her eyes got (as big) as plates* 19. movió las ramas de un arbusto, *she moved the branches of a bush* 20. allí encontró la entrada de una cueva, *there she found the entrance to a cave* 21. gritó, *she screamed* 22. ¡Roberto, ven! *Robert, come!* 23. ¡Mira lo que encontré! *Look what I found!*

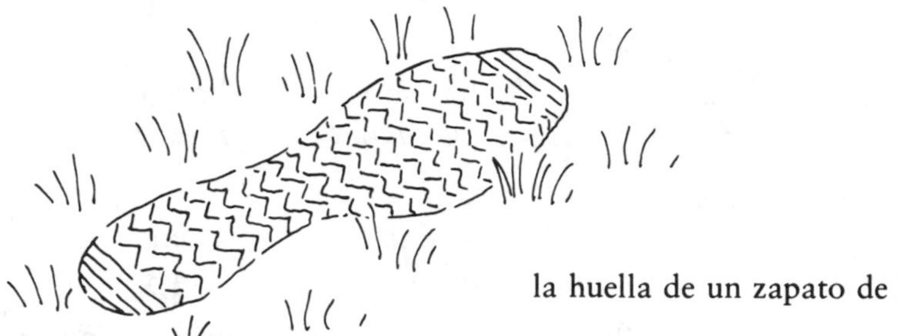

la huella de un zapato de hombre

9.7 *Detective Story (Part 6)*

CLASS: Your teacher will read the Detective Story below for you. Sight-read in the book. Listen carefully.

ROBERTO Y MARÍA, DETECTIVES

Roberto y María salieron a buscar al ladrón en el coche de un amigo. Pasaron por muchas calles, y por fin salieron de la ciudad. Después de media hora, llegaron al lugar donde había desaparecido el ladrón. Buscaron por todas partes entre los árboles y las rocas. Pero no encontraron nada.

Roberto dijo: "Vamos a la casa, aquí no hay nada." Pero María persistió. Le dijo a Roberto: "Media hora más, por favor," y Roberto aceptó.

María comenzó a buscar entre unas rocas inmensas. De pronto, vio la huella de un zapato de hombre cerca de unos arbustos. El corazón le comenzó a latir muy aprisa y los ojos se le pusieron como platos. Movió las ramas de un arbusto, y allí encontró la entrada de una cueva. Gritó. "¡Roberto, ven! ¡Ven! ¡Mira lo que encontré!" (To be continued)

9.8 *Reading a Paragraph*

CLASS: Your teacher will point out individual students who will read a WHOLE paragraph in the story above. Read as smoothly as you can.

9.9 *Translating Exercise (optional)*

CLASS: Your teacher will point out individual students who will read one sentence in the story above and translate it into English.

9.10 *Exercises*

A. Answer these questions:

1. ¿Trae usted su libro a la clase? 2. ¿Trae usted una pluma a la clase? 3. ¿Viene usted a la clase tarde? 4. ¿Trae usted su cuaderno a la clase? 5. ¿Escribe usted en el cuaderno? 6. ¿Viene usted a la clase con Roberto? 7. ¿Trae usted un canario a la clase? 8. ¿Estudia español el canario? 9. ¿Estudia español el presidente? 10. ¿Estudia usted español? 11. ¿Hace usted ensalada para la cena? 12. ¿Hace usted sándwiches para los niños? 13. ¿Hace usted limonada para los estudiantes en la clase? 14. ¿Hace usted muchas cosas interesantes? 15. ¿Sale de la clase tarde? 16. ¿Hace usted cosas locas? 17. ¿Tiene usted una bicicleta? 18. ¿Tiene usted un canario? 19. ¿Tiene muchos discos? 20. ¿Tiene usted un suéter azul? 21. ¿Viene usted a la clase en taxi? 22. ¿Viene usted a la clase en autobús? 23. ¿Viene usted a la clase los sábados? 24. ¿Tiene usted un avión? 25. ¿Tiene usted un elefante en su casa?

B. Translate these sentences into Spanish:

1. They sell bread in the bakery. 2. My cousin brings me many things. 3. The butcher cuts the meat in the butcher shop. 4. The baker doesn't sell meat. 5. I don't sell jackets. 6. I leave late.

Review the four forms of THE.

	Singular	Plural
feminine:	la, *the*	las, *the*
masculine:	el, *the*	los, *the*
Examples:	la casa. *the house*	las casas, *the houses*
	el coco, *the coconut*	los cocos, *the coconuts*

SLANG: COCO is slang for "head."
Repeat: loco en el coco, *crazy in the coconut (head).*

HOW TO FORM THE SUPERLATIVE

To form the Superlative, use the word THE (EL, LA, LOS, LAS) before the comparative.

Example: el más caro (masc.), *the most expensive*
la más alta (fem.), *the tallest*

USE OF THE SUPERLATIVE

Learn:

el más alto DE, *the tallest of, in, on*
Alberto es el más alto de la clase.
Alberto is the tallest in (of) the class.
Es la rosa más bonita del jardín.
It's the prettiest rose in (of) the garden.

9.11 *Exercise*

Translate these (singular) superlatives:

1. the tallest (masc.) 2. the most expensive (masc.) 3. the prettiest (fem.) 4. the tallest (fem.) 5. the most expensive (fem.) 6. the biggest (masc.) 7. Alberto is the tallest in the class. 8. It's the prettiest rose in the garden.

LESSON 10

Stem-changing Verbs: ***E*** *to* ***IE***

THE STEM

The STEM of a verb is what is left over after removing the ending. For example, in the verb PINTAR *(to paint)*, AR is the Infinitive ending. PINT is the stem.

10.1 *Exercise*

CLASS: Give the stems of the following verbs (remove AR, ER, or IR from the Infinitive).

Examples:

INFINITIVES	ENDINGS	STEMS
cantar, *to sing*	ar	cant
vender, *to sell*	er	vend
vivir, *to live*	ir	viv
1. dormir, *to sleep*	___	______
2. sentir, *to feel*	___	______
3. pensar, *to think*	___	______
4. cerrar, *to close*	___	______
5. entender, *to understand*	___	______

STEM-CHANGING VERBS: E to IE

There are some verbs which have changes in the STEM. These are STEM-CHANGING VERBS. Example: The stem of TENER *(to have)* is TEN. In the Present Tense, the letter E in the stem TEN changes to IE: TIENE, you have, he has, she has, it has.

STEM CHANGE
E ⟶ IE

PENSAR, *to think*

I think	PIENSO	PENSAMOS	*we think*
you think *he, she thinks*	PIENSA	PIENSAN	*you (pl.) think* *they think*

Familiar form: tú PIENSAS, *you think (familiar)*

The STEM has changed in the following way:

PEN (STEM)

PIEN	PEN
PIEN	PIEN

Notice that the WE form and the Infinitive are regular. In all the other forms, the E changes to IE. Notice where E changes to IE in the Present Tense:

IE	e
IE	IE

The E changing verbs change to IE as in the chart above.

REMEMBER: In all verbs and in all tenses the good, old WE form tends to remain regular. It is regular in all the verbs in this lesson.

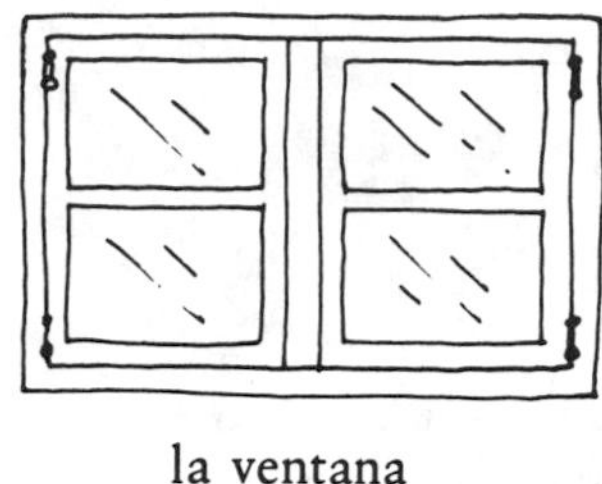

la ventana

la puerta

10.2 *Exercise*

CLASS: Repeat the four forms of each verb, in unison, after your teacher says them in Spanish. Use no English, *por favor.*

I	YOU, HE, SHE, IT	WE	YOU (pl.), THEY
1. pensar, *to think*			
pienso	piensa	pensamos	piensan
I think	*you think*	*we think*	*they think*
2. cerrar, *to close*			
cierro	cierra	cerramos	cierran
I close	*you close*	*we close*	*they close*
3. querer, *to want*			
quiero	quiere	queremos	quieren
I want, love	*you want*	*we want*	*they want*
4. sentir, *to feel*			
siento	siente	sentimos	sienten
I feel	*you feel*	*we feel*	*they feel*
5. perder, *to lose*			
pierdo	pierde	perdemos	pierden
I lose	*you lose*	*we lose*	*they lose*

STUDENT: Could you do the Exercise above with your books closed? Your teacher will give you an Infinitive. You give the four forms of the verb, as above. Close your books.

El tren llega a las ocho.
The train arrives at eight.

10.3 *Remember These Words*

CLASS: Repeat these words and phrases, in unison, after your teacher says them in Spanish. Do not use English. Only look at the meaning of each word.

¿a qué hora? *at what time?*
a las ocho, *at eight o'clock*
esta noche, *tonight*
sándwiches de pollo, *chicken sandwiches*
ensalada de papas, *potato salad*
veinte personas, *twenty people*
todos mis amigos, *all my friends*
música buena, *good music*
discos buenos, *good records*
flores, *flowers*
tulipanes, *tulips*
margaritas, *daisies*
todos, *everybody, all*

¿viene? *are you coming? do you come?*
¿Por qué no viene a la fiesta? *Why don't you come to the party?*
¿a qué hora viene? *at what time are you coming?*
vengo con mi primo, *I'm coming with my cousin*
¿quién viene? *who is coming?*
¿cuántos vienen? *how many are coming?*
todos mis amigos vienen, *all my friends are coming*
para todos, *for everybody*

NOTICE that VIENE expresses both the Present Tense and the Present Progressive. It means both "he comes" and "he is coming."

10.4 *Speaking Exercise*

CLASS: Answer these questions when your teacher calls on you. Read the answers in the book.

1. ¿Viene a la fiesta esta noche?
   Sí, vengo a la fiesta.
   No, no vengo a la fiesta.

2. ¿A qué hora viene?
   Vengo a las ocho. Vengo con mi primo.
3. ¿Tiene música buena para la fiesta?
   Sí, tengo unos discos muy buenos.
4. ¿Tiene una ensalada?
   Sí, tengo dos ensaladas. Una ensalada de pollo y una ensalada de papas.
5. ¿Tiene flores para la fiesta?
   Sí, tengo tulipanes y margaritas.
6. ¿Quién viene a la fiesta?
   Roberto y Alberto vienen a la fiesta.
7. ¿Viene Bárbara?
   Sí, Bárbara viene con Jorge.
8. ¿Cuántos vienen?
   Vienen veinte personas. Todos mis amigos vienen.

CLASS: Could you do the Exercise above with books closed?

10.5 *Creating Sentences*

CLASS: Repeat the words in the three columns below after your teacher says them in Spanish. Then, each student will combine words from the three columns to form a complete sentence. Create your own sentences.

A.

I	II	III
¿Quién *(who)* ¿Cuándo *(when)* Alicia *(Alice)* Pablo *(Paul)*	VIENE *is coming* *are you coming?* *is he, she coming?* *is coming* NO VIENE *isn't coming*	a la clase a la fiesta a mi casa mañana *(tomorrow)* esta noche *(tonight)* esta tarde el sábado *(on Saturday)* el domingo *(on Sunday)*

REMEMBER that VIENE means "you are coming" and "you come."

B.

I	II	III
		a la fiesta?
		a la casa?
		a la clase?
¿Por qué no	VIENE	mañana?
why don't you	*come*	el sábado?
why doesn't he	VA	el domingo?
why doesn't she	*go*	el lunes?
		más tarde? *(later)*
		más temprano? *(earlier)*

el pan

10.6 *Exercise*

Fill in the blanks below with the correct form of the Present Tense of CERRAR *(to close)*.

1. El carnicero ________ la carnicería.
2. Yo ________ la ventana en la clase.
3. Nosotros ________ la tienda tarde.
4. Alberto y Julia ________ el banco a las tres.
5. ¿A qué hora ________ usted la tienda?
6. Los estudiantes ________ los libros.
7. Luis ________ la puerta en la clase.
8. Nosotros ________ los libros después de la clase.
9. ¿A qué hora ________ la panadería?
10. ¿________ usted la zapatería los sábados?

QUERER, *to want, to love*

The verb QUERER is important because it is used in so many ways. Examples:

1. te quiero, *I love you*
2. ¿Quieres pan? *Do you want (any) bread? (familiar)*

3. No quiero nada. *I don't want anything.*
4. Quiero nadar. *I want to swim.*
5. no quiero, *I don't want to*
6. Nosotros queremos ir a la playa. *We want to go to the beach.*

PRESENT TENSE

QUERER, *to want, to love*

I want, I love	QUIERO	QUEREMOS	*we want, love*
you want, love *he, she, it wants, loves*	QUIERE	QUIEREN	*you (pl.) want, love* *they want, love*

Familiar form: tú quieres, *you want, love (familiar)*

te quiero
(I love you)

IMPERFECT TENSE

I wanted, loved	QUERÍA	QUERÍAMOS	*we wanted, loved*
you, he, she, it wanted, loved	QUERÍA	QUERÍAN	*you (pl.) wanted, loved* *they wanted, loved*

Familiar form: tú querías, *you wanted, loved (familiar)*

REMEMBER that when a verb is followed by a noun referring to a person, you insert a personal A before the noun. The A doesn't mean anything.

10.7 *Creating Sentences*

CLASS: Repeat the words in the next columns after your teacher says them in Spanish. Then, each student will combine words from the columns to form a complete sentence.

A.

I	II
QUIERO *I love* Roberto quiere *Robert loves* Susana quiere *Susan loves* QUERÍA *I, you, he, she loved*	a mi tío, *my uncle* a mi abuelo, *my grandfather* a mi abuela, *my grandmother* a mi tía, *my aunt* a mis primos, *my cousins* a Marta a Carlos a David

B.

I	II	III
QUIERO *I want* ¿QUIERE *Do you want* *Does he, she, want* ¿QUIEREN *Do you (pl.) want* *Do they want* QUERÍA *I, you, he, she wanted*	IR, *to go*	a la playa, *to the beach* al cine, *to the movies* al juego, *to the game* a la tienda, *to the store* al concierto, *to the concert* al teatro, *to the theater* al campo, *to the country* a la fiesta, *to the party* a casa, *home* a tu casa, *to your house (familiar)* al circo, *to the circus* al centro, *downtown* a un día de campo, *on a picnic*

C.

I	II	III
quiero *I want* ¿Quiere *Do you want* *does he,* *she want*	ver, *to see* oír, *to hear*	una buena película, *a good film* la comedia, *the play* el programa (masc.), *the program* a Juan, *John* a su abuelo, *your grandfather* a Ana, *Anne*

10.8 *Vocabulary*

For the Detective Story below.

CLASS: Repeat each word and sentence, in unison, after your teacher says it in Spanish.

1. María encontró la entrada de una cueva. *Mary found the entrance of a cave.* 2. Gritó: "¡Ven!" *She shouted: "Come!" (familiar)* 3. Roberto corrió a la cueva. *Robert ran to the cave.* 4. Allí él y María encontraron una candela. *There he and Mary found a candle.* 5. pronto, *quickly.* 6. unos fósforos, *some matches* 7. una cajetilla de cigarros, *a pack of cigarettes* 8. Roberto dijo, *Robert said* 9. ¡Vámonos pronto! *Let's go right away (quickly)!* 10. Es posible que el ladrón venga. *It's possible that the thief will come.* 11. corrieron al coche, *they ran to the car* 12. fueron a la estación de policía, *they went to the police station* 13. Allí María describió la cueva. *There, Mary described the cave.* 14. les dio a los detectives, *she gave to the detectives* 15. en pocas horas los detectives aprenhendieron al ladrón, *in a few hours the detectives arrested the thief* 16. el jefe de policía, *the police chief* 17. le presentó una medalla, *(he) presented her a medal* 18. por su excelente trabajo, *because of your excellent work* 19. fue posible, *it was possible* 20. Roberto le dio un abrazo a su hermana, *Robert gave his sister a hug* 21. estaba feliz, *she was happy, overjoyed* 22. esa noche, *that night* 23. los amigos de María le dieron una fiesta, *Mary's friends gave her a party* 24. para celebrar su

triunfo, *to celebrate her triumph* 25. llevaron refrescos, *they took refreshments* 26. cantaron y tocaron las guitarras, *they sang and played the guitars* 27. todos estuvieron contentísimos, *they were all very, very happy* 28. abrazaron a María con mucho cariño, *they hugged Mary with much affection* 29. ¡VIVA MARÍA!, *Long live Mary!*

10.9 *Detective Story (Part 7)*

CLASS: Your teacher will read the Detective Story below for you. Sight-read in the book. Listen carefully.

ROBERTO Y MARÍA, DETECTIVES

María encontró la entrada de una cueva. Gritó: "¡Roberto, ven!" Roberto corrió a la cueva, y allí él y María encontraron una candela, unos sándwiches, unos fósforos, y una cajetilla de cigarros. Roberto dijo: "¡Vámonos pronto! Es posible que el ladrón venga."

Corrieron al coche y fueron a la estación de policía a toda velocidad. Allí, María describió la cueva, y les dio a los detectives los fósforos y la cajetilla de cigarros.

En pocas horas los detectives aprehendieron al ladrón. El jefe de policía invitó a María a la estación, y le presentó una medalla. Le dijo: "María, usted es fantástica. Por su excelente trabajo de detective fue posible aprehender al ladrón." Roberto le dio un gran abrazo a su hermana. María estaba feliz.

Esa noche los amigos de María le dieron una gran fiesta para celebrar su triunfo. Llevaron sándwiches, refrescos, dulces y flores. Cantaron y tocaron las guitarras. Bailaron. Todos estuvieron contentísimos. Besaron y abrazaron a María con mucho cariño y con admiración.

¡VIVA MARÍA!

10.10 *Reading a Paragraph*

CLASS: Your teacher will point out individual students who will read a whole paragraph in the story above. Read as smoothly as you can.

10.11 *Translating Exercise (optional)*

CLASS: Your teacher will point out individual students who will read one sentence in the story above, and translate it into English.

10.12 *Speed Reading Exercise*

CLASS: Your teacher will guide you in reading sentences from the Hearing Exercise in Lesson 8. Read as fast as you can.

PROGRESS TEST

A. Give the correct form of the Imperfect Tense of the following verbs. End each verb in ABA or ÍA.

1. invitar, *to invite:* Roberto ________ 2. vender, *to sell:* nosotros ________ 3. vivir, *to live:* el actor ________ 4. pintar, *to paint:* el artista ________ 5. hacer, *to do, to make:* el carpintero ________ 6. llevar, *to wear:* el ladrón ________ 7. correr, *to run:* Susana ________ 8. escribir *to write:* el estudiante ________ 9. vivir, *to live:* usted ________ 10. hablar, *to talk:* mi tío ________ 11. comprar, *to buy:* papá ________ 12. sufrir, *to suffer:* yo ________ 13. tener, *to have:* Carlos ________ 14. estar, *to be (location):* el coche ________ 15. querer, *to want, to love:* yo ________ 16. salir, *to go out:* Alberto ________ 17. curar, *to cure:* el doctor ________ 18. subir, *to go up:* Alfredo ________ 19. dormir, *to sleep:* yo ________ 20. terminar, *to finish:* mi tía ________

B. Give the correct form of the Preterite Tense of each of the following verbs. AR verbs end in É for me, Ó for others. ER and IR verbs end in Í for me, IÓ for others (singular).

1. comprar, yo ________ 2. exportar, usted ________ 3. recibir, María ________ 4. visitar, Roberto ________ 5. escribir, yo ________

C. Answer these questions:

1. ¿Dónde estaba el tren? 2. ¿Dónde estaba el dinero? 3. ¿Dónde estaba el coche? 4. ¿LLevaba pantalones grises el ladrón? 5. ¿Escribía Shakespeare? 6. ¿Hacía sillas el carpintero? 7. ¿Corría Luis en la clase? 8. ¿Cantaba mucho el canario? 9. ¿Recibía muchas cartas el presidente? 10. ¿Quién compraba todo? 11. ¿Estaba en el hospital el doctor? 12. ¿Era inteligente la doctora? 13. ¿Venía a la clase el profesor? 14. ¿Está usted escribiendo frases? 15. ¿Está usted nadando en la clase? 16. ¿Están jugando tenis sus amigos? 17. ¿Está trabajando el carpintero? 18. ¿Está sufriendo usted? 19. ¿Corrió al garaje el ladrón? 20. ¿Vio María al ladrón? 21. ¿Describió María al ladrón? 22. ¿Corrió en su pijama Roberto? 23. ¿Cuántos años tenía María? 24. ¿Escribió la descripción el policía? 25. ¿Estamos estudiando español en la clase?

LESSON 11

Stem-changing Verbs: ***O*** *to* ***UE***

STEM-CHANGING VERBS. O to UE

There are some Stem-changing verbs in which the letter O changes to UE. Example:

VOLVER, *to return*

I return	VUELVO	VOLVEMOS	*we return*
you return *he, she returns*	VUELVE	VUELVEN	*you (pl.) return* *they return*

Familiar form: tú vuelves, *you return*

Notice that the WE form and the Infinitive are regular. In the other forms, the O changes to UE. Notice where O changes to UE:

UE	o
UE	UE

El perro no muerde.
The dog does not bite.

11.1 *Exercise*

CLASS: Repeat each verb below after your teacher says it in Spanish. Read the verbs across each line. No English please.

	INFINITIVE	I	YOU, HE, SHE, IT
	Examples:		
	volver, *to get back*	vuelvo, *I get back*	vuelve, *she gets back*
	poder, *to be able*	puedo, *I can*	puede, *she can*
1.	contar, *to count*	cuento, *I count*	cuenta, *she counts*
2.	morder, *to bite*	muerdo, *I bite*	muerde, *it bites*
3.	recordar, *to remember*	recuerdo, *I remember*	¿Recuerda? *Do you remember?*
4.	encontrar, *to find*	encuentro, *I find*	encuentra, *he finds*
5.	poder, *to be able*	puedo, *I can*	puede, *you can*
6.	envolver, *to wrap*	envuelvo, *I wrap*	envuelve, *you wrap*
7.	jugar, *to play (a game)*	juego, *I play*	juega, *you play*

NOTE: CONTAR means both "to count" and "to tell" (a story). In JUGAR, *to play,* the U changes to UE.

CLASS: Could you do the exercise above with books closed? Your teacher will give you the Infinitive, and you give the "I" form and the YOU, HE, SHE form.

THE DOUBLE NEGATIVE

In Spanish we use the double negative. We do not say "I don't know anything." We say instead, "No sé nada." (I don't know nothing), "No recuerdo nada" (I don't remember nothing). This is the correct grammatical form in Spanish.

¿Recuerdas? *Do you remember?*

11.2 *Remember These Words*

CLASS: Repeat these words and phrases, in unison, after the teacher says them in Spanish. Do not use English. Only look at the meaning of each word.

la dirección, *the address*
la página, *the page*
esta noche, *tonight*
mañana, *tomorrow*
aquí, *here*
béisbol, *baseball*
vóleibol, *volleyball*
un concierto, *a concert*
conmigo, *with me*
el poema, *the poem*
el nombre, *the name*
nada, *nothing*
el juego, *the game*
a las doce, *at twelve o'clock*
el sábado, *on Saturday*
el domingo, *on Sunday*
fútbol, *soccer*
el número de teléfono, *the phone number*

Voy a un concierto, *I'm going to a concert*
¿Recuerda? *Do you remember?*
recuerdo, *I remember*
¿Juega vóleibol? *Do you play volleyball?*
Juego todos los días. *I play everyday.*
Juego los sábados. *I play on Saturdays.*
¿Puede estudiar conmigo? *Can you study with me?*
¿Puede estar aquí? *Can you be here?*
¿Puede ir a la fiesta? *Can you go to the party?*
Aquí está. *Here it is.*

NOTE: PUEDO *(I can)* is used with any Infinitive.

Examples: puedo ir, *I can go*
no puedo ir, *I can't go*
puedo jugar, *I can play*
puedo trabajar, *I can work*
no puedo venir a la fiesta, *I can't come to the party*
no puedo salir, *I cannot go out*

juego con mis amigos, *I play with my friends*
¿Cuánto cuesta el boleto? *How much does the ticket cost?*
el poema que aprendí, *the poem that I learned*
es el doctor Wong, *it's doctor Wong*

el boleto

11.3 *Speaking Exercise*

CLASS: Answer these questions when your teacher calls on you. Read the answers in the book.

1. ¿Recuerda usted la lección?
   Sí, recuerdo la lección muy bien.
2. ¿Recuerda usted el poema?
   Sí, recuerdo el poema que aprendí en la clase.
3. ¿Recuerda la dirección de Alberto?
   Sí, recuerdo la dirección de Alberto.
4. ¿Recuerda el número de teléfono de Susana?
   Sí, recuerdo el número de teléfono de Susana.
7. ¿Recuerda usted el nombre del doctor?
   Sí, recuerdo el nombre del doctor. Es el doctor Wong.
8. ¿Qué recuerda usted?
   ¡No recuerdo nada!
9. ¿Puede estudiar esta noche?
   No. No puedo estudiar esta noche. Voy a un concierto.
10. ¿Puede ir al cine mañana?
    Sí, puedo ir al cine mañana.
11. ¿Puede ir al juego de fútbol el domingo?
    Sí, puedo ir al juego de fútbol el domingo.
12. ¿Cuánto cuesta el boleto?
    No cuesta mucho.
13. ¿Puede estar aquí a las doce?
    Sí, puedo estar aquí a las doce.
14. ¿Juega usted béisbol?
    Sí, juego béisbol en el parque.
15. ¿Juega vóleibol?
    Sí, juego vóleibol con mis amigos, pero no juego muy bien.

CLASS: Could you do this exercise with books closed?

11.4 *Creating Sentences*

CLASS: Match up the words below to form sentences:

¿Juega usted *Do you play* Juego *I play* ¿Sabe jugar *Do you know how to play* Sé jugar *I know how to play*	tenis vóleibol bridge fútbol béisbol con mis amigos con los niños *(with the children)*	en el club en el parque en casa en el jardín con mi familia con mis amigos con ella, *with her* en el gimnasio *(in the gym)*
¿Puede *Can you* Puedo *I can* No puedo *I can't*	ir, *go* estudiar, *study* salir, *go out* jugar, *play* ver, *see* oír, *hear* comprar, *buy* venir, *come*	al cine esta noche esta tarde tenis el programa bien dulces a la fiesta

11.5 *Everyday Expressions*

CLASS: Repeat each sentence, in unison, after your teacher says it in Spanish.

No sé nada. *I don't know anything (nothing).*
No recuerdo nada. *I don't remember anything.*
¿Cuánto cuesta? *How much does it cost?*
No puedo ir. *I can't go.*
¿Recuerda? *Do you remember?*
¿Sabe? *Do you know?*
La cuenta, por favor. *The check, please (in a restaurant).*
Es un cuento interesante. *It's an interesting story.*
¿Cuándo vuelve? *When do you get back?*

11.6 *Exercise*

Answer these questions:

1. ¿Recuerda usted la dirección de Alberto? 2. ¿Recuerda el número de teléfono de Gloria? 3. ¿Puede estudiar esta noche? 4. ¿Cuesta mucho el boleto? 5. ¿Juega usted tenis? 6. ¿Cuándo vuelve usted? 7. ¿Puede salir esta noche? 8. ¿Puede ir conmigo a la fiesta mañana? 9. ¿Puede venir a mi casa esta noche? 10. ¿Puede usted ir a la luna esta noche?

LESSON 12

Irregular Verbs, Present Tense

LIST OF IRREGULAR VERBS
PRESENT TENSE

Five verbs are regular in the Present Tense, except for the "I" form (GO ending).

CLASS: Repeat these verbs after your teacher says them in Spanish.

	I	YOU, HE, SHE, IT	WE	YOU (Pl.), THEY
1.	traer, *to bring*			
	traigo	trae	traemos	traen
	I bring	*you bring*	*we bring*	*they bring*
2.	hacer, *to do, to make*			
	hago	hace	hacemos	hacen
	I do	*you do*	*we do*	*they do*
3.	poner, *to put, to set the table*			
	pongo	pone	ponemos	ponen
	I put	*you put*	*we put*	*they put*
4.	caer, *to fall*			
	caigo	cae	caemos	caen
	I fall	*you fall*	*we fall*	*they fall*
5.	salir, *to go out, to leave*			
	salgo	sale	salimos	salen
	I go out	*you go out*	*we go out*	*they go out*

Two GO verbs are stem-changing (E to IE).

6. tener, *to have*

tengo	tiene	tenemos	tienen
I have	*you have*	*we have*	*they have*

7. venir, *to come*

vengo	viene	venimos	vienen
I come	*you come*	*we come*	*they come*

In OÍR, *to hear,* the letter I of the third persons changes to Y.

8. oír, *to hear*

oigo	oye	oímos	oyen
I hear	*you hear*	*we hear*	*they hear*

NOTE: Use TENGO QUE *(I have to)* with any Infinitive: Tengo que ir al banco. *I have to go to the bank.* Tengo que estudiar. *I have to study.*

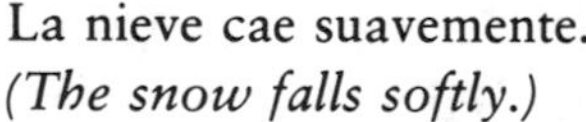

La nieve cae suavemente.
(The snow falls softly.)

IMPORTANT: Irregular verbs are the most necessary words in speaking any language. They are the basic roots of our most ancient civilization. You cannot "live" in Spanish without irregular verbs. Therefore, there is nothing to do but to sit down and study these verbs as you have studied nothing else in learning Spanish. Study them with all your might.

A wise man in ancient Greece said: "Before the gates of excellence, lies sweat."

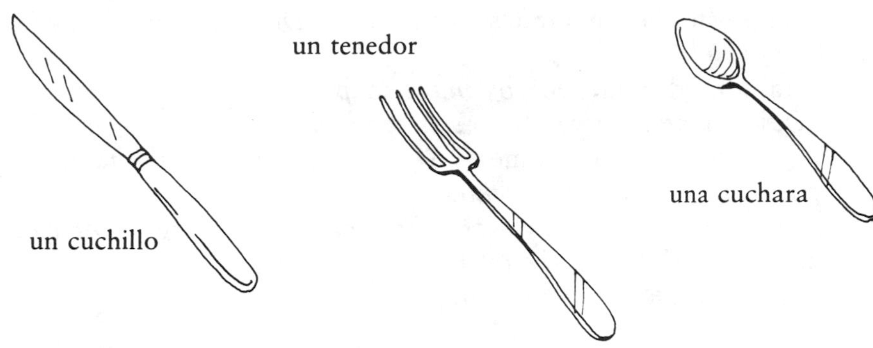

12.1 *Remember These Words*

CLASS: Repeat these words and phrases, in unison, after your teacher says them in Spanish.

un cuchillo, *a knife*
un tenedor, *a fork*
una cuchara, *a spoon*
una servilleta, *a napkin*
su abuelo, *your grandfather*
unos dulces, *some candy*
un diccionario, *a dictionary*
un paraguas, *an umbrella*
sal, *salt*
pimienta, *pepper*
platos, *plates*
con frecuencia, *frequently*
un día de campo, *a picnic*
azúcar, *sugar*
mi libro, *my book*
la cama, *the bed*

los sábados, *on Saturdays*
¿A qué hora salen ustedes? *At what time do you leave?*
Salimos a las ocho. *We leave at eight o'clock.*
sopa buena, *good soup*
sándwiches buenos, *good sandwiches*
la nieve, *the snow*
suave, *soft*
suavemente, *softly*
mi cuaderno, *my notebook*
un periódico, *a newspaper*
todas las mañanas, *every morning*
muchas cosas, *many things*

los sábados por la noche, *on Saturday nights*
Luis sale todas las noches, *Louis goes out every night*
hago muchas cosas, *I do many things*
¿Hace ejercicios en la clase de gimnasia? *Do you do exercises in gym class?*
un satélite, *a satellite*
¿Qué trae Susana? *What does Susan bring?*
no traigo un periódico, *I don't bring a newspaper*
traigo mi libro, *I bring my book*

¿Hace usted la cama todas las mañanas? *Do you make the bed every morning?*
¿Hace usted sopa? *Do you make soup?*
¿Quién pone la mesa? *Who sets the table?*
¿Qué pone usted en la mesa? *What do you put on the table?*
poner, *to put, to set (the table)*
¿Qué trae Susana a la clase? *What does Susan bring to the class?*
la guía de teléfonos, *the telephone directory*
Eso es ridículo. *That's ridiculous.*

12.2 *Speaking Exercise*

CLASS: Your teacher will call on individual students to answer a question. Read the answer in the book.

1. ¿Qué trae Susana a la clase?
   Susana trae un diccionario a la clase.
2. ¿Qué trae Carlos a la clase?
   Carlos trae un libro a la clase.
3. ¿Trae usted dulces a la clase?
   No, no traigo dulces a la clase. Traigo mi libro a la clase.
4. ¿Trae un periódico a la clase?
   No, no traigo un periódico a la clase. Traigo mi cuaderno.
5. ¿Hace usted la cama todas las mañanas?
   Sí, hago la cama todas las mañanas.
6. ¿Hace usted sopa buena?
   Sí, hago sopa deliciosa.
7. ¿Hace sándwiches buenos?
   Sí, hago sándwiches deliciosos.
8. ¿Quién pone la mesa?
   Yo pongo la mesa.
9. ¿Qué pone usted en la mesa?
   En la mesa, pongo platos, azúcar, servilletas, cuchillos, tenedores, cucharas, sal, pimienta, y flores.
10. ¿Sale usted los sábados en la noche?
    Sí, salgo los sábados en la noche.
11. ¿Sale mucho Luis?
    Sí, Luis sale todas las noches.
12. ¿A qué hora salen ustedes?
    Salimos a las ocho de la mañana.

13. ¿Qué hace usted los sábados?
    Hago muchas cosas los sábados.
14. ¿Hace usted ejercicios en la clase de gimnasia?
    Sí, hago ejercicios en la clase de gimnasia.
15. ¿Trae usted la guía de teléfonos a la clase?
    No. Eso es ridículo. No traigo la guía de teléfonos a la clase. Traigo el libro de español a la clase.

12.3 *Creating Sentences*

CLASS: Match up the words below to form sentences.

¿Traigo
Shall I bring(?)

Traemos
We bring

¿Traemos
Shall we bring(?)

¿Traes (familiar)
Will you bring(?)

fruta
pan
refrescos
los libros
carne
tomates

al día de campo
del supermercado
para los niños
a la clase
para la cena
para la ensalada

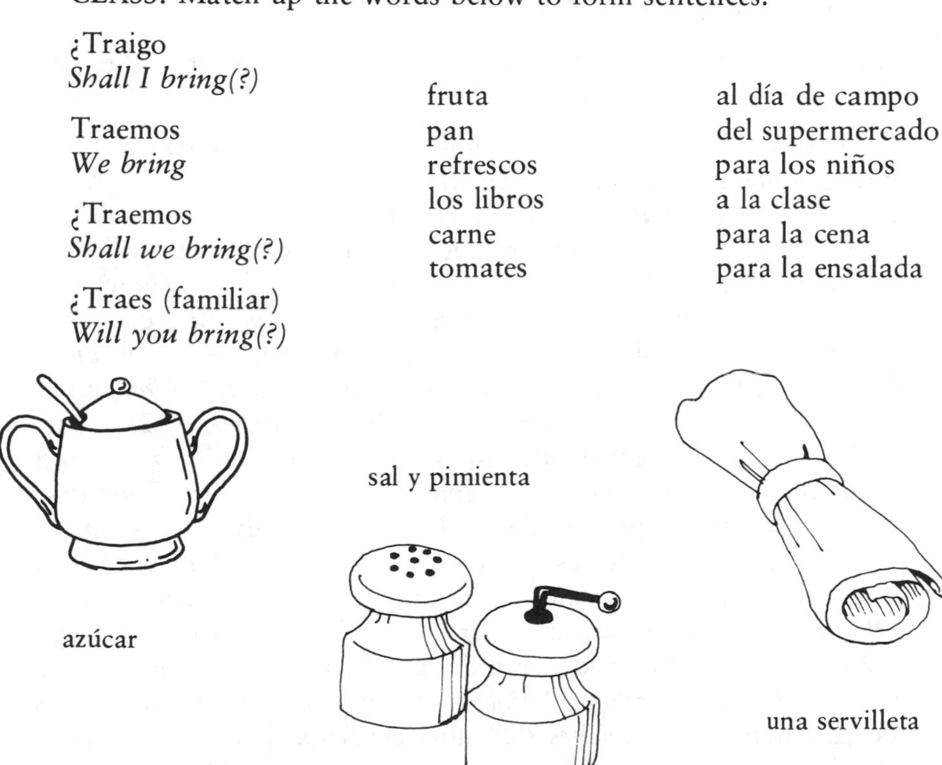

12.4 *Creating Sentences*

CLASS: Repeat the words in the next two columns after your teacher says them in Spanish. Then, combine words from each column to form a complete sentence. Create your own sentences.

Vengo, *I'm coming*
¿Viene? *Are you coming?*
Venimos, *we are coming*
Vienen, *they are coming*
¿Quién viene? *Who is coming?*
¿Por qué no viene? *Why don't you come?*
¿Cuándo viene? *When are you coming? When is he, she, it coming?*

al día de campo, *to the picnic*
a la playa, *to the beach*
a la fiesta, *to the party*
al concierto, *to the concert*
a mi casa, *to my house*
al cine, *to the movies*
al museo, *to the museum*
a la clase, *to the class*

12.5 *Vocabulary*

For the Conversation below.

CLASS: Repeat each word or phrase, in unison, after your teacher says it in Spanish.

1. ¿Vienes a la fiesta? *Are you coming to the party? (familiar)* 2. esta noche, *tonight* 3. con mucho gusto, *with much pleasure* 4. ¿A qué hora vienes? *At what time are you coming? (fam.)* 5. a las ocho, *at eight o'clock* 6. ¿Tienes música buena para la fiesta? *Have you good music for the party?* 7. Tengo discos muy buenos. *I have very good records* 8. ¿Tienes una guitarra para la fiesta? *Have you a guitar for the party?* 9. Lo siento, pero no tengo guitarra. *I'm sorry, but I haven't.* 10. ¿Traigo la guitarra de mi primo? *Shall I bring my cousin's guitar?* 11. ¡Ay sí, por favor! *Oh, yes, please!* 12. Bueno, *O.K.* 13. Nos vemos. *I'll be seeing you (We'll be seeing each other).* 14. más tarde, *later (more late)* 15. Adiós. *Good-bye.* 16. ¿Tienes dulces para la fiesta? *Have you candy for the party?* 17. Tengo muchos dulces. *I have a lot of candy (much candy).* 18. ¿Tienes suficientes sándwiches? *Have you enough sandwiches?* 19. Tengo muchos sándwiches para todos. *I have many sandwiches for everybody.* 20. sándwiches de rosbif con lechuga y mayonesa, *roast beef sandwiches with lettuce and mayonnaise* 21. sándwiches de jamón, *ham sandwiches* 22. una ensalada de pollo, *a chicken salad* 23. una ensalada de papas, *a potato salad* 24. ¿Qué traigo para la fiesta? *What shall I bring for the party?* 25. ¿Por qué no traes un pollo a la parrilla? *Why don't you bring a grilled chicken?*

Familiar form: Add a letter S to the YOU form.
Examples: tú vienes, *you come (familiar)*
tú traes, *you bring (familiar)*

12.6 *Conversation*

CLASS: Your teacher will point out students to take the roles of Susana and Alberto. Play your role as well as you can. Let's see if you are a good actor.

LA FIESTA

Susana —¿Vienes a mi fiesta esta noche?
Alberto—Sí, con mucho gusto.
Susana —¿A qué hora vienes?
Alberto—A las ocho. ¿Tienes música buena para la fiesta?
Susana —Sí, tengo unos discos muy buenos.
Alberto—¿Tienes una guitarra para la fiesta?
Susana —No. Lo siento, pero no tengo una guitarra.
Alberto—¿Traigo la guitarra de mi primo?
Susana —¡Ay sí, por favor!
Alberto—Bueno, nos vemos más tarde. Adiós.

Two other students will take the roles below.

Juan —¿Tienes dulces para la fiesta?
Susana—Sí, tengo muchos dulces.
Juan —¿Tienes suficientes sándwiches?
Susana—Sí, tengo muchos sándwiches para todos.
Juan —¿Tienes sándwiches de rosbif?
Susana—Sí, sándwiches de rosbif con lechuga y mayonesa.
Juan —¿Tienes sándwiches de jamón?
Susana—Sí, tengo muchos sándwiches de jamón.
Juan —¿Tienes una ensalada?
Susana—Tengo dos ensaladas. Una ensalada de pollo y una ensalada de papas.
Juan —¿Qué traigo para la fiesta?
Susana—¿Por qué no traes un pollo a la parrilla?
Juan —Sí, con mucho gusto. Bueno, adiós. Nos vemos más tarde.

12.7 *Exercises*

Answer these questions:

1. ¿Trae usted un diccionario a la clase? 2. ¿Hace usted sopa buena? 3. ¿Tiene usted un satélite en su garaje? 4. ¿Pone usted sal y pimienta en la mesa? 5. ¿Pone usted la mesa en su casa? 6. ¿Pone usted servilletas en la mesa? 7. ¿Pone usted un elefante en la mesa? 8. ¿Pone usted platos en la mesa? 9. ¿Toma usted gasolina para el almuerzo? 10. ¿Oye usted a los estudiantes en la clase? 11. ¿Oye usted música en la clase? 12. ¿Oímos español en la clase?

Translate these sentences into Spanish.

13. Gloria is coming to the party. 14. Are you coming to the class? 15. Albert comes to my house. 16. I hear interesting programs on the radio. 17. I set the table. 18. The snow falls softly. 19. They go out on Saturdays. 20. I put forks on the table. 21. They put spoons on the table. 22. Do you put flowers on the table? 23. We put knives on the table. 24. Do you want to go to the park with me? 25. Do you want to go to the moon?

REPEAT: 1. no tengo tiempo, *I haven't time* 2. no puedo, *I can't* 3. no puedo ir, *I can't (to) go.* 4. no quiero ir, *I don't want to go.* 5. tengo que ir al banco, *I have to go to the bank.*

LESSON 13

Irregular Verbs, Present Tense (continued)

LIST OF IRREGULAR VERBS
PRESENT TENSE

REMEMBER how important Irregular Verbs are.

NOTE: The first eight irregular verbs are listed in Lesson 12. Now we continue with the rest of the list.

VER, *to see,* is almost regular. It should be "vo" in the "I" form, but it is not. VEO is *I see.*

1. ver, *to see*

veo	ve	vemos	ven
I see	*you see*	*we see*	*they see*

Then come the little OY brothers, which are regular except for the OY ending, and the accents on ESTÁ and ESTÁN.

2. estar, *to be (location)*

estoy	está	estamos	están
I am	*you are*	*we are*	*they are*

3. ir, *to go*

voy	va	vamos	van
I go	*you go*	*we go*	*they go*

4. dar, *to give*

doy	da	damos	dan
I give	*you give*	*we give*	*they give*

One little OY brother is completely different from all the others, but you already know it:

5. ser, *to be*

soy	es	somos	son
I am	*you are*	*we are*	*they are*

There are two other important verbs which are irregular (different):

6. decir, *to say*

digo	dice	decimos	dicen
I say	*you say*	*we say*	*they say*

7. saber, *to know*

sé	sabe	sabemos	saben
I know	*you know*	*we know*	*they know*

13.1 *Creating Sentences*

CLASS: Repeat the words in the two columns below after your teacher says them in Spanish. Then, combine words from each column to form a complete sentence. Create your own sentences.

A.

Sé
I know
¿Sabe usted
Do you know(?)
Juan sabe
John knows
Alicia sabe
Alice knows
Sabemos
We know
Saben
They know
No sé
I don't know
No saben
They don't know

la dirección, *the address*
el número de teléfono, *the phone number*
la lección, *the lesson*
las frases, *the sentences*
el vocabulario, *the vocabulary*
las palabras, *the words*
la palabra, *the word*
el verbo, *the verb*
los verbos, *the verbs*
la respuesta, *the answer*
el número, *the number*
cuánto es, *how much it is*
cuánto cuesta, *how much it costs*
si tiene tiempo, *if he, she, has time*

B.

Julia dice	que es interesante, *that it's interesting*
Julia says	que es bueno, *that it's good (masc.)*
Pedro dice	que es malo, *that it's bad (masc.)*
Peter says	que eres simpático, *that you (fam.) are nice*
Dicen	que es imposible, *that it's impossible*
They say	que no puede, *that he can't, that she can't*
Mis amigos dicen	que no quiere, *that he, she doesn't want to*
My friends say	que no sabe, *that he, she doesn't know*

Remember these words:

CLASS: Repeat these words, in unison, after the teacher says them in Spanish.

las respuestas, *the answers*
los estudiantes, *the students*
muy bien, *very well*
interesante, *interesting*
la dirección, *the address*
un concierto, *a concert*

¿ve usted? *do you see?*
¿va usted? *are you going?*
somos, *we are, are we?*
¿qué dice? *what do you say? what does he (she) say?*
¿qué dice Juan? *what does John say?*
ir, *to go*
¿qué dicen? *what do they say?*
¿saben? *do they know?* saben, *they know*
¿sabemos? *do we know?* sabemos, *we know*
voy, *I'm going, I go*
dice, *you say; he, she says*
eres mi amigo, *you (fam.) are my friend*
es muy tarde, *it's very late*
quiere ir, *he, she wants to go*

13.2 *Speaking Exercise*

CLASS: Answer these questions when your teacher calls on you. Read the answers in the book.

1. ¿Va usted a la clase esta tarde?
   Sí. Voy a la clase esta tarde.
2. ¿Va usted a una fiesta esta noche?
   Sí. Voy a una fiesta esta noche.
3. ¿Va usted al cine esta tarde?
   No. No voy al cine esta tarde. Voy a la clase.
4. ¿Somos estudiantes excelentes?
   Sí. Somos estudiantes fantásticos.
5. ¿Qué dice Julia?
   Julia dice que la clase es interesante.
6. ¿Qué dice Pedro?
   Pedro dice que es imposible ir.
7. ¿Qué dicen?
   Dicen que no saben la dirección.
8. ¿Saben las respuestas?
   Sí. Saben las respuestas.
9. ¿Sabemos la lección en la clase?
   Sí. Sabemos la lección en la clase.
10. ¿Qué dice Ana?
    Ana dice que es muy tarde y quiere ir a casa.

13.3 *Exercises*

A. CLASS: Give your teacher the "I" form of a verb below. End the verb in GO.

1. tener, *to have*	________ *I have*
2. venir, *to come*	________ *I come*
3. hacer, *to do, to make*	________ *I do, I make*
4. poner, *to put, to set (the table)*	________ *I put, I set (the table)*
5. traer, *to bring*	________ *I bring*
6. salir, *to go out, leave*	________ *I go out, I leave (a place)*
7. oír, *to hear*	________ *I hear*
8. decir, *to say*	________ *I say*

Oigo el radio. *I listen to the radio.*

B. Give your teacher the WE form of a verb below. End the verb in MOS.

1. poner, *to put, set* ________ *we put, set (the table)*
2. traer, *to bring* ________ *we bring*
3. tener, *to have* ________ *we have*
4. hacer, *to do, to make* ________ *we do, we make*
5. salir, *to go out, leave* ________ *we go out, leave (a place)*
6. venir, *to come* ________ *we come*
7. oír, *to hear* ________ *we hear*
8. decir, *to say* ________ *we say*

13.4 *Vocabulary*

For the Conversation below

CLASS: Repeat these words, in unison, after your teacher says them in Spanish.

1. ¿Qué vas a hacer? *What are you going to do?* 2. esta tarde, *this afternoon* 3. Voy a limpiar la casa. *I'm going to clean the house.* 4. ¿No quieres ir al parque? *Don't you want to go to the park?* 5. No puedo. *I can't.* 6. Tengo que limpiar la casa. *I have to clean the house.* 7. ¿Por qué no vas al parque? *Why don't you go to the park?* 8. conmigo, *with me* 9. Te digo que no puedo. *I tell you that I can't.* 10. te, (to) *you (familiar)* 11. pero, *but* 12. esta noche, *tonight* 13. algo, *something* 14. puedo hacer algo, *I can do something* 15. ¿Quieres ir al cine? *Do you want to go to the movies?* 16. ¿quieres? *do you want? (familiar)* 17. Te invito. *I invite you (I'll pay).* 18. ¡Ay, sí! *Oh, yes!* 19. muchas gracias, *thank you very much* 20. ¿Por qué no vamos? *Why don't we go?* 21. ¿Por qué no vamos a ver la película? *Why don't we go to see the film?* 22. la película, *the film* 23. Dicen que es una comedia excelente. *They say that it's an excellent*

comedy. 24. ¡Qué buena idea! *What a good idea!* 25. el sábado, *on Saturday* 26. ¿Y tú? *And you? (familiar)* 27. el domingo, *on Sunday* 28. mi tía, *my aunt* 29. ¿Quieres ir? *Do you want to go?* 30. un concierto, *a concert* 31. por la noche, *at night* 32. Vamos al concierto. *Let's go to the concert.*

13.5 *Conversation*

CLASS: These are two natural, everyday conversations about making plans for the weekend. Your teacher will select students, two by two, who will go to the front of the class, and conduct a conversation about making plans. Take your book with you. First, read a block in the book. Then, close the book and repeat the same conversation on your own. Say anything you want, but only in Spanish. Use your acting skills.

MAKING PLANS FOR THE WEEKEND

First student —¿Qué vas a hacer esta tarde?
Second student—Voy a limpiar la casa.
First student —¿No quieres ir al parque?
Second student—No puedo. Tengo que limpiar la casa.
First student —¿Por qué no vas al parque conmigo?
Second student—Te digo que no puedo. Pero esta noche puedo hacer algo. ¿Quieres ir al cine conmigo? Te invito.
First student —¡Ay, sí! Muchas gracias. ¿Por qué no vamos a ver la película en el Teatro Central? Dicen que es una comedia excelente.
Second student—Sí. ¡Qué buena idea!

First student —¿Qué vas a hacer el sábado?
Second student—Voy al cine. ¿Y tú?
First student —Voy al teatro.
Second student—¿Qué vas a hacer el domingo?
First student —Voy a visitar a mi tía.
Second student—¿No quieres ir al parque?
First student —No. Quiero visitar a mi tía.
Second student—¿Quieres ir a un concierto esta noche?
First student —Sí. Esta noche sí puedo.

REMEMBER:

1. In general, the PLURAL of words which do not end in A, E, I, O, U is formed by adding ES to the singular (nouns, adjectives):

SINGULAR	PLURAL
flor, *flower*	flores, *flowers*
animal, *animal*	animales, *animals*
tenedor, *fork*	tenedores, *forks*

2. In general, adverbs are formed by adding MENTE to adjectives (LY = MENTE).

suave, *soft*	suavemente, *softly*
natural, *natural*	naturalmente, *naturally*
general, *general*	generalmente, *generally*

13.6 *Exercise*

CLASS: Create sentences with the words in the columns below:

VOY, *I go*
I'm going
NO VOY, *I don't go*
I'm not going
¿VA, *do you go (?)*
¿VAMOS, *are we going (?)*
shall we go (?)
VAMOS, *Let's go*
we are going
VAN, *they are going*

a la playa, *to the beach*
a nadar, *swimming (to swim)*
a la piscina, *to the swimming pool*
con usted, *with you*
contigo, *with you (familiar)*
con él, *with him*
con ella, *with her*
con ellos, *with them (masc.)*
con ellas, *with them (fem.)*
todos los días, *every day*
los sábados, *on Saturdays*
a pescar, *to fish (fishing)*
juntos, *together*

WORD BUILDER

You can convert most English words which end in IVE or RY into Spanish by ending them in the letter O.
Examples: IVE = IVO productivo, activo
RY = RIO canario, extraordinario

Most English words which end in OR, AL, BLE are alike in English and in Spanish.

Examples: OR = OR color, superior
AL = AL capital, central
BLE = BLE terrible, posible

Luis va a salir. *Louis is going out.*

13.7 *Exercise*

Translate these sentences into Spanish:

1. We are going to the picnic. 2. When? 3. I don't know. 4. We are going on Sunday. 5. When are they going? 6. Shall I go with him? 7. We go every day. 8. Let's go swimming. 9. Shall I go with you? 10. Shall I go with Marta? 11. I'm not going swimming. 12. Shall we go together?

Your teacher will dictate. Give these words in Spanish.

13. the action. 14. the film. 15. necessary. 16. the dictionary. 17. the emotion. 18. with me. 19. tomorrow. 20. Gee whiz!

LESSON 14

The Command (Imperative)

THE COMMAND

1. To form the singular regular Command:
   End AR verbs in the letter E
   End ER and IR verbs in the letter A
   Examples: comprar, *to buy.*
   Compre pan. *Buy (some) bread.*
   escribir, *to write*
   Escriba la lección. *Write the lesson.*
2. Stress the next to the last syllable of the Command, just as you do in the Present Tense: COM-pre, es-CRI-ba.

14.1 *Pronunciation Exercise*

Pronounce the Command form of the following verbs:

	INFINITIVE	COMMAND
1.	estudiar, *to study*	es-TU-die, *study*
2.	vender, *to sell*	VEN-da, *sell*
3.	escribir, *to write*	es-CRI-ba, *write*
4.	lavar, *to wash*	LA-ve, *wash*
5.	planchar, *to iron*	PLAN-che, *iron*
6.	ayudar, *to help*	a-YU-de, *help*
7.	mandar, *to send*	MAN-de, *send*
8.	aprender, *to learn*	a-PREN-da, *learn*
9.	mirar, *to look at*	¡MI-re! *Look!*
10.	llevar, *to take*	LLE-ve, *take*
11.	esperar, *to wait for, to hope*	es-PE-re, *wait for*
12.	saludar, *to greet, to say hello to*	sa-LU-de, *greet*

Llévеme al aeropuerto, por favor.

USE OF PRONOUNS IN THE COMMAND

Pronouns are added on to the singular, affirmative Command to form one word. Examples:

Escríbame. *Write to me.*
Espéreme. *Wait for me.*
Míreme. *Look at me.*
Prométame. *Promise me.*
Ayúdeme. *Help me.*

Invítelo. *Invite him.*
Espérelo. *Wait for him.*
Espérela. *Wait for her.*
Ayúdela. *Help her.*
Mírelo. *Look at him.*

NOTE: There is a written accent on the third syllable from the end when it is stressed. Examples: de-mo-CRÁ-ti-co, a-YÚ-de-me.

14.2 *Hearing Exercise*

CLASS: Repeat each sentence, in unison, after your teacher says it in Spanish.

1. Cómpreme un periódico. *Buy me a newspaper.*
2. Mire la mariposa. *Look at the butterfly.*
3. Escriba las frases. *Write the sentences.*
4. Invítelo a la fiesta. *Invite him to the party.*
5. Invítela al baile. *Invite her to the dance.*
6. Visítenos pronto. *Visit us soon.*
7. Cánteme una canción. *Sing me a song.*
8. Lléveme al cine. *Take me to the movies.*
9. Lléveme al aeropuerto. *Take me to the airport.*
10. Ayúdeme, por favor. *Help me, please.*
11. Mándeme un par de botas. *Send me a pair of boots.*
12. Mándeme una bufanda. *Send me a scarf.*
13. Lave la ropa. *Wash the clothes.*
14. No grite tanto. *Don't scream so much.*
15. Espéreme. *Wait for me.*
16. Venga conmigo. *Come with me.*
17. Salude a Carlos. *Say hello to Carlos.*

IRREGULAR VERBS IN THE COMMAND FORM

All the irregular GO verbs in the Present Tense become GA verbs in the Command.

Examples:	vengo, *I come*	venga, *come*
	oigo, *I hear, I listen*	oiga, *listen*

la mariposa

14.3 *Command Exercise*

CLASS: Your teacher will call on you to read the three forms of a verb, as indicated.

	INFINITIVE	PRESENT TENSE	COMMAND
1.	traer *to bring*	traigo *I bring*	traiga *bring*
2.	hacer *to do, to make*	hago *I do, I make*	haga *do, make*
3.	poner *to put, to set*	pongo *I put, I set*	ponga *put, set*
4.	salir *to go out, leave*	salgo *I go out, I leave*	salga *go out, leave*
5.	tener *to have*	tengo *I have*	tenga *have*
6.	venir *to come*	vengo *I come*	venga *come*
7.	oír *to hear, to listen*	oigo *I hear, I listen*	oiga *hear, listen*
8.	decir *to say, to tell*	digo *I say, I tell*	diga *tell*

CLASS: Now, your teacher will give you an Infinitive, and you give the I form of the Present Tense, and the Command (as above). Close your books.

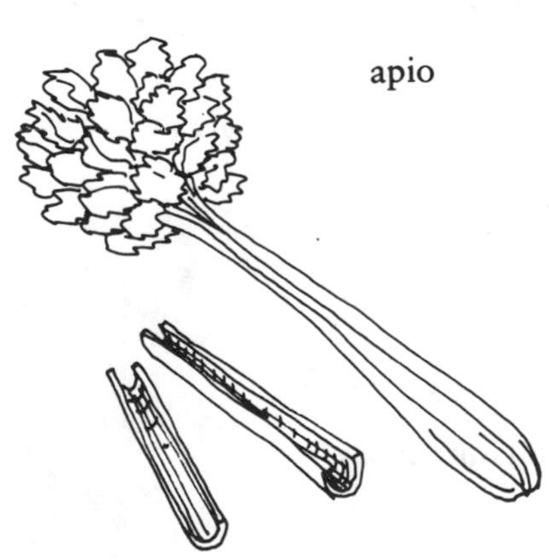

apio

lechuga

14.4 *Creating Sentences*

CLASS: Your teacher will ask you to match up the words in the columns below, to form sentences.

Traiga *Bring*	un lápiz chocolates un regalo
Tráigame *Bring (to) me*	un disco un vaso de agua, *a glass of water*
Tráigale *Bring (to) him* *Bring (to) her*	un vaso de leche, *a glass of milk* un sándwich de jamón, *a ham sandwich* un refresco, *a refreshment* chorizos, *sausages*
Tráiganos *Bring (to) us*	apio, *celery* cebollas, *onions*
Tráigales *Bring (to) them*	chicle, *chewing gum* unas toallas, *some towels* jabón, *soap*

14.5 *Remember These Words*

CLASS: Repeat these words and phrases, in unison, after your teacher says them in Spanish. Do not use English. Only look at the meaning of each word.

huevos, *eggs*
apio, *celery*
jamón, *ham*
leche, *milk*
pan, *bread*
una docena, *a dozen*
chorizos, *sausages*
limones, *lemons*
peras, *pears*
la tienda, *the store*
una docena de huevos, *a dozen eggs*
toallas blancas, *white towels*
una bolsa, *a purse, a bag*
para su tía, *for your aunt*
una botella, *a bottle*
un periódico, *a newspaper*
una manzana, *an apple*
lechuga, *lettuce*
supermercado, *supermarket*
la tienda de música, *the music store*
Voy al supermercado. *I'm going to the supermarket.*
¿Traigo apio? *Shall I bring celery?*
¿Qué traigo? *What shall I bring? (What do I bring?)*
traiga, *bring*
¿Qué más? *What else?*
¿Qué más traigo? *What else shall I bring? (do I bring?)*
Traiga toallas blancas. *Bring (some) white towels.*
una botella de perfume para mi tía, *a bottle of perfume for my aunt*
Venga conmigo. *Come with me.*

una bolsa

una botella de perfume

14.6 *Speaking Exercise*

CLASS: Answer these questions when your teacher calls on you. Read the answers in the book.

Examples: Voy al supermercado. ¿Qué traigo?
I'm going to the supermarket. What shall I bring?
Traiga pan, por favor.
Bring some bread, please.

1. ¿Qué traigo?
   Traiga pan, jamón y leche, por favor.
2. ¿Qué más traigo?
   Traiga una docena de huevos, por favor.
3. ¿Traigo fruta?
   Sí, traiga manzanas, peras y limones.
4. ¿Traigo apio?
   Sí, traiga apio y lechuga.
5. Voy a la tienda. ¿Qué traigo?
   Traiga dos toallas blancas y una bolsa para su tía.
6. Voy a la tienda de música. ¿Qué traigo?
   Traiga un caset y un disco popular.
7. ¿Traigo un periódico?
   Sí, por favor, traiga un periódico.
8. ¿Traigo chorizos?
   Sí, traiga chorizos.
9. ¿Traigo una botella de perfume para mi tía?
   Sí, traiga una botella de perfume para su tía.

CLASS: Could you answer the questions with books closed?

STEM-CHANGES IN THE COMMAND

Almost all stem-changes in the Command are the same as those of the "I" form in the Present Tense.
Examples:

recuerdo, *I remember*	¡Recuerde! *Remember!*
pienso, *I think*	¡Piense! *Think!*
cuento, *I count, tell (story)*	cuente, *tell (story)*

Cuénteme un cuento. *Tell me a story.*

THE PLURAL COMMAND

1. To make the US form of the Command, add MOS to the singular form of the Command.
   Examples: trabajemos, *let us work*
   compremos, *let's buy*
   hagamos, *let's make, let's do*

2. To make the YOU (pl.) form of the Command, add the letter N to the singular form of the Command.
   Examples: compren pan, *buy bread (you, pl.)*
   vengan temprano, *come early (you, pl.)*

Tráigame una ensalada, por favor.

14.7 *Exercise*

CLASS: Give the YOU plural form of the following Commands (add the letter N to the singular).

Examples:		
	venga, *come*	vengan, *come (pl.)*
	compre, *buy*	compren, *buy (pl.)*

	SINGULAR	PLURAL
1.	estudie, *study*	________
2.	escriba, *write*	________
3.	traiga, *bring*	________
4.	venga, *come*	________
5.	haga, *do, make*	________
6.	oiga, *listen*	________
7.	piense, *think*	________
8.	recuerde, *remember*	________
9.	duerma bien, *sleep well*	________
10.	vaya, *go (irregular)*	________

REMEMBER: When you command more than one person, give the plural command.

14.8 *Conversation*

CLASS: Your teacher will select two students to take the roles of waiter and customer. Act naturally. Other students could make up their own dialogue.

EN EL RESTAURANTE

First Student —¿Qué quiere usted (comer)?
Second Student—Yo quiero rosbif y papas. No tengo tenedor. Tráigame uno, por favor.
First Student —¿Quiere usted ensalada?
Second Student—Sí, por favor. Tráigame una ensalada de lechuga y tomates.
First Student —¿Le traigo un vaso de agua?
Second Student—No, gracias. Tráigame un refresco de limón, por favor.

14.9 *Translate the following commands into Spanish (optional):*

1. Speak Spanish. 2. Write the lesson. 3. Look! 4. Sell the house. 5. Send the package. 6. Learn the words. 7. Write the letter. 8. Bring the book to the class. 9. Write to me. 10. Wait for me. 11. Help me. 12. Invite him. 13. Invite her. 14. Sing me a song. 15. Take me to the movies. 16. Send me a pair of boots, please. 17. Come to the park with me. 18. Listen! (hear) 19. Tell me everything. 20. Bring me a glass of water, please. 21. Bring (some) sausages. 22. Go to the store. 23. Buy me chocolates. 24. Come (pl.) to the house. 25. Sleep well.

NOTE: LE means TO him, TO her, TO you

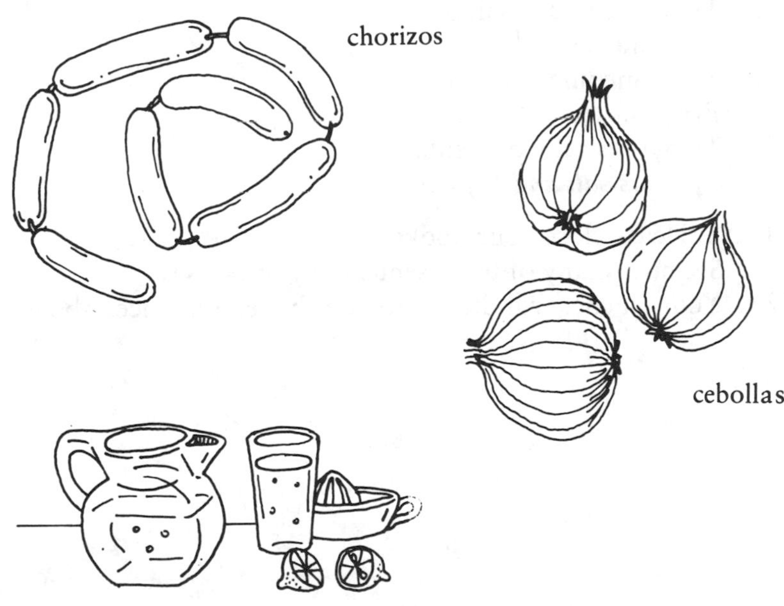

14.10 *Speed Reading Exercise*

CLASS: Read the Spanish sentences below very fast. Can you read five sentences in one breath?

1. Tráigame un vaso de agua, por favor.
   Bring me a glass of water, please.
2. Tráigale café, por favor.
   Bring her some coffee, please.
3. Tráigale un sándwich de atún, por favor.
   Bring him a tuna fish sandwich, please.
4. Tráigale un vaso de leche, por favor.
   Bring her a glass of milk, please.
5. Tráigame chocolate, por favor.
   Bring me some chocolate, please.
6. Tráigame lo mismo, por favor.
   Bring me the same thing, please.
7. Tráigale sopa de pollo, por favor.
   Bring her chicken soup, please.
8. Tráigame una ensalada.
   Bring me a salad.
9. Tráigame una cucharita.
   Bring me a teaspoon.
10. Tráiganos sal y pimienta.
    Bring us salt and pepper.

CLASS: Please close your books.

1. See how many of these sentences you can say.
2. Your teacher will dictate to you the ten sentences above.

LESSON 15

The Familiar Command
Direct and Indirect Object Pronouns

DIRECT AND INDIRECT OBJECT PRONOUNS

DIRECT OBJECT PRONOUNS

me	ME	NOS	*we, us*
you, it (masc.), him	LO	LOS	*you (masc. pl.), them (masc.)*
you, it (fem.), her	LA	LAS	*you (fem. pl.), them (fem.)*

Familiar form: te, *you (familiar)*

Examples:
Lo vi. *I saw him.*
Lo invité. *I invited him.*
Los visité. *I visited them.*
Nos invitó. *He invited us.*
La vi. *I saw her.*
La invité. *I invited her.*
Las invité. *I invited them.*
Lo vi. *I saw it (masc.)*

INDIRECT OBJECT PRONOUNS

to me	ME	NOS	*to us*
to you, *to him, to her*	LE	LES	*to you (pl.)* *to them*

Familiar form: te, *TO you (familiar)*

Examples:

Le mandé el paquete. *I sent the package TO him.*
I sent (to) him the package.

Tráigale el libro. *Bring the book TO him.*
Bring (to) him the book.

NOTICE: LE is used for persons.

POSITION OF PRONOUNS

1. Pronouns usually go before the verb.
   Examples: No lo veo. *I don't see him (it).*
   Lo invité. *I invited him.*
   La visité. *I visited her.*
   Le mandé un libro. *I sent him (her) a book.*
   Nos compró un regalo. *He bought us a present.*

2. Add Object Pronouns to the Infinitive to make one word.
   Examples:
   invitarla, *to invite her* Quiero invitarla. *I want to invite her.*
   comprarlo, *to buy it (masc.)* Quiero comprarlo. *I want to buy it.*

3. Add Object Pronouns to the Command to make one word.
   Examples:
   Cómpreme unos chocolates. *Buy me some chocolates.*
   Tráigame el libro. *Bring me the book.*
   Tráigale el dinero. *Bring (to) him, her the money.*

REMEMBER: 1. ¿Invitó usted? *Did you invite?*
2. ¿Visita usted? *Do you visit?*
3. ¿Va usted a la playa? *Are you going to the beach?*

15.1 *Speaking Exercise*

CLASS: Your teacher will point out individual students for an answer. Read the answer in the book.

1. ¿Invitó usted a Carlos a la fiesta?
   Sí, lo invité *(Yes, I invited him).*
2. ¿Invitó usted a Luisa?
   Sí, la invité.
3. ¿Invitó usted a María y a Marta?
   Sí, las invité.
4. ¿Ve usted a Julia?
   Sí, la veo.
5. ¿Vio usted a sus tíos ayer?
   Sí, los vi.
6. ¿Visitó usted a sus abuelos?
   Sí, los visité.

7. ¿Nos invitaron a la fiesta?
   Sí, nos invitaron.
8. ¿Va usted al concierto?
   Sí. Carlos me invitó.
9. ¿Van ustedes a la playa?
   Sí. David nos invitó.

CLASS: Answer the above questions with books closed.

15.2 *Creating Sentences with Pronouns (direct object)*

CLASS: Combine words from the two columns to create your own sentences.

Invítelo
Invite him

Invítela
Invite her

Tráigalo
Bring him

Tráigala
Bring her

Llévenos
Take us

Llévelos
Take them (masc. or masc. and fem.)

Mándelos
Send them (masc.)

a la fiesta, *to the party*
a la casa, *to the house, home*
al día de campo, *to the picnic*
a la playa, *to the beach*
al campo, *to the country*
a la coveción, *to the convention*
a la cena, *to dinner*
al almuerzo, *to lunch*
al desayuno, *to breakfast*
al concierto, *to the concert*
al museo, *to the museum*
al cine, *to the movies*
al ballet, *to the ballet*
a la ópera, *to the opera*
al restaurante, *to the restaurant*
al juego, *to the game*
al baile, *to the dance*

REMEMBER: LO, *him, you, it (masc.)*
LA, *her, you, it (fem.)*
LE, *to him, to her, to you.*

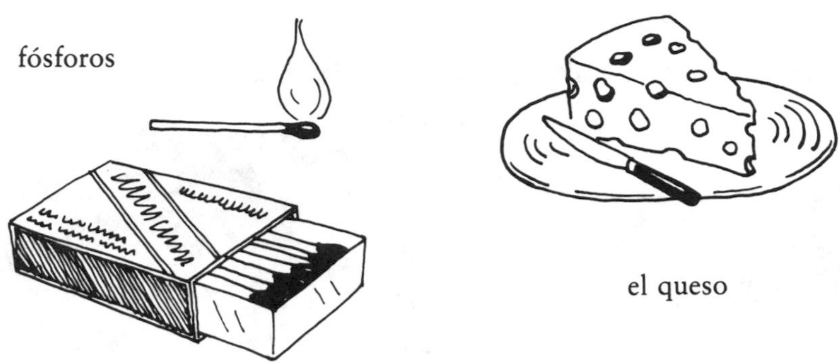

NOTE: Verbs which end in CO in the Present "I" form change to QUE in the Command form.

Example:

TOCO, *I play (an instrument)*
TOQUE la guitarra, por favor. *Play the guitar, please.*

Regular verbs that end in GO in the Present Tense change to GUE in the Command form.

Example:

LLEGO, I arrive.
LLEGUE a tiempo, por favor. *Get here/there (arrive) on time, please.*

REMEMBER: HAY, *there is, is there?*
there are, are there?
Examples: Hay una fiesta esta noche. *There is a party tonight.*
No hay clases. *There aren't any classes.*

EVERYDAY EXPRESSIONS

¿Hay una pluma roja? *Is there a red pen?*
Hay muchas flores rojas. *There are many red flowers.*
¿Hay leche? *Is there any milk?*
No hay agua caliente. *There is no hot water.*
¿Hay boletos para esta noche? *Are there tickets for tonight?*

No hay nada. *There isn't anything (nothing).*
No hay nadie. *There isn't anybody (nobody).*
¿Hay italianos en su clase? *Are there any Italians in your class?*
Hay muchos estudiantes en la fiesta. *There are a lot of students at the party.*
¿Hay queso? *Is there any cheese?*
¿Hay chiles? *Are there any hot peppers?*
¿Hay carne? *Is there any meat?*
¿Hay chile con carne? *Is there any meat with hot peppers?*
Sí, hay mucho. *Yes, there is a lot.*

15.3 *Exercise*

Translate these commands into Spanish.

1. Invite him to the beach. 2. Invite her to the museum. 3. Bring them (masc.) to the restaurant. 4. Take us to the game. 5. Take her to the class. 6. Take me to the station. 7. Invite them (masc.) to the picnic. 8. Bring her to the beach. 9. Visit us tomorrow. 10. Take us to the airport.

15.4 *Creating Sentences with Pronouns (indirect object)*

CLASS: Combine words from the two columns to create your own sentences.

Tráigame
Bring me (to me)

Tráigale
Bring him (to him)
Bring her (to her)

Tráiganos
Bring us (to us)

Deme
give me

Dele
give (to) him, her

el paquete, *the package*
el regalo, *the present*
un vaso de agua, *a glass of water*
un vaso de leche, *a glass of milk*
un sándwich de jamón, *a ham sandwich*
un refresco, *a refreshment*
chicle, *(some) chewing gum*
la llave, *the key*
un paraguas, *an umbrella*
unos fósforos, *some matches*
una camisa, *a shirt*
un par de zapatos, *a pair of shoes*
aretes, *earrings*
un anillo, *a ring*
un collar, *a necklace*

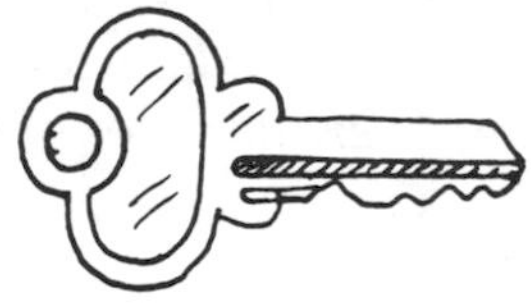

la llave

15.5 *Exercise*

Translate these Commands into Spanish:

1. Bring me a glass of milk, please. 2. Bring us some matches, please. 3. Bring (to) her the key, please. 4. Give (to) her a present. 5. Bring them some chewing gum. 6. Give me the package, please. 7. Take a shirt to him. 8. Send me a pair of shoes, please. 9. Give (to) her the earrings. 10. Buy her a necklace.

THE FAMILIAR COMMAND

1. To form the Familiar Command, end AR verbs in A, and ER and IR verbs in E.

Examples:	FAMILIAR COMMAND
comprar, *to buy*	Compra el libro. *Buy the book.*
mirar, *to look*	¡Mira! *Look!*
correr, *to run*	Corre. *Run.*
escribir, *to write*	Escríbeme. *Write to me.*

2. To form the Familiar Command of some GO verbs, drop the GO.

Examples:	
vengo, *I come*	Ven conmigo. *Come with me*
digo, *I say, I tell*	Di. *Tell.* Dime. *Tell me.*
salgo, *I go out*	Sal. *Go out.*
pongo, *I put, I set*	Pon la mesa. *Set the table.*
tengo, *I have*	Ten esto. *Have this. Take this.*

Other Familiar Commands are different:

traigo, *I bring*	Trae. *Bring.*
oigo, *I hear, listen*	¡Oye! *Listen!*
hago, *I do, make*	Haz esto. *Do this.*

Cómprale el anillo.
Buy her the ring (familiar).

¡Míralo!
Look at it! (familiar)

EVERYDAY COMMANDS

Vuelva pronto. *Come back soon.*
Recuerde. *Remember!*
Perdón. *Pardon me.*
Quédese. *Stay (yourself). Stay here.*
Quédese conmigo. *Stay with me.*
Ayúdeme, por favor. *Help me, please.*
Venga conmigo. *Come with me.*
Ven con ella. *Come with her (familiar).*
Óyeme. *Listen (hear) to me (familiar).*
Ponlo en la mesa. *Put it on the table (familiar).*
Dime tu dirección. *Tell me your address (familiar).*

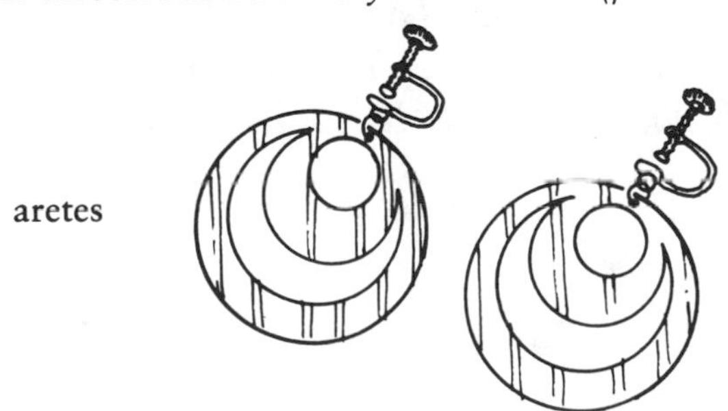

aretes

15.6 *Exercises*

A. Translate these Commands (optional):

1. Invite him to the house. 2. Bring her to the dance. 3. Take us to the hospital. 4. Give me a ham sandwich, please. 5. Take them (masc.) to the park. 6. Send her to the bank. 7. Bring him an umbrella. 8. Give her the money. 9. Bring me the salt, please. 10. Give me (some) chocolates. 11. Buy her a bottle of perfume. 12. Take us to the country. 13. Say "hello" to Robert. 14. Bring him to the party. 15. Give me a glass of water, please. 16. Take us to the ballet. 17. Give me the book. 18. Send them the package. 19. Give me the dictionary, please.

REMEMBER: When the word IT stands for a masculine noun, use the word LO. When IT stands for a feminine noun, use LA.

B. CLASS: Give the correct pronoun below. Read the complete sentence.

1. ¿Invitó a Roberto? Sí, ______ invité. 2. ¿Invitó a Julia? Sí, ______ invité. 3. ¿Visitó a sus tíos? Sí, ______ visité. 4. ¿Vio a Luisa? Sí, ______ vi. 5. ¿Compró el suéter? Sí, ______ compré. 6. ¿Compró la casa? No. No ______ compré. 7. ¿Compró el abrigo? Sí, ______ compré. 8. ¿Le escribe cartas? No. No ______ escribo muchas cartas. 9. ¿Invitó a María y a Roberto? Sí, ______ invité. 10. ¿Nos invitaron? Sí, ______ invitaron.

REMEMBER: LE does not represent things.

Tráigala. *Bring her. Bring it (fem.).*
Tráigalo. *Bring him. Bring it (masc.).*
Tráigale. *Bring TO HIM. Bring TO HER.*

Tráigale la guitarra (a María).
Bring the guitar to her. Bring her the guitar.
Tráigala. *Bring it (the guitar).*

LESSON 16

How to form the Present Subjunctive
Use of the Present Subjunctive

HOW TO FORM THE PRESENT SUBJUNCTIVE

1. AR verbs end in the letter E in the Present Subjunctive.
2. ER, IR, and IRREGULAR verbs end in the letter A.

The following rule shows you how to form virtually every Present Subjunctive in the Spanish language.

RULE: Take the "I" form of the Present Tense (Indicative).

1. For AR verbs, change the final letter O to E.
2. For other verbs (ER, IR, IRREGULAR verbs), change the final letter O to A.

Examples:

Present (Indicative) "I" form	Present Subjunctive
AR: compro, *I buy*	compre, *buy*
E to IE: cierro, *I close*	cierre, *close*
U to UE: cuento, *I count*	cuente, *count*
ER: vendo, *I sell*	venda, *sell*
IR: escribo, *I write*	escriba, *write*
E to IE: pierdo, *I lose*	pierda, *lose*
O to UE: puedo, *I can*	pueda, *can*
IRREGULAR: vengo, *I come*	venga, *come*

USE OF THE PRESENT SUBJUNCTIVE

The Subjunctive is used with expressions of request and preference.
Examples:
QUIERO QUE. *I want you to. I want him, her, it to.*
ESPERO QUE. *I hope that you will. I hope that he, she, it will.*
OJALÁ QUE (Oh Allah that). *I certainly hope that you, he, she, it will.*

Examples:

Quiero que traiga unas flores. *I want you to bring some flowers.*
Espero que venga a la fiesta. *I hope that you will come to the party.*
Ojalá que tenga tiempo. *I certainly hope that you will have time.*

16.1 *Remember These Words*

CLASS: Repeat these words, in unison, after your teacher says them in Spanish.

conmigo, *with me*
el paquete, *the package*
lo, *it (masc.)*
a las nueve, *at nine o'clock*
pronto, *soon*
nos, *us*

quiero que trabaje, *I want you to work*
quiero que mande, *I want you to send*
quiero que venga, *I want you to come*
quiero que espere, *I want you to wait*
espero que venga, *I hope that he will come*
espero que venda, *I hope that you sell*
espero que traiga, *I hope that he will bring*
ojalá que lo vea, *I certainly hope that she will see it*
espero que escriba, *I hope that he will write*
espero que vaya, *I hope that he will go (exception to the Subjunctive rule)*

IMPORTANT: Object pronouns go before the Subjunctive forms.

Example: Quiero que me espere, *I want you to wait for me.*

NOTE: To maintain the same sound in the Present Subjunctive, there are changes in spelling.

Present Indicative	Present Subjunctive
TOCO, *I play*	Quiero que toque el piano. *I want you (him, her) to play the piano.*
PAGO, *I pay*	Ojalá que me pague mañana. *I hope he pays me tomorrow.*

16.2 *Reading Exercise*

CLASS: Repeat each sentence, in unison, after your teacher says it in Spanish.

1. Quiero que trabaje conmigo mañana.
   I want you to work with me tomorrow.
2. Quiero que mande el paquete.
   I want you to send the package.
3. Quiero que venga a las nueve.
   I want you to come at nine o'clock.
4. Quiero que me espere.
   I want you to wait for me.
5. Espero que venga a la fiesta.
   I hope that you (he, she) will come to the party.
6. Espero que venda la casa pronto.
   I hope that you will sell the house soon.
7. Espero que Roberto traiga a María a la fiesta.
   I hope that Robert will bring María to the party.
8. Ojalá que mi tío nos visite.
   I certainly hope that my uncle will visit us.
9. Ojalá que lo vea.
   I certainly hope that you will see it.
10. Ojalá que me escriba.
    I certainly hope that he (she) will write to me.
11. Ojalá que no pierda la llave.
    I certainly hope that he will not lose the key.
12. Espero que vaya al juego conmigo.
    I hope that you will go to the game with me.

16.3 *Exercise (optional)*

Your teacher will dictate some of the sentences above, or will ask you to translate them into English, one at a time.

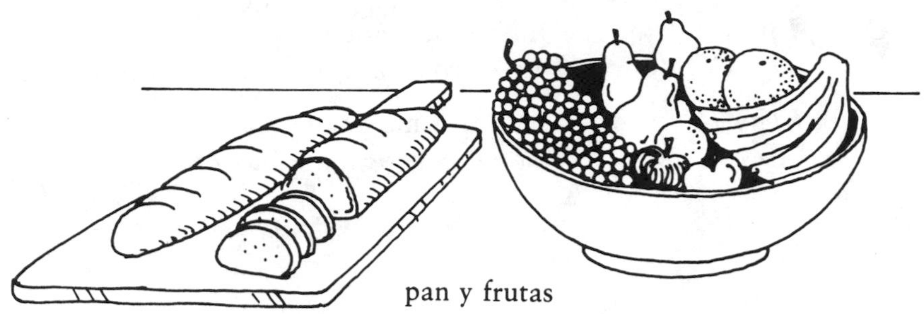

pan y frutas

LEARN these:

¿Quiere que trabaje con usted? *Do you want me to work with you?*
¿Quiere que mande el paquete? *Do you want me to send the package?*
¿Quiere que venda la casa? *Do you want me to sell the house?*
¿Quiere que compre una revista? *Do you want me to buy a magazine?*
Sí, quiero que compre una revista. *Yes, I want you to buy a magazine.*

16.4 *Speaking Exercise*

CLASS: Your teacher will point out individual students who will answer a question. Read the answer in the book.

1. ¿Quiere que trabaje con usted? Sí, quiero que trabaje conmigo.
2. ¿Quiere que mande el paquete? Sí, quiero que mande el paquete.
3. ¿Quiere que venda la bicicleta? Sí, quiero que venda la bicicleta.
4. ¿Quiere que venga mañana? Sí, quiero que venga mañana.
5. ¿Quiere que compre pan? Sí, quiero que compre pan y frutas.
6. ¿Quiere que compre una revista? Sí, quiero que compre una revista.
7. ¿Quiere que venga a la fiesta? Sí, quiero que venga a la fiesta.
8. ¿Quiere que espere a Julia? Sí, quiero que espere a Julia.
9. ¿Quiere que traiga la guitarra a la fiesta? Sí, quiero que traiga la guitarra a la fiesta.
10. ¿Quiere que lo vea? *(Do you want me to see it?)* Sí, quiero que lo vea.

11. ¿Quiere que escriba la carta? Sí, quiero que escriba la carta.
12. ¿Quiere que prepare sopa para la cena? Sí, quiero que prepare sopa para la cena.
13. ¿Quiere que vaya al cine con usted? Sí, quiero que vaya al cine conmigo.
14. ¿Quiere que vaya a la fiesta con usted? Sí, quiero que vaya a la fiesta conmigo.
15. ¿Quiere que haga dulces? *(Do you want me to make some candy?)* ¡Ay sí! Quiero que haga dulces.

CLASS: Your teacher will ask you one of the questions above. Answer it. Close your book, of course.

Vengan conmigo.

16.5 *Exercise*

CLASS: Your teacher will read the three indicated forms of each of the verbs below. Repeat each line of verbs, in unison, after the teacher says it in Spanish. Read across the page.

INFINITIVES	PRESENT (Indicative, I form)	PRESENT SUBJUNCTIVE and COMMAND
1. venir *to come*	vengo *I come*	venga *come*
2. traer *to bring*	traigo *I bring*	traiga *bring*
3. hacer *to do, to make*	hago *I do, I make*	haga *do, make*
4. oír *to hear, to listen*	oigo *I hear, I listen*	oiga *hear, listen*
5. ver *to see*	veo *I see*	vea *see*
6. mirar *to look*	miro *I look*	mire *look*
7. terminar *to finish*	termino *I finish*	termine *finish*
8. mandar *to send*	mando *I send*	mande *send*
9. aprender *to learn*	aprendo *I learn*	aprenda *learn*
10. esperar *to wait, to hope*	espero *I wait, I hope*	espere *wait, hope*
11. escribir *to write*	escribo *I write*	escriba *write*
12. trabajar *to work*	trabajo *I work*	trabaje *work*

CLASS: Could you do the Exercise above with books closed? Your teacher will give you the Present Tense (Indicative) form of a verb (from the middle column). You give the Present Subjunctive (as in the third column). Close your books.

16.6 *Creating Sentences*

CLASS: Combine words from the three columns to form your own sentences.

		chocolates
	venga, *come*	una ensalada
Quiero que	traiga, *bring*	después de la clase
I want you, him, her to	escriba, *write*	un regalo
Espero que	mande, *send*	a la fiesta
I hope that you, she, he will	estudie, *study*	a María
	compre, *buy*	mucho
	reciba, *receive*	un regalo
Ojalá que	vaya, *go*	la lección
I certainly hope that you, he, she will	invite, *invite*	la bicicleta
	haga, *do, make*	mi carta
	espere, *wait*	al cine
		a Susana

Esperen aquí, por favor.

THE PLURAL PRESENT SUBJUNCTIVE

To form the plural of the Present Subjunctive, add the letter N to the singular form for THEY-THEM, and add MOS for the WE-US form.

Examples: Singular	Plural
venga, *come*	vengan, *come (they, you pl.)*
venga, *come*	vengamos, *come (we, us)*
vaya, *go*	vayan, *go (they, you pl.)*

Quiere que vengamos a la fiesta. *She wants us to come to the party.*
Quiere que vengan a la fiesta. *She wants them to come to the party.*
Quiere que vayan al banco. *She wants them to go to the bank.*

revistas

16.7 *Reading Exercise*

CLASS: Repeat these sentences, in unison, after your teacher says them in Spanish.

1. Quiero que vengan a la fiesta.
   I want them to come to the party.
2. Quiero que me manden el paquete.
   I want them to send me the package.
3. Ojalá que traigan al nene.
   I certainly hope that they bring the baby (boy).
4. Quiero que traigan a la nena.
   I want them to bring the baby (girl).
5. Ojalá que lleguen a tiempo.
   I certainly hope that they will arrive on time.
6. Ojalá que terminen pronto.
   I certainly hope that they will finish soon.
7. Espero que terminen a tiempo.
   I hope that you (pl.) will finish on time.
8. Espero que nos visiten.
   I hope that they visit us.

REMEMBER: Action is never expressed in the Subjunctive. The Subjunctive never happens in the present. It expresses what you want or hope that somebody will do. But it never tells what someone did or is doing.

16.8 *Speed Reading Exercise*

CLASS: The teacher will guide you in reading LESSON 14 (14.2) as a Speed Reading Exercise. Read aloud, as quickly as you can.

OTHER USES OF THE PRESENT SUBJUNCTIVE

Use the Present Subjunctive after these expressions when they refer to the future:

1. PARA QUE, *so that*
2. HASTA QUE, *until (that)*
3. AUNQUE, *even though*
4. CON TAL QUE, *provided that*
5. CUANDO, *when*

Examples:

para que termine, *so that you finish*
hasta que venga, *until he comes*
aunque no venga, *even if he doesn't come*
con tal que espere, *provided he waits*
cuando venga, *when she comes*

16.9 *Exercise*

A. Answer these questions (optional):

1. ¿Quiere que trabaje esta noche? 2. ¿Quiere que termine esta noche? 3. ¿Quiere que mande el dinero? 4. ¿Quiere que escriba la carta? 5. ¿Quiere que aprenda la lección? 6. ¿Quiere que traiga el disco? 7. ¿Quiere que traiga el dinero? 8. ¿Quiere que trabaje con usted? 9. ¿Quiere que compre chocolates? 10. ¿Quiere que compre una revista? 11. ¿Quiere que venga a la fiesta? 12. ¿Quiere que venga mañana? 13. ¿Quiere que hable con Alberto? 14. ¿Quiere que espere a Roberto? 15. ¿Quiere que prepare la ensalada hoy? 16. ¿Quiere que vaya al supermercado? 17. ¿Quiere que haga el trabajo? 18. ¿Quiere que vaya al banco? 19. ¿Quiere que vaya Juan a la fiesta?

B. Translate these sentences into Spanish:

20. I hope that he will buy chocolates. 21. I hope that she will receive my letter. 22. I hope that he will bring the money. 23. I certainly hope that he will come with Susan. 24. I certainly hope that he will go to the bank. 25. I certainly hope that they will come. 26. I certainly hope that they will receive my letter.

16.10 *Speed Reading Exercise*

CLASS: Read the Spanish sentences below very fast. Can you read all ten sentences in one breath?

1. Quiero que vaya al parque.
   I want you (him,her) to go to the park.
2. Quiero que vaya al banco.
   I want you to go to the bank.
3. Quiero que vaya al teatro.
   I want you to go to the theater.
4. Quiero que vaya a la tienda.
   I want you to go to the store.
5. Quiero que vaya a la fiesta.
   I want you to go to the party.
6. Quiero que venga a mi casa.
   I want you to come to my home.
7. Quiero que venga a la clase.
   I want you to come to the class.
8. Quiero que venga hoy.
   I want you to come today.
9. Quiero que venga mañana.
   I want you to come tomorrow.
10. Quiero que compre sal.
    I want you to buy some salt.

CLASS: Please close your books.

1. See how many of the sentences above you can say.
2. Your teacher will dictate to you the ten sentences above.

LESSON 17

Reflexive Verbs

REFLEXIVE PRONOUNS

myself	ME	NOS	*ourselves*
yourself *himself* *herself*	SE	SE	*yourselves* *themselves*

Familiar form: TE, *yourself*

1. Verbs which take Reflexive Pronouns, such as MYSELF, YOURSELF, are known as Reflexive Verbs because the action reflects back upon the subject.
   Example: me peso, *I weigh myself*
2. There are many Reflexive Verbs in Spanish which are not reflexive in English.
3. Reflexive Pronouns come before the verb. Exceptions: add pronouns onto the Infinitive and the Command to form one word.
   Examples: bañarse, *to bathe (oneself)* (Infinitive)
   báñese, *bathe (yourself)* (Command)
   me bañé, *I bathed (myself)*

Most of the verbs which you use when you speak of getting ready for a party are reflexive.

Learn these verbs:

1.	levantarse *to get up (oneself)*	me levanté *I got up (myself)*	se levantó *he got up (himself)*
2.	bañarse *to bathe (oneself)*	me bañé *I bathed (myself)*	se bañó *he bathed (himself)*
3.	peinarse *to comb (oneself)*	me peiné *I combed (myself)*	se peinó *he combed (himself)*
4.	afeitarse *to shave (oneself)*	me afeité *I shaved (myself)*	se afeitó *he shaved (himself)*
5.	lavarse *to wash (oneself)*	me lavé *I washed (myself)*	se lavó *he washed (himself)*
6.	sentarse *to sit down (oneself)*	me senté *I sat down (myself)*	se sentó *he sat down (himself)*
7.	ponerse *to put on (oneself)*	me puse *I put on (myself)*	se puso *he put on (himself)*
8.	quitarse *to take off (oneself)*	me quité *I took off (myself)*	se quitó *he took off (himself)*

IMPORTANT: Do not use MY, HIS, HER, OUR, YOUR or THEIR with reflexive verbs. Use THE instead. Example: el abrigo, *my, your, his, her coat.*

17.1 *Remember These Words*

CLASS: Repeat these words and phrases, in unison, after your teacher says them in Spanish. Do not use English. Only look at the meaning of each word.

dientes, *teeth*
la ropa, *the clothes*
camisa, *shirt*
calcetines, *socks*
las joyas, *the jewels*
muy lindo, *very lovely*
contentos, *happy (pl.)*
estufa, *stove, heater*

ropa interior, *underwear*
zapatos, *shoes*
medias, *stockings*
un vestido, *a dress*
perfume francés, *French perfume*
un collar de perlas, *a pearl necklace*
encantados, *delighted (pl.)*
la bata, *the bathrobe*

¿Qué hizo Bernardo? *What did Bernard do?*
se levantó, *you, he, she got up*
se bañó, *you, he, she bathed*
se lavó los dientes, *you, he, she "washed" your, his, her teeth*
se peinó, *you, he, she combed your, his, her hair*
se puso, *you, he, she put on*
se quitó los zapatos, *he took off his shoes*
después de levantarse, *after getting up (to get up)*
¿Y después? *And afterwards (after that)?*
después de bañarse, *after bathing (to bathe)*
después de peinarse, *after combing your, his, her hair*
¿Fueron a la fiesta Bernardo y Susana? *Did Bernard and Susan go to the party?*
¿Se sentó usted? *Did you sit down?*
Me senté. *I sat down.*
¿Están contentos? *Are they happy?*
Están encantados. *They are delighted.*

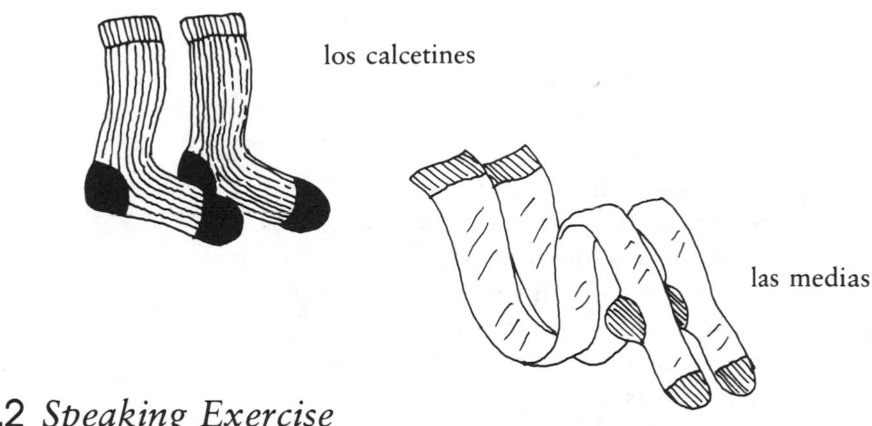

17.2 *Speaking Exercise*

CLASS: Your teacher will point out individual students who will answer these questions. Read the answers in the book.

1. ¿Qué hizo Bernardo? *(What did Bernard do?)*
   Bernardo se levantó. *(Bernard got up).*
2. ¿Qué hizo después de levantarse?
   Se bañó.
3. ¿Qué hizo después de bañarse?
   Se lavó los dientes.
4. ¿Qué hizo después de lavarse los dientes?
   Se peinó.

un collar de perlas

la corbata

5. ¿Qué hizo después de peinarse?
   Se puso la ropa interior.
6. ¿Y después?
   Se puso los pantalones.
7. ¿Y después?
   Se puso la camisa.
8. ¿Y después?
   Se puso los calcetines.
9. ¿Y después?
   Se puso los zapatos.
10. ¿Se puso las medias Susana?
    Sí. Susana se puso las medias y los zapatos.
11. ¿Se puso un vestido Susana?
    Sí, Susana se puso un vestido muy bonito.
12. ¿Se puso perfume Susana?
    Sí, Susana se puso un perfume francés.
13. ¿Se puso joyas Susana?
    Sí. Se puso un anillo muy lindo y un collar de perlas.
14. ¿Fueron a la fiesta Susana y Bernardo?
    Sí, Bernardo y Susana fueron a la fiesta.
15. ¿Están contentos Susana y Bernardo?
    Sí. Están encantados.

CLASS: Could you answer the questions above with books closed?

Practice these verbs: yo me peiné, *I combed (my hair);* yo me bañé *(I bathed);* yo me puse, *I put on;* yo me lavé las manos, *I washed my hands*.

los zapatos

17.3 *Exercise*

CLASS: Change the verbs and reflexive pronouns below into the first person singular.

Example: David se levantó. Yo me levanté. *I got up.*

HE, SHE	I	
1. Susana se peinó.	Yo ________	*I combed (my hair).*
2. Alberto se bañó.	Yo ________	
3. Alberto se puso un suéter.	Yo ________	
4. Susana se levantó.	Yo ________	
5. Bernardo se lavó las manos.	Yo ________	
6. Susana se puso los zapatos.	Yo ________	
7. Carlos se sentó.	Yo ________	

Carlos se baña

17.4 *Creating Sentences*

CLASS: Combine words from the two columns to form complete sentences.

me puse *I put on*	el abrigo
Susana se puso *Susan put on*	los guantes, *my, her, his gloves, etc.*
me quité *I took off*	los zapatos, *my shoes, his shoes, etc.*
Alicia se quitó *Alice took off*	un anillo, *a ring*
¿Se puso *Did you, he, she put on*	perfume
	un collar de perlas, *a pearl necklace*
	agua de Colonia, *cologne*
	los calcetines, *my, his, her socks*
	los pantalones, *my, his, her slacks*
	un traje gris, *a gray suit*
	la ropa interior, *my, his, her underwear*
	las joyas, *my, her jewels*
	los patines, *my, his, her skates*

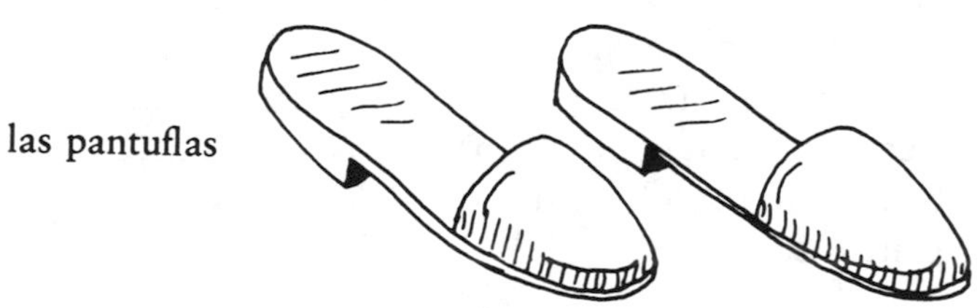
las pantuflas

17.5 *Exercise*

Answer these questions:

1. ¿Se levantó usted tarde? *(Did you get up late?)* _________
2. ¿Se bañó usted? _________
3. ¿Se puso usted las pantuflas? _________
4. ¿Se puso usted la bata? _________
5. ¿Se lavó usted los dientes? _________
6. ¿Se peinó usted? _________
7. ¿Se quitó el abrigo? _________
8. ¿Se puso los zapatos? _________
9. ¿Se puso la ropa? _________

17.6 *Vocabulary*

For the Conversation below

CLASS: Repeat these words and sentences, in unison, after your teacher says them in Spanish.

1. tu, *your (familiar)* 2. tu cumpleaños, *your birthday* 3. mi, *my* 4. Tuve un día lindo. *I had a lovely day.* 5. mis tíos, *my aunt and uncle* 6. vinieron a mi casa, *came to my house* 7. para el desayuno, *for breakfast* 8. Me cantaron "Feliz Cumpleaños." *They sang "Happy Birthday" to me.* 9. y me dieron unos discos fantásticos, *and they gave me some fantastic records* 10. ¿Qué hiciste para el almuerzo? *What did you do for lunch?* 11. mi papá me llevó, *my father took me* 12. tomamos un almuerzo delicioso, *we had a delicious lunch* 13. Tu fiesta ayer estuvo linda. *Your party yesterday was lovely.* 14. Gracias. ¿Qué te gustó? *Thank you. What did you like?* 15. Me gustó mucho la música. *I liked the music very much.* 16. Carlos toca la guitarra muy bien. *Charles plays the guitar very well.* 17. Y me gustaron las canciones de Susana. *And I liked Susan's songs.* 18. Me divertí mucho. *I had a lot of fun.* 19. ¿Te gustó el radio que recibí? *Did you like the radio that I received?* 20. ¿Quién te lo dio? *Who gave it to you?* 21. Carlos me lo dio. *Charles gave it to me.* 22. Carlos es muy amable. *Charles is very kind.* 23. Tuve un cómpleaños fantástico. *I had a fantastic birthday.* 24. Estoy muy contenta. *I am very happy (fem.).*

NOTE: If what you liked is singular, use ME GUSTÓ, *I liked.* If what you liked is plural, use ME GUSTARON, *I liked, (they) pleased me.* Examples:
Me gustó el radio. *I liked the radio.*
Me gustaron las canciones. *I liked the songs.*

17.7 *Conversation*

CLASS: Your teacher will call on individual students, two at a time, to ask and answer the questions in the following blocks. This is a chance for you to show your acting skills.

MY BIRTHDAY

First student —¿Qué hiciste en tu cumpleaños?
Second student—Tuve un día lindo. Mis tíos vinieron a mi casa para el desayuno. Me cantaron "Feliz Cumpleaños," y me dieron unos discos fantásticos.
First student —¿Qué hiciste para el almuerzo?
Second student—Mi papá me llevó a un restaurante, y tomamos un almuerzo delicioso.
First student —¿Qué hiciste por la tarde?
Second student—Jugué tenis.

First student —Tu fiesta ayer estuvo linda.
Second student—Gracias. ¿Qué te gustó?
First student —Me gustó mucho la música. Carlos toca la guitarra muy bien. Y me gustaron las canciones de Susana. Bailé mucho. Me divertí mucho.
Second student—¿Te gustó el radio que recibí?
First student —Sí. Es fantástico. ¿Quién te lo dio?
Second student—Carlos me lo dio.
First student —Carlos es muy amable.
Second student—Tuve un compleaños fantástico. Estoy muy contenta (contento).

17.8 *Exercise*

Answer these questions:

1. ¿Se levantó Bernardo? 2. ¿Se bañó Bernardo? 3. ¿Se peinó Bernardo? 4. ¿Se puso los zapatos Bernardo? 5. ¿Se puso las medias Susana? 6. ¿Se puso un vestido Susana? 7. ¿Se puso perfume Susana? 8. ¿Se puso un collar de perlas Susana? 9. ¿Se peinó usted? 10. ¿Se levantó tarde usted? 11. ¿Se puso usted los zapatos? 12. ¿Se puso usted un suéter? 13. ¿Se quitó usted el sué-

ter? 14. ¿Se quitó usted los zapatos en la clase? 15. ¿Se quitó los guantes Susana? 16. ¿Se quitó usted el abrigo? 17. ¿Se puso usted las pantuflas? 18. ¿Se quitó usted las pantuflas? 19. ¿Se sentó usted en el sofá? 20. ¿Se sentó usted en la estufa?

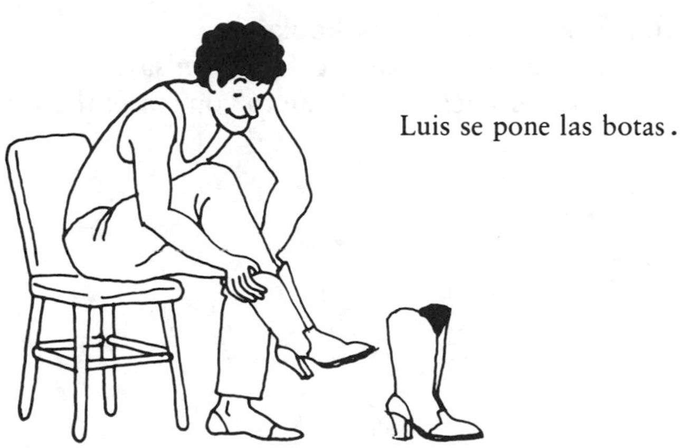

Luis se pone las botas.

17.9 *Speed Reading Exercise*

CLASS: Read the Spanish sentences below very fast. Can you read ten sentences in one breath? Is there anyone in the class who can read more than ten sentences in one breath?

1. Me puse la ropa. *I put on my clothes.*
2. Me puse la bata. *I put on my bathrobe.*
3. Me puse las botas. *I put on my boots.*
4. Me puse los zapatos. *I put on my shoes.*
5. Me puse el abrigo. *I put on my coat.*
6. Me puse el anillo. *I put on my ring.*
7. Se puso los pantalones. *He put on his pants.*
8. Se puso los guantes. *He put on his gloves.*
9. Se puso perfume. *She put on perfume.*
10. Se puso el vestido. *She put on her dress.*
11. Se puso las medias. *She put on her stockings.*
12. Se puso la ropa interior. *She put on her underwear.*
13. Se quitó el collar. *She took off her necklace.*
14. Se quitó la corbata. *He took off his necktie.*

15. Se quitó las pantuflas. *He took off his slippers.*
16. Me quité el sombrero. *I took off my hat.*
17. Me levanté tarde. *I got up late.*
18. Me bañé. *I took a bath.*
19. Me lavé las manos. *I washed my hands.*
20. Me lavé la cara. *I washed my face.*

CLASS: Please close your books.

1. See how many sentences you can say.
2. Your teacher will dictate to you ten of the sentences above.

LESSON 18

The Present Perfect Tense
The Past Perfect Tense

THE PRESENT PERFECT TENSE (**AR** verbs)

HABLAR, *to talk*

HE HABLADO *I have talked*	HEMOS HABLADO *we have talked*
HA HABLADO *you have talked*	HAN HABLADO *they have talked*

Familiar form: HAS HABLADO, *you have talked (fam.)*

Auxiliary Verb
HABER, *to have*
(used only with other verbs)

HE *(I have)*	HEMOS *(we have)*
HA *(you have)*	HAN *(they have)*

Familiar form: HAS, *you have (fam.)*

NOTE: This is an auxiliary or helping verb. Do not use it except in combination with the Past Participle of other verbs.

THE PAST PARTICIPLE (**AR** verbs)

In order to form the past participle of AR verbs, remove AR from the infinitive and add ADO.

Examples:

estudiar, *to study*	estudiado, *studied*
progresar, *to progress*	progresado, *progressed*
trabajar, *to work*	trabajado, *worked*

REMEMBER: The letter H is ALWAYS absolutely silent in Spanish.

18.1 *Exercise*

CLASS: Give the singular of the Present Perfect Tense of the following verbs: (Remove AR from the Infinitive and add ADO.)

INFINITIVE	I form	YOU, HE, SHE, IT form
Example:		
invitar, *to invite*	he invitado, *I have invited*	ha invitado *you have invited*
1. visitar, *to visit*	________	________
2. reservar, *to reserve*	________	________
3. terminar, *to finish*	________	________
4. ganar, *to win, earn*	________	________
5. depositar, *to deposit*	________	________
6. dar, *to give*	________	________
7. mandar, *to send*	________	________
8. esperar, *to wait*	________	________
9. cambiar, *to change*	________	________
10. pescar, *to fish*	________	________
11. pagar, *to pay*	________	________

CLASS: Could you do the Exercise above with books closed? Your teacher will give you the Infinitve. You give the singular of the Present Perfect Tense.

THE PAST PARTICIPLE (of **ER** and **IR** verbs)

The ending of the Past Participle of ER and IR verbs is IDO.
Examples: he recibido, *I have received*
ha venido, *he, she, it has come*
ha salido, *he, she, it has left, gone out*
he ido, *I have gone*

18.2 *Exercise*

CLASS: Give the singular of the Present Perfect Tense of the following verbs. (Remove ER or IR from the Infinitive, and add IDO.)

	INFINITIVE	I form	YOU, HE, SHE, IT form
	Example:		
	vivir, *to live*	he vivido *I have lived*	ha vivido *he, she has lived*
1.	recibir, *to receive*	________	________
2.	venir, *to come*	________	________
3.	salir, *to leave, go out*	________	________
4.	comprender, *to understand*	________	________
5.	aprender, *to learn*	________	________
6.	decidir, *to decide*	________	________
7.	correr, *to run*	________	________
8.	vender, *to sell*	________	________
9.	sufrir, *to suffer*	________	________
10.	ir, *to go*	________	________
11.	ofrecer, *to offer*	________	________

CLASS: Could you do the Exercise above with books closed?

1. There are a few Past Participles that have a written accent.
   Examples: oír, *to hear* — he oído, *I have heard*
   leer, *to read* — he leído, *I have read*
2. In the verb IR *(to go)*, you remove the whole verb and the ending is the Past Participle.
   Example: ir, *to go* — he ido, *I have gone* — ha ido, *he, she, it has gone*

¿Has pagado la cuenta?
Have you paid the bill?

18.3 *Exercise*

CLASS: Give the correct Past Participle in the sentences below. (Remove AR, ER, or IR from the Infinitive, and add ADO or IDO.) Read the complete sentence.

Examples: Yo he (terminar) terminado la lección.
I have finished the lesson.
Alberto ha (recibir) recibido la carta.
Albert has received the letter.

1. María ha (preparar) ________ la cena.
2. Yo he (estudiar) ________ la lección.
3. Luis ha (depositar) ________ el dinero en el banco.
4. Bernardo no ha (terminar) ________ la lección.
5. Yo he (leer) ________ el libro.
6. Yo he (aprender) ________ el vocabulario.
7. Margarita ha (trabajar) ________ mucho.
8. Alberto ha (contestar) ________ la carta.
9. María ha (recibir) ________ muchas cartas.
10. Yo he (oir) ________ el disco.
11. Roberto ha (comprar) ________ una revista.
12. Roberto ha (decidir) ________ todo.
13. Yo he (correr) ________ en el parque.
14. Yo he (pagar) ________ la cuenta en la tienda.
    I have paid the bill in the store.

18.4 *Remember These Words*

CLASS: Repeat these words and phrases, in unison, after your teacher says them in Spanish. Do not use English. Only look at the meaning of each word.

todavía, *yet*
las oraciones, *the sentences*
naturalmente, *naturally*
todo, *everything*
la cuenta, *the bill*
las preguntas, *the questions*
no soy idiota, *I am not an idiot*
muchas cartas, *many letters*
todas las cartas, *all the letters*

mi disco nuevo, *my new record*
muchos otros, *many other(s)*
música clásica, *classical music*
música popular, *popular music*
son lindos, *they are beautiful, lovely*
unos son, *some are*
otros son, *others are*

¿ha terminado? *have you finished?*
no he terminado todavía, *I have not finished yet*
he leído la lección, *I have read the lesson*
¿ha contestado las preguntas? *have you answered the questions?*
he aprendido todo, *I have learned everything*
¿ha recibido cartas? *have you received letters?*
he contestado las cartas, *I have answered the letters*
he oído su disco, *I have heard your record*
¿ha comprado otros discos? *have you bought other records?*
¿ha visto una película? *have you seen a film (movie)?*
he pagado la cuenta *I have paid the bill*
La cuenta, por favor. *The check, please (in a restaurant).*

NOTE: There are a few Past Participles which are irregular.

Example: HECHO, *done, made*
¿Qué ha hecho? *What have you done?*
No he hecho nada. *I haven't done anything.*
hecho en México, *made in Mexico*

DICHO, *said*
No he dicho nada. *I haven't said anything.*
Dicho y hecho. *Said and done.*

¿Has visto la película?
Have you seen the movie?

18.5 *Speaking Exercise*

CLASS: Your teacher will point out individual students who will answer these questions. Read the answers in the book.

1. ¿Ha contestado las preguntas?
   Sí, he contestado las preguntas.
2. ¿Ha aprendido todo?
   Sí, he aprendido todo.
3. ¿Qué ha hecho? *What have you done?*
   He leído la lección, he aprendido el vocabulario y he contestado las preguntas. He terminado todo.
4. ¿Ha recibido muchas cartas?
   Sí, he recibido muchas cartas.
5. ¿Ha leído las cartas?
   Sí, he leído las cartas.
6. ¿Ha comprendido todas las cartas?
   Sí, naturalmente. No soy idiota.
7. ¿Ha oído mis discos nuevos?
   Sí, he oído sus discos nuevos. Son lindos.
8. ¿Ha comprado otros discos?
   Sí, he comprado muchos otros discos.
9. ¿Son de música clásica o de música popular?
   Unos son de música clásica y otros son de música popular.
10. ¿Ha visto un programa interesante?
    Sí. He visto un programa muy interesante.
11. ¿Ha visto a Juan?
    Sí. He visto a Juan.
12. ¿Qué ha dicho Carlos?
    Carlos no ha dicho nada todavía.

CLASS: Could you answer the questions above with books closed?

FAMILIAR FORMS

When a verb has an auxiliary, you make the familiar form by adding the letter S to the auxiliary.

Examples: ¿Has terminado? *Have you finished? (familiar)*
Vas a terminar pronto. *You are going to finish soon. (familiar)*
Estás trabajando demasiado. *You are working too much. (familiar)*
Estabas hablando. *You were speaking. (familiar)*
¿Vas al banco? *Are you going to the bank? (familiar)*

18.6 *Vocabulary*

For the Conversation below.

CLASS: Repeat these words and sentences, in unison, after your teacher says them in Spanish.

1. buenas tardes, *good afternoon* 2. ¿Cómo estás? *How are you? (familiar)* 3. ¿Y tú? *And you? (familiar)* 4. ¿Está Alberto? *Is Albert here (there)?* 5. Ha salido. *He has gone out.* 6. ¿Quieres oír unos discos? *Do you want to hear some records?* 7. ¡Qué buena idea! *What a good idea!* 8. ¿Has oído mi disco nuevo? *Have you heard my new record? (familiar)* 9. ¿Has comprado otros discos? *Have you bought other records? (familiar)* 10. unos son de música clásica, y otros son de música popular, *some are of classical music, and others are of popular music* 11. ¿Vamos al cine? *Shall we go to the movies?* 12. No puedo. *I can't.* 13. No he terminado la lección. *I haven't finished the lesson.* 14. ¿Has leído el cuento? *Have you read the story?* 15. pero no he contestado las preguntas, *but I haven't answered the questions.* 16. ¿Has aprendido el vocabulario? *Have you learned the vocabulary?* 17. no lo he aprendido muy bien, *I haven't learned it very well* 18. ¿Por qué no estudias? *Why don't you study? (familiar)* 19. y vamos al cine después, *and we'll go to the movies afterwards* 20. Bueno. *O.K.* 21. ¿Me esperas? *Will you (do you) wait for me?* 22. Te espero. *I wait for you. I'll wait for you.* 23. ¡Apúrate! *Hurry up! (familiar)*

18.7 *Conversation*

CLASS: Your teacher will select students to take the roles of Alicia and Daniel in the next Conversations. Read your role clearly, and with as much expression as possible.

UNA VISITA

Alicia—Buenas tardes, Daniel. ¿Cómo estás?
Daniel—Bien, gracias. ¿Y tú?
Alicia—Bien, gracias.
Daniel—¿Está Alberto?
Alicia—No. Ha salido.
Daniel—¿Quieres oír unos discos?
Alicia—Sí. ¡Qué buena idea! ¿Has oído mi disco nuevo?
Daniel—Sí, es lindo. ¿Has comprado otros discos?
Alicia—Sí. Esta tarde compré muchos discos.
Daniel—¿Son de música clásica o de música popular?
Alicia—Unos son de música clásica, y otros son de música popular.

Daniel—¿Vamos al cine?
Alicia—No puedo. No he terminado la lección todavía.
Daniel—¿Has leído el cuento?
Alicia—Sí, pero no he contestado las preguntas.
Daniel—¿Has aprendido el vocabulario?
Alicia—Sí, pero no lo he aprendido muy bien.
Daniel—¿Por qué no estudias, y vamos al cine después?
Alicia—Bueno. ¿Me esperas?
Daniel—Sí. Te espero. ¡Apúrate!

la carta

los discos

18.8 *Speed Reading Exercise*

CLASS: The teacher will guide you in reading LESSON 16 (16.2) as a Speed Reading Exercise. Read aloud, as quickly as you can.

THE PAST PERFECT TENSE

To form the Past Perfect Tense, combine the following auxiliary verbs with the Past Participle.

AUXILIARY VERB

I had	HABÍA	HABÍAMOS	*we had*
you had *he, she, it had*	HABÍA	HABÍAN	*you (pl.) had* *they had*

Familiar form: HABÍAS, *you had*

Examples: había salido, *I had gone out*
había entrado, *I had come in*

18.9 *Exercises*

A. Read these sentences aloud (Spanish only):

1. Había terminado cuando entró.
   I had finished when he came in.
2. Había comenzado la lección cuando llegó.
   I had begun the lesson when he arrived.
3. Había preparado la cena cuando llegó.
   I had prepared dinner when he arrived.
4. Había hecho el trabajo cuando vino.
   I had done the work when he came.

B. Answer these questions:

1. ¿Ha preparado usted la lección? 2. ¿Ha contestado usted las preguntas? 3. ¿Ha contestado usted las cartas? 4. ¿Ha comprado usted discos? 5. ¿Ha comprado usted pan? 6. ¿Ha comprado usted un suéter? 7. ¿Ha pagado usted la cuenta? 8. ¿Ha aprendido usted la lección? 9. ¿Ha recibido usted muchas cartas? 10. ¿Ha aprendido usted todo? 11. ¿Ha terminado? 12. ¿Ha oído usted un programa interesante? 13. ¿Ha leído usted un libro interesante? 14. ¿Ha salido Ricardo? 15. ¿Ha aprendido usted el vocabulario? 16. ¿Ha visto usted un programa interesante?

18.10 *Speed Reading Exercise*

CLASS: Read the Spanish sentences below very fast. Can you read seven sentences in one breath? Is there anyone in the class who can read more than seven? Could you read ten or fifteen?

1. No he terminado todavía. *I haven't finished yet.*
2. No he pagado la cuenta. *I haven't paid the bill.*
3. No he contestado la carta. *I haven't answered the letter.*
4. No he visitado a mi tía. *I haven't visited my aunt.*
5. No han llegado todavía. *They haven't arrived yet.*
6. No han comenzado todavía. *They haven't begun yet.*
7. No han mandado el paquete. *They haven't sent the package.*
8. No ha salido hoy. *He, she hasn't gone out today.*
9. No ha dicho nada. *He hasn't said anything.*
10. No lo he oído. *I haven't heard it.*
11. No lo he leído. *I haven't read it.*
12. No lo han traído. *They haven't brought it.*
13. No lo he visto. *I haven't seen it.*
14. No lo ha hecho. *He hasn't done it.*
15. No he dicho nada. *I haven't said anything.*

CLASS: Please close your books.

1. See how many of the sentences above you can say.
2. Your teacher will dictate to you ten of the sentences above.

LESSON 19

Irregular Verbs, Preterite Tense

THE PRETERITE TENSE OF IRREGULAR VERBS
Endings of the Preterite Tense of Irregular Verbs

I	E	IMOS	*we*
you, he she, it	O	IERON	*you (pl.) they*

Familiar form: ISTE

IRREGULAR VERBS IN THE PRETERITE TENSE

LEARN these verbs. Repeat the four forms of each verb aloud several times.

1. tener, *to have*

tuve	tuvo	tuvimos	tuvieron
I had	*you had*	*we had*	*they had*

2. estar, *to be*

estuve	estuvo	estuvimos	estuvieron
I was	*you were*	*we were*	*they were*

19.1 *Reading Exercise*

CLASS: Repeat these sentences, in unison, after your teacher says them in Spanish.

1. Tuve una fiesta el sábado. *I had a party on Saturday.*
2. Antonio tuvo un accidente. Pobre Antonio. *Anthony had an accident. Poor Anthony.*
3. Tuvimos una conversación interesante. *We had an interesting conversation.*
4. Tuvieron mucho trabajo. *They had a lot of work.*

19.2 *Creating Sentences*

CLASS: Match up the words in the columns below to form your own sentences.

Tuve	una fiesta	el sábado
I had	un examen, *a test*	ayer, *yesterday*
	visitas, *visitors*	el domingo, *on Sunday*
Antonio tuvo	una cita, *an appointment*	anoche, *last night*
Anthony had	un resfriado, *a cold*	hoy, *today*
¿Tuvo	mucho trabajo, *much work*	la semana pasada,
Did you have	una conversación interesante	*last week*

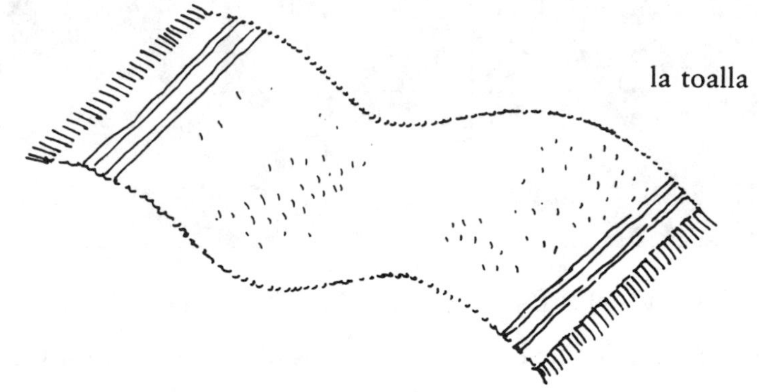

	estudiar, *to study*	a Juan, *John*
	lavar, *to wash*	aceite, *oil*
Tuve que	comprar, *to buy*	la sala, *the living room*
I had to	encontrar, *to meet*	cartas, *letters*
¿Tuvo que	limpiar, *to clean*	anoche, *last night*
Did you have to	escribir, *to write*	la ropa, *the clothes*
Tuvimos que	salir, *to go out*	ayer, *yesterday*
We had to	ir, *to go*	al banco, *to the bank*
	venir, *to come*	al despacho, *to the office*
	hacer, *to make*	el almuerzo, *lunch*

Learn the words in ALL of the columns above.

19.3 *Exercise*

Answer these questions in the "I" form.

1. ¿Tuvo usted mucho trabajo la semana pasada?
2. ¿Tuvo que ir al banco?
3. ¿Estuvo en San Francisco la semana pasada?

4. ¿Tuvo que estudiar anoche?
5. ¿Estuvo en casa hoy?
6. ¿Dónde estuvo ayer?
7. ¿Tuvo visitas el domingo?
8. ¿Tuvo que hacer el almuerzo?
9. ¿Tuvo un resfriado la semana pasada?
10. ¿Tuvo una conversación interesante con Juan?

LEARN these verbs. Repeat the four forms of each verb several times.

1. venir, *to come*

vine	vino	vinimos	vinieron
I came	*you came*	*we came*	*they came*

2. hacer, *to make*

hice	hizo	hicimos	hicieron
I made	*you made*	*we made*	*they made*

3. decir, *to say*

dije	dijo	dijimos	dijeron
I said	*you said*	*we said*	*they said*

4. traer, *to bring*

traje	trajo	trajimos	trajeron
I brought	*you brought*	*we brought*	*they brought*

Notice that DIJERON and TRAJERON (above) do not end in IERON, but in ERON.

19.4 *Creating Sentences*

CLASS: Match up the words in the columns below to form complete sentences.

Vine
I came

Vinieron
They came

Alicia vino
Alice came

a la clase
al despacho, *to the office*
al parque, *to the park*
a la fiesta, *to the party*
a mi casa, *to my house*
a la tienda, *to the store*
al campo, *to the country*

ayer, *yesterday*
hoy, *today*
con Juan, *with John*
solo, *alone (masc.)*
con Sara, *with Sarah*
a tiempo, *on time*
tarde, *late*
esta tarde, *this afternoon*

I	II	III
Hice *I made*	café	esta mañana
Alicia hizo *Alice made*	una ensalada	hoy
	la sopa, *soup*	para la cena, *for dinner*
	sándwiches	para el almuerzo, *for lunch*
	la cama, *bed*	esta tarde, *this afternoon*

I	II
Dije *I said*	que era bonito, *that it was pretty*
Antonio dijo *Anthony said*	que era tarde, *that it was late*
Luisa dijo *Louise said*	que era delicioso, *that it was delicious*
	que era imposible, *that it was impossible*
	que era terrible, *that it was terrible*
	que era amarillo, *that it was yellow*
	que era bueno, *that it was good*
	que era fantástico, *that it was fantastic*

I	II	III
Traje *I brought*	el libro, *the book*	a la casa, *home*
Trajimos *We brought*	a Juan, *John*	al parque, *to the park*
Trajeron *They brought*	a María, *Mary*	a la playa, *to the beach*
	a mi tía, *my aunt*	a la clase, *to the class*
	flores, *flowers*	a la fiesta, *to the party*
	al nene, *the baby boy*	al campo, *to the country*
	a la nena, *the baby girl*	para mi cumpleaños, *for my birthday*
	el perro, *the dog*	para la fiesta, *for the party*
	un regalo, *a present*	en el coche, *in the car*

el gato

el perro

19.5 *Exercise*

Answer these questions in the "I" form.

1. ¿Vino usted a la clase con Juan?
2. ¿Vino a la clase anoche?
3. ¿Hizo usted una ensalada para el almuerzo?
4. ¿Hizo café esta mañana?
5. ¿Trajo usted flores para la fiesta?
6. ¿Trajo usted el perro al parque?
7. ¿Hizo usted sopa hoy?

Translate these sentences into Spanish:

8. Robert said that it was good.
9. Anthony said that it was terrible.
10. Louis said that it was fantastic.

Juan tuvo un resfriado el mes pasado.

LEARN these verbs. Repeat the four forms of each verb several times.

1. poder, *to be able*

pude	pudo	pudimos	pudieron
I could	*you could*	*we could*	*they could*

2. poner, *to put, to set (the table)*

puse	puso	pusimos	pusieron
I put	*you put*	*we put*	*they put*

Notice that the verb IR, *to go*, is completely irregular:

3.

fui	fue	fuimos	fueron
I went	*you went*	*we went*	*they went*

19.6 *Creating Sentences*

Combine words from the three columns to form your own sentences.

Puse *I put (past)* Pusimos *We put (past)* Pusieron *they put (past)* Sara puso *Sara put (past)*	la llave, *the key* el coche, *the car* la fruta, *the fruit* las toallas, *the towels* las flores, *the flowers* los libros, *the books* el paraguas, *the umbrella* el abrigo, *the coat* el aceite, *the oil* el contrato, *the contract* los huevos, *the eggs*	en la mesa, *on the table* en el baño, *in the bathroom* en el florero, *in the vase* en el garaje, *in the garage* en la cocina, *in the kitchen* en la sala, *in the living room* en el closet, *in the closet* en el sillón, *on the arm-chair* en el escritorio, *on the desk* en el refrigerador en el sartén, *in the frying pan*

NOTE: PUDE, *I could,* is used with Infinitives.

Pude *I could* No pude *I couldn't* No pudimos *We couldn't* No pudieron *They couldn't*	traer, *bring* hacer, *do* terminar, *finish* venir, *come* salir, *go out* pintar, *paint* oír, *hear* recordar, *remember* llegar, *arrive* dejar, *leave (a thing)* mandar, *send*	la guitarra, *the guitar* al despacho, *to the office* esta noche, *tonight* la silla, *the chair* el programa, *the program* el trabajo, *the work* la lección, *the lesson* el número, *the number* la carta, *the letter* a tiempo, *on time* el paquete, *the package*

Learn the words in ALL of the columns above.

la silla

el paraguas

19.7 *Exercise*

Give the Preterite THEY form of the following verbs.

Example: venir, *to come* — vinieron, *they came*

1. comprender, *to understand* ______
2. insistir, *to insist* ______
3. vender, *to sell* ______
4. ver, *to see* ______
5. venir, *to come* ______
6. hacer, *to make, to do* ______
7. poner, *to put* ______
8. tener, *to have* ______
9. estar, *to be* ______
10. poder, *to be able to* ______

EXCEPTIONS: Three important verbs do not end in IERON in the Preterite Tense. Learn these three verbs very well.

1. decir, *to say* — dijeron, *they said*
2. traer, *to bring* — trajeron, *they brought*
3. ir, *to go* — fueron, *they went*

Fueron a las montañas. *They went to the mountains.*

19.8 *Exercise*

Answer these questions in the "I" form.

1. ¿Fue al cine con David? 2. ¿Puso flores en la sala? 3. ¿Puso el coche en la sala? 4. ¿Fue a la fiesta anoche?

Translate these sentences into Spanish.
5. Pedro came to my house. 6. I couldn't go to the party. 7. They went to Mexico. 8. I couldn't remember the number. 9. They couldn't leave the package. 10. We couldn't go. 11. They couldn't go. 12. They came. 13. They made. 14. They couldn't finish. 15. They had. 16. They didn't bring the umbrella. 17. They said. 18. They were in San Francisco last week. 19. They went to Panamá. 20. They saw Luisa in the park.

LESSON 20

How to form the Past Subjunctive
Use of the Past Subjunctive

HOW TO FORM THE PAST SUBJUNCTIVE

The following rule shows you how to form the Past Subjunctive of virtually every verb in the Spanish language (regular AR, ER, IR verbs and irregular verbs).

RULE: Take the Preterite THEY form of a verb. Remove the final ON, and add the letter A.

Examples:	Preterite THEY form	Past Subjunctive
AR:	compraron, *they bought*	comprara
ER:	vendieron, *they sold*	vendiera
IR:	escribieron, *they wrote*	escribiera
IRREGULAR:	tuvieron, *they had*	tuviera
	vinieron, *they came*	viniera
	trajeron, *they brought*	trajera
	fueron, *they went*	fuera

USE OF THE PAST SUBJUNCTIVE

These expressions are followed by the past subjunctive.

1. QUERÍA QUE, *I wanted you (him, her) to*
2. ESPERABA QUE, *I hoped that you (he, she) would*
3. DIJO QUE, He, she said that you (he, she) should

NOTE: DIJO QUE requires the Subjunctive ONLY when it is followed by a suggested action.

Examples:

1. Quería que comprara flores. *I wanted you to buy flowers.*
2. Esperaba que viniera a la fiesta. *I hoped that you would come to the party.*
3. Juan dijo que pintara la casa. *John said that you should paint the house.*

20.1 *Hearing Exercise*

CLASS: Repeat each sentence, in unison, after your teacher says it in Spanish.

1. Quería que comprara una chaqueta. *I wanted you to buy a jacket.*
2. Quería que fuera al cine. *I wanted you to go to the movies.*
3. Quería que Luis trajera fruta. *I wanted Louis to bring fruit.*
4. Esperaba que tuviera una fiesta. *I hoped that you would have a party.*
5. Esperaba que María comprara una bicicleta. *I hoped that Mary would buy a bicycle.*
6. Juan dijo que fuera a su casa. *John said that you should go to his house.*

Quería que sacara la basura.
I wanted him to take out the garbage.

20.2 *Creating Sentences*

Combine these words to make complete sentences.

QUERÍA QUE		
I wanted you to		
He wanted you to	llegara, *arrive*	a Roberto, *Robert*
She wanted you to	visitara, *visit*	a tiempo, *on time*
Roberto quería que	invitara, *invite*	hoy, *today*
Robert wanted you to	fuera, *go*	a Susana, *Susan*
Mi tío quería que	pintara, *paint*	la basura, *the garbage*
My uncle wanted you to	sacara, *take out*	la silla, *the chair*

ESPERABA QUE	estudiara, *study*	los platos, *the dishes*
I hoped that you would	lavara, *wash*	la ropa, *the clothes*
I hoped that she would	secara, *dry*	un lápiz, *a pencil*
I hoped that he would	comprara, *buy*	a Juan, *John*
He hoped that you would	dejara, *leave*	el paquete, *the package*
She hoped that you would	tomara, *drink*	a María, *Mary*
Alicia esperaba que	invitara, *invite*	la lección, *the lesson*
Alice hoped that you would	visitara, *visit*	el refresco, *the refreshment*

DIJO QUE		
He said that you should		a la estación
She said that you should	fuera	las manos, *your hands*
Gloria dijo que	vendiera	a David
Gloria said that you should	invitara	la cara, *your face*
María dijo que	visitara	la silla
Mary said that you should	pintara	a su casa
Mary said that he should	limpiara, *clean*	el radio
Mary said that she should	viniera, *come*	a Susana
	se lavara, *wash*	la casa

REMEMBER: The action never happens in the subjunctive.

20.3 *Exercise*

Translate these sentences into Spanish.

1. I wanted you to invite Susan.
2. Robert wanted you to work today.
3. I hoped that you would send the package.
4. He wanted you to paint the chair.
5. She wanted you to arrive on time.
6. I hoped that you would buy the house.
7. He said to paint (that you should paint) the table.
8. Alice said to buy (that you should buy) clothes.
9. He wanted you to wash the dishes.
10. He hoped that you would go to the party.

DAR, *to give*

DAR, *to give,* is a strange verb. It is an AR verb, but it has ER endings in the Preterite Tense and the Past Subjunctive.
dar, *to give*

Preterite Tense:	di *I gave*	dio *you gave*	dimos *we gave*	dieron *they gave*
	Familiar form: DISTE, *you gave*			
Past Subjunctive:	diera, *give*			

> 1. The singular Past Subjunctive ending of regular ER and IR verbs, and of irregular verbs is IERA.
> 2. To form the Past Subjunctive of ER and IR verbs, and of irregular verbs, remove ON from the Preterite THEY form, and add the letter A.

20.4 *Exercise*

Give the Past Subjunctive form of the following verbs (remove ON from the Preterite THEY form and add the letter A).

1. vendieron, *they sold* ________
2. aprendieron, *they learned* ________
3. escribieron, *they wrote* ________
4. salieron, *they went out* ________
5. tuvieron, *they had* ________
6. estuvieron, *they were* ________
7. anduvieron, *they rode, walked* ________
8. vinieron, *they came* ________
9. hicieron, *they did, made* ________
10. trajeron, *they brought* ________
11. vieron, *they saw* ________
12. pusieron, *they put, set (table)* ________
13. conocieron, *they met, knew (a person)* ________
14. oyeron, *they heard* ________
15. dieron, *they gave* ________

STUDENT: Your teacher will give you the THEY form of the Preterite of a verb, you give the Past Subjunctive (as above). Close your book.

20.5 *Creating Sentences*

STUDENT: Learn the words in the columns below.

CLASS: Combine the words in the three columns below to form complete sentences.

Quería que
I wanted you to
He wanted you to
She wanted you to

Esperaba que
I hoped that you would

Dijo que
He said to
He said that you should

escribiera, *write*
hiciera, *do, make*
comprara, *buy*
empacara, *pack*
trajera, *bring*
fuera, *go*
viniera, *come*
llegara, *arrive*

el trabajo, *the work*
biftec, *beefsteak*
la valija, *the suitcase*
las cartas, *the letters*
las flores, *the flowers*
al juego, *to the game*
a la fiesta, *to the party*
al concierto, *to the concert*
a mi casa, *to my house*
a la tienda, *to the store*
al supermercado, *to the supermarket*
a la farmacia, *to the drugstore*

Ella quería que le trajera flores.
She wanted me to bring her flowers.

20.6 *Speaking Exercise*

Answer these questions. Read the answers in the book.

1. ¿Qué quería Juan? *What did John want?*

   Quería que viniera a la fiesta.
   He wanted me to come to the party.

2. ¿Qué quería Carlos? *What did Carlos want?*

   Quería que comprara el libro.
   He wanted me to buy the book.

3. ¿Qué quería Gloria? *What did Gloria want?*

Quería que pintara la casa.
She wanted me to paint the house.

4. ¿Qué quería David?

Quería que fuera al cine con él.
He wanted me to go to the movies with him.

CLASS: Could you answer these questions with books closed?

20.7 *Exercise*

Translate these sentences into Spanish.

1. He said that you should go to the drugstore. 2. Robert wanted you to pack the suitcase. 3. I wanted you to write the letters. 4. She wanted you to bring the flowers. 5. I hoped that you would do the work. 6. I wanted you to give me the money. 7. She wanted you to give her a ring. 8. She said to buy some bedroom slippers. 9. He hoped that you would go to the concert. 10. He wanted you to go to the game.

20.8 *Creating Sentences*

Quería que
I wanted you to

Esperaba que
I hoped that you would

Dijo que
She said that you should

diera, *give*
me diera, *give me*
le diera, *give him, give her*

una fiesta, *a party*
el libro, *the book*
el dinero, *the money*
el lápiz, *the pencil*
la pluma, *the pen*
un disco, *a record*
un anillo, *a ring*
un beso, *a kiss*

USE OF THE PAST SUBJUNCTIVE

The Past Subjunctive expresses "iffy" wishes.
Examples: ¡Si comprendiera! *If you would (only) understand!*
¡Si fuera posible! *If it were possible!*

¡Si yo fuera rey! *If I were a king!*

EVERYDAY EXPRESSIONS

¡Si fuera rey! *If I were king!*
¡Si no fuera tarde! *If it weren't late!*
¡Si tuviera dinero! *If I had money!*
¡Si tuviera tiempo! *If I had time!*
¡Si fuera posible! *If it were only possible!*
¡Si fuera verdad! *If it were only true!*
¡Si supiera! *If you only knew!*
¡Si pudiera! *If I only could!*

REMEMBER: There is no action in the Subjunctive. The Past Subjunctive doesn't express what people do or did. It expresses the hopes of humanity.

TEACHER'S GUIDE

This book is designed to convince students that the Spanish language is well within their grasp. They are led gently from the familiar to the unknown. Confident students learn much faster than those who are insecure. Furthermore, confidence brings happiness. Insecurity is depressing.

It took years of research to discover, bit by bit, which are the interesting words that students can learn easily, and then use in sentences almost at once.

The sections Remember These Words and Reading Exercise in each lesson are designed to develop the "ear." When the teacher says each word in these sections clearly, and with enthusiasm, the students will imitate the clarity and the verve. They will quickly learn to speak with animation and enthusiasm, as Spanish is actually spoken. And they will enjoy their own enthusiasm.

THE TEACHER IS ALL

Therefore, the teacher is the director, who orchestrates the class, not with notes, but with words. And think how many more words there are than notes!

Orchestrating a class is no easy matter. That is why the first few words the teacher says in each class must be like trumpet calls. They must bring the class instantly to attention. After the first few forceful seconds, the class is with you, learning, off to a great start.

YOUR GOLDEN OPPORTUNITY

The sections Remember These Words and Reading Exercise, in each lesson, give you a golden opportunity to impart character to each individual word and sentence. Remember that the class will say what you say IN THE WAY YOU SAY IT.

The teacher breathes life into the Spanish language. It does not become a living language until you begin to say words with enthusiasm. You not only give the class its character, you give each individual word its life.

When you say the word "avión" so that it zooms off into space, you implant an image onto the students' mind, and a new sound and meaning into their consciousness. The students will remember your voice and your expression long after they have left the Spanish class, sometimes for many years.

The students will remember HOW you say words, and say them as you say them. When you have an enthusiastic intonation, students will copy it, since they feel helpless without your guidance. You are, in effect, giving each student a word.

You can reinforce this when the students speak. If a student pronounces the word "terrible" in a lazy way, you can say: "That doesn't sound terrible. Say 'terrible' so that it sounds simply terrible." Or you may say: "Think of a fast take off, and then say avión." This not only teaches students a word, it gives them acting skill. It will make people listen. It will help each student to become an entity.

Your guidance will breathe life into words, and into the students in the class.

The Remember These Words section in each lesson is designed to introduce vocabulary, to teach the students the words they will use in the lesson. Some of these same words may be in the Words to Remember section of other lessons. This is to refresh the students' memory, to repeat a word which may be difficult to retain, or to help the students to form a BASIC VOCABULARY which they will have at their constant command. Students tend to forget words which are not repeated. Repetition is greatly important if the student is to retain material learned previously. Many methods do not emphasize retention. But without retention the students simply cannot form a BASIC VOCABULARY. Without a BASIC VOCABULARY, students cannot speak, understand, read or write Spanish.

STEPS TO FOLLOW IN EACH LESSON

Each lesson in the book has basically the same sections. Therefore, if you are familiar with the procedure in Lesson 1, it will be easy to follow the steps in all the other lessons. The material in the book becomes more advanced and more varied, but the lessons retain the same sections. Following is a suggestion for a step by step procedure in each lesson. Lesson 1 has been used as an example.

LESSON 1

Step 1 *Guidelines*

Lesson One begins with a guideline in a box. The guidelines contain the main grammatical points of the language. The student who knows all of the guidelines will have a fine grounding in grammar. Read the guidelines aloud, and have the students repeat words, or answer questions, as indicated.

You will notice that the guidelines are all in blocks and, therefore, stand out readily on the page. Whenever you want to do a grammar review, just look for the guidelines, that is, the blocked sections.

Step 2 *Remember These Words*

Ask the students to sight-read the Spanish words and their English translations, one by one. Ask the class to repeat each Spanish word, in unison, immediately after you say it. This is an important moment, as it is the precise time at which you begin to breathe life into the Spanish language.

If the students have any difficulty in pronouncing a word, it is a good idea to repeat it. You may also ask the students to copy these Spanish words into their notebooks.

Without leadership, the student is unaware of the importance of each word, and of the beauty and vivaciousness of the Spanish language. You, and ONLY YOU can impart to the students what a joy it is to speak Spanish. You can give each student an extraordinary achievement: the ability to speak a foreign language. Teaching Spanish is a beautiful thing. It enriches the lives of your students. It gives them a sense of being international, citizens of the world. It gives them new horizons.

After the students have absorbed the words in Remember These Words, proceed to the next section.

Step 3 *Hearing Exercise*

The student is ready to form complete sentences. Read the sentences in this section, and have all the class repeat each sentence, in unison, immediately after you say it. This exercise trains the students to hear and understand sentences. The students will imitate your inflection and forcefulness.

Step 4 *Speaking Exercise*

In order to keep the full attention of the class, it is important to point to students at random for an answer. Pointing to students, instead of calling out names, usually saves much time, and keeps them at full attention, for students never know when you will call on them. It prevents them from looking out the window, or whispering among themselves.

If it is at all possible, repeat this exercise with books closed. This will prove to students that they can understand Spanish "on the wing."

Step 5 *Dictation*

DICTATION is a wonderful exercise for a class. It helps students to connect Spanish sounds to their corresponding letters. It is a good idea for the teacher to select words from the Remember These Words section and sentences from the Hearing Exercise, and dictate them to the class.

There is a marked improvement in any class when the teacher dictates four or five words and two or three sentences during each session.

After the dictation, the students exchange what they have written with those who are sitting in front of them. Then, one student takes the same dictation again on the blackboard. The class corrects any errors on the blackboard, and the errors in their neighbor's dictation. It helps if the teacher circulates in the class, and gives a little supervision to the correction of the papers.

When the students KNOW that there is a dictation coming up in every class, they pay attention more carefully to the Remember These Words and the Hearing Exercises. Another advantage is that dictation tends to create a spirit of camaraderie in the class.

Step 6 *Creating Sentences*

The Creating Sentences exercise is one of the most important in the book, because it helps students to absorb new verb forms, and to blend them with vocabulary they already know. The students learn to combine new grammatical forms, and to apply them to everyday conversation. Thus, they assimilate new material easily, and learn to use it correctly.

The students also learn to form logical sentences when they combine words and phrases which are not in logical order. With a controlled, small possibility of error, they can enjoy the satisfaction of creating their own sentences. Students gain a sense of freedom and confidence.

This exercise also gives teachers a selected vocabulary which the students already know, and which combines with new grammatical forms. This aids the teachers in making up numerous questions of their own, keeping the students on familiar ground.

It is a good idea for teachers to ask nonsensical questions in order to teach students to avoid the pitfalls of illogical answers. This is a humorous and refreshing exercise. It adds zest and inventiveness to the class.

Step 7

The exercises and grammatical expositions which follow Step 6 are self-explanatory.

Step 8 *Word Builder*

Read the introduction and guidelines aloud for the students. Emphasize the great number and importance of IÓN words. Help the students to pronounce these words correctly. They must learn to stress the final ON very firmly.

It is a good idea to interrupt this lesson and other lessons, and ask the students, at random, to translate a few IÓN words into Spanish in order to keep them fresh in their memory. These form a large part of the BASIC VOCABULARY which students will use in everyday conversation.

If it is at all possible, have the students review all of the Word Builder exercises from *Open Door to Spanish*, Book One. These exercises can be reviewed, one by one, over the course of several class sessions.

The Word Builder exercises give the students the feeling of "creating" words, because they have never seen or heard these Spanish words before. But they have used similar words in English all of their lives.

Step 9

The sections which follow the Word Builder are self-explanatory.

Step 10 *The Stories*

The stories are a completely different form of exercise from all the others in the book. In the stories, the students must try to guess the meaning of that which they don't know, because of its position in the sentence, or because it is similar to English. Before each story, there is a vocabulary which contains a list of words to be used. A quick reading of this vocabulary will help the students to understand the story better.

The stories teach the students to thrust into unknown, or only partially known written Spanish, and try to guess the meaning of any sentence they may encounter. This teaches students to read and understand material which is beyond their knowledge. They cannot speak beyond their knowledge, but they certainly can learn to read beyond their knowledge.

The stories are exercises in teaching students how to guess at the meaning of the printed word. Their guesses may sometimes be wrong, but they will be able to guess enough to get the substance of the unfamiliar printed word. Each story stretches the students' ability to read the printed word. Students learn not to be defeated by that which they do not understand well, but to give it the old school try and guess at its meaning. This gives them a sense of VICTORY over the language.

Step 11 *Conversation*

The Conversation sections are among the most important in the book, because they teach students how to "create" conversations in which they use new grammatical forms. In these conversations the students learn to "turn over" the grammar they have just learned, and assimilate it into ordinary conversation.

The introductions to the Conversations direct the students to close their books, and begin to improvise. The sooner they cut loose from the written word, the sooner they will learn to speak Spanish.

Most students love to improvise. They are stimulated by speaking on their own. However, there is a pitfall here. Students begin to ask the teacher for new words. "How do you say this?" Or, "How do you say that?" Here, the teacher must resist temptation, and politely refuse to give the students new words. The whole point of the Conversations is for the students to learn to combine new grammatical forms with the words which they ALREADY KNOW!

Teachers who introduce new vocabulary into the Conversations are inviting chaos. One of the most important advantages of using the Madrigal method is that students progress on familiar ground. The author uses the "eyedropper" method, in which students learn one thing at a time, and learn it very well. The students must learn to blend the new material with that which they already know, and assimilate it into their speech. They are not ready to learn ANYTHING which is new, until they have absorbed what is in each lesson, and can use it passably in conversation. The main objective is to practice Spanish in conversation.

SPANISH-ENGLISH VOCABULARY

Abbreviations: adj. = adjective; aux. = auxiliary; f. = feminine; imp. = imperfect; m. = masculine; pl. = plural; pret. = preterite; refl. = reflexive; sing. = singular.

A

a, *to; the personal* A *comes before persons; it doesn't mean anything.*
a la, *f. at the, to the*
  a la luz, *by the light*
abandonar, *to abandon*
abogado, *m. lawyer*
abrazar, *to hug, to embrace*
abrigo, *m. coat*
abril, *April*
abrir, *to open*
absolutamente, *absolutely*
abuela, *f. grandmother*
abuelita, *f. dear grandmother*
abuelito, *m. dear grandfather*
abuelo, *m. grandfather*
abuelos, *m. & f. pl. grandparents*
abundante, *abundant*
acá, *here*
  ven acá, *come here*
accidental, *accidental*
accidente, *m. accident*
acción, *f. action*
aceite, *m. oil*
  aceite de oliva, *olive oil*
aceptar, *to accept*
activa, *f. active*
actividad, *f. activity*
activo, *m. active*
acto, *m. act*
actor, *m. actor*
acumulador, *f. battery*
además, *besides, furthermore*
adhesivo, *m. adhesive*
adiós, *good bye*
administración, *f. administration*
admiración, *f. admiration*
admirar, *to admire*
¿adónde?, *(to) where?*
adoptar, *to adopt*
adoraba *(imp.), adored, used to adore*
adorar, *to adore*
adulación, *f. praise, adulation*
aeropuerto, *m. airport*
afectar, *to affect*
afeitarse, *to shave (oneself)*
África, *Africa*
agencia, *f. agency*
agente, *m. agent*
agonía, *f. agony*
agosto, *August*
agresivo, *m. aggressive*
agua, *f. (m. article) water*
¡ah!, *ah!*
ahora, *now, at this moment*
aire, *m. air*
ajustar, *to adjust*
ajuste, *adjust (command)*
al, *m. to the*
  al poco tiempo, *in a short time*
alarmar, *to alarm*
alas, *f. pl. wings*
Alberto, *Albert*
alegría, *f. gaiety*
algo, *something*
Alicia, *Alice*
allí, *there*

allí está, *there it is*
almuerzo, *m. lunch*
alquilar, *to rent*
alta, *f. high, tall*
altas, *f. pl. tall, high*
alto, *m. high, tall*
altura, *f. height, altitude*
amable, *m. & f. kind, amiable*
amarillo, *m. yellow*
ambición, *f. ambition*
ambulancia, *f. ambulance*
América, *f. America*
América Central, *Central America*
América del Sur, *South America*
americana, *f. American*
americano, *m. American*
amiga, *f. friend*
amigo, *m. friend*
amor, *m. love*
Ana, *f. Ann, Anne*
andar, *to walk, to ride*
andar en tren, *to ride a train*
anduvimos, *we walked; we rode*
anillo, *m. ring*
animal, *m. animal*
aniversario, *m. anniversary*
anoche, *last night*
antes, *before*
antibiótico, *m. antibiotic*
Antonio, *m. Anthony*
año, *m. year*
apio, *m. celery*
aplaudir, *to applaud*
aprehender, *to arrest*
aprender, *to learn*
aprendido, *learned*
aprisa, *fast*
apurarse, *to hurry, to hurry up (refl.)*
apúrate, *hurry up (familiar command)*
apúrese, *hurry up (command)*
aquí, *here*
árbol, *m. tree*
arbolito, *m. little tree*
arbusto, *m. bush*
aretes, *m. pl. earrings*
aristocracia, *f. aristocracy*
aristocrática, *f. aristocratic*
aristocrático, *m. aristocratic*
arquitecto, *m. architect*
arquitectura, *f. architecture*
arroz, *m. rice*
artículo, *m. article*
artista, *m. & f. artist*
así, *thus, in this way*
asiento, *m. seat*
aspecto, *m. look, aspect*
aspirina, *f. aspirin*
astronauta, *m. astronaut*
atención, *f. attention*
aterrizar, *to land (in an airplane)*
Atlántico, *m. Atlantic*
atómica, *f. atomic*
atómico, *m. atomic*
atracción, *f. attraction*
atractiva, *f. attractive*
atractivo, *m. attractive*
atrapar, *to trap*
atrocidad, *f. atrocity*
atún, *m. tuna fish*
audaz, *m. & f. bold, audacious, daring*
aumentar, *to increase*
aunque, *even if, even though*
auto, *m. car, auto*
autobús, *m. bus*
aviación, *f. aviation*
avión, *m. airplane*
ay, *oh, ouch*
ayer, *yesterday*
ayudar, *to help, to aid*
ayúdeme, *help me (command)*
ayudó, *he, she, it helped*
me ayudó, *he, she, it helped me*
azúcar, *m. sugar*
azul, *blue*
azules, *m. & f. pl. blue*

B

bailar, *to dance*
baile, *m. dance*
bajo, *low, short (stature)*
ballet, *m. ballet*
banco, *m. bank*
banda, *f. band (musical)*
banquero, *m. banker*
bañarse, *to bathe (oneself)*
baño, *m. bath, bathroom*
baño de sol, *sun bath*
barba, *f. beard*
Bárbara, *f. Barbara*
barrer, *to sweep*
barriendo, *sweeping*
basura, *f. garbage*

béisbol, *m. baseball*
bella, *f. beautiful*
bello, *m. beautiful*
Bernardo, *Bernard*
besar, *to kiss*
beso, *m. kiss*
  un beso, *a kiss*
biblioteca, *f. library*
bicicleta, *f. bicycle*
bien, *well, fine*
biftec, *m. beefsteak*
billete, *m. ticket*
blanca, *f. white*
blanco, *m. white*
blusa, *f. blouse*
boda, *f. wedding*
boleto, *m. ticket*
bolsa, *bag, purse*
bonita, *f. pretty*
bonito, *m. pretty*
botas, *f. pl. boots*
botella, *f. bottle*
bridge, *m. bridge (game)*
brillar, *to shine*
buen, *m. good*
buena, *f. (sing.) good*
buenas, *f. (pl.) good*
buenas noches, *good evening, good night*
buenas tardes, *good afternoon*
bueno, *m. (sing.) good, hello (phone)*
buenos, *m. (pl.) good*
  Buenos Aires, *(good airs), capital of Argentina*
  buenos días, *good morning*
bufanda, *f. scarf*
buscar, *to look for, to search*

C

caballito, *m. little horse*
caballo, *m. horse*
cabaña, *f. cabana, cabin*
cabeza, *f. head*
cable, *m. cable*
cablegrama, *m. cablegram*
cada, *each*
caer, *to fall*
café, *m. coffee*
calcetines, *m. socks*
caían, *fell, used to fall*
caja, *f. box*
cajetilla, *f. pack, packet*
calle, *f. street*
calor, *m. heat*
  hace calor, *it's hot*
  tengo calor, *I'm warm, hot*
cama, *f. bed*
cambiado, *changed*
cambiar, *to change*
caminaban *(imp.), they walked, used to walk*
caminar, *to walk*
camino, *m. road; I walk*
camión, *m. truck*
camisa, *f. shirt*
campo, *m. country (not nation)*
  día de campo, *m. picnic*
canal, *m. canal*
canario, *m. canary*
canasta, *f. basket*
canción, *f. song*
candela, *f. candle*
candor, *m. candor*
cansada, *f. tired*
cansado, *m. tired*
cantar, *to sing*
cánteme, *sing to me*
canto, *m. song*
capacidad, *f. capacity*
capitalista, *m. capitalist*
cara, *f. face*
Caracas, *Caracas*
carácter, *m. character*
¡caramba!, *Gee whiz!, Gosh!, Darn!*
caramelos, *m. pl. hard candy*
cargador, *m. red-cap, porter*
caridad, *f. charity*
cariño, *m. affection*
Carlos, *Charles*
Carmen, *f. Carmen*
carne, *f. meat*
carnicería, *f. butcher shop*
carnicero, *m. butcher*
Carolina, *f. Caroline*
carpintero, *m. carpenter*
carrera, *f. career, race*
carta, *f. letter*
cartero, *m. mailman*
casa, *f. house*
  en casa, *at home*
  Casa Blanca, *White House*

casaron *(refl.)*,
se casaron, *they got married*
casarse, *to get married (house themselves)*
caset, *m. & f. cassette*
casi, *almost*
casita, *little house*
casó *(refl.)*,
se casó, *got married*
catorce, *fourteen*
causar, *to cause*
cebolla, *f. onion*
celebración, *f. celebration*
celebrar, *to celebrate*
cena, *f. supper*
central, *m. & f. central*
centro, *m. middle, center, downtown*
cerca, *close, near*
cerca de, *close to*
cereal, *m. cereal*
cero, *m. zero*
cero, *m. zero*
cerrado, *closed*
cerradura, *f. lock*
cielo, *m. sky*
cien, *one hundred*
ciencia, *f. science*
científico, *m. scientific*
cinco, *five*
cincuenta, *fifty*
cine, *m. movies*
cinturón, *m. belt, seat belt*
circulación, *f. circulation*
cita, *f. date, appointment*
ciudad, *f. city*
civilización, *f. civilization*
claro, *m. clear, of course*
clase, *f. class*
clásico, *m. classical*
cliente, *m. & f. client*
closet, *m. closet*
club, *m. club*
coche, *m. car*
cocina, *f. kitchen*
cocinar, *to cook*
cocinera, *f. cook, chef*
cocinero, *m. cook, chef*
coctel, *m. cocktail*
colección, *f. collection*
collar, *m. necklace*
colombiana, *f. Colombian*
colombiano, *m. Colombian*
Colonia, *f. cologne*
agua de Colonia, *cologne*
colonial, *m. & f. colonial*
color, *m. color*
combinación, *f. combination*
combinar, *to combine*
comedia, *f. comedy*
comenzado, *begun*
comenzar, *to begin*
comenzó, *began*
comer, *to eat*
comercial, *commercial*
comida, *f. meal, dinner*
comisión, *f. commission*
como, *as, like; I eat*
¿cómo?, *how?*
¿cómo no?, *how not?, of course!*
cómodo, *m. comfortable*
compañero, *m. campanion*
compañía, *f. company*
comparar, *to compare*
compasión, *f. compassion*
compensación, *f. compensation*
competente, *m. & f. competent*
completamente, *completely*
completo, *m. complete*
complicada, *complicated*
composición, *f. composition*
comprar, *to buy*
compras, *f. pl. purchases, shopping*
voy de compras, *I'm going shopping*
fui de compras, *I went shopping*
comprender, *to understand*
comprendido, *understood*
comprensión, *f. understanding, comprehension*
comprendo, *I understand*
compresión, *f. compression*
compro, *I buy*
comprometidos, *m. & f. pl. engaged*
comunicación, *f. communication*
comunicar, *to communicate*
comunidad, *f. community*
con, *with*
concentración, *f. concentration*
concentrar, *to concentrate*
concierto, *m. concert*
conclusión, *f. conclusion*
condición, *f. condition*
conductor, *m. conductor (train)*
conectar, *to connect*

conferencia, *f. conference, lecture*
confusión, *f. confusion*
congreso, *m. congress*
conmigo, *with me*
conocer, *to know (a person), to meet*
conocido, *known*
bien conocido, *well known*
conozco, *I know (persons)*
consecutivo, *m. consecutive*
conservativo, *m. conservative*
consistir, *to consist*
constante, *m. & f. constant*
constitución, *f. constitution*
constructiva, *f. constructive*
constructivo, *m. constructive*
contacto, *m. contact*
contar, *to count, to tell (a story)*
contenta, *f. happy*
contentísimo, *m. very, very happy*
contento, *m. happy*
contestado, *answered*
contestar, *to answer, to reply*
contigo, *with you (familiar)*
continente, *m. continent*
continuar, *to continue*
continuó, *you, he, she, it continued*
contra, *against*
contraria, *f. contrary*
contrario, *m. contrary*
contrato, *m. contract*
contribución, *f. contribution*
convencer, *to convince*
convención, *f. convention*
conveniente, *m. & f. convenient*
conversación, *f. conversation*
conversar, *to converse*
cooperar, *to cooperate*
copiar, *to copy*
corbata, *f. necktie*
corre, *run (familiar command)*
correcta, *f. correct*
correcto, *m. correct*
correr, *to run*
corrido, *run*
cortar, *to cut*
cosa, *f. thing*
coser, *to sew*
costar, *to cost*
¿cuánto cuesta? *how much does it cost?*
creación, *f. creation*
creativo, *m. creative*
creer, *to believe, to think*
crema, *f. cream*
creo, *I think*
¿crees? *(familiar), do you think?*
¿qué crees? *what do you think?*
criminal, *criminal*
criminales, *m. & f. pl. criminals*
crisis, *f. crisis*
crítica, *f. criticism*
cuaderno, *m. notebook*
cual, *which*
¿cuál?, *which?*
cuales, *m. & f. which, whom*
cuando, *when*
¿cuándo?, *when*
¿cuánto?, *how much?*
¿cuánto cuesta?, *how much does it cost?*
¿cuántos?, *how many?*
cuarenta, *forty*
cuarenta y uno, *forty-one*
cuarto, *m. quarter, room*
cuatro, *four*
cuatrocientos, *four hundred*
cubano, *m. Cuban*
cubrir, *to cover*
cuchara, *f. spoon*
cuchillo, *m. knife*
cuenta, *f. bill, check (in a restaurant)*
cuente, *count (command)*
cuente conmigo, *count on me*
cuénteme, *tell me (a story)*
cuento, *m. story; I tell (a story); I count*
cuero, *m. leather*
cuesta, *it costs, does it cost?*
¿cuánto cuesta?, *how much does it cost?*
cueva, *f. cave*
cuidar, *to take care of*
cuide, *take care of (command)*
cuídese, *take care of yourself*
cultivar, *to cultivate*
cultural, *cultural,*
cumpleaños, *m. sing. birthday*
cumplir, *to fulfill*
cuota, *f. quota*
curar, *to cure*
curiosa, *f. curious*
curiosidad, *f. curiosity*
curioso, *m. curious*
curva, *f. curve*

CH

chaqueta, *f. jacket*
chicle, *m. chewing gum*
chile, *m. chili, chili peppers*
chileno, *m. Chilean*
chiquita, *f. little*
  la chiquita, *the little girl*
chiquito, *m. little*
  el chiquito, *the little boy*
chistoso, *m. funny*
chocolate, *m. chocolate (drink)*
chocolates, *m. chocolates (candy)*
chofer, *m. driver, chauffeur*
chorizo, *m. sausage*
chuleta, *f. chop*
  chuleta de puerco, *pork chop*

D

da, *give (familiar command)*
dado, *given*
dame, *give me (familiar command)*
dámelo, *give it to me (familiar command)*
Daniel, *m. Daniel, Dan*
dar, *to give*
  le voy a dar, *I'm going to give you, him, her*
David, *m. David*
de, *of, from, about, than*
  más de, *more than*
debajo, *under*
debemos, *we owe*
decente, *m. & f. decent*
decidido, *decided*
decidir, *to decide*
decir, *to say, to tell*
decisión, *f. decision*
declaración, *f. declaration*
decoración, *f. decoration*
defectivo, *m. defective*
defecto, *m. defect*
defensivo, *m. defensive*
déjalo, *let him be (familiar)*
del, *m. of the*
delgado, *m. slender, thin*
deliciosa, *f. delicious*
delicioso, *m. delicious*
demasiado, *m. too much*
demasiados, *m. pl. too many*
démelo, *give it to me (command)*
democracia, *f. democracy*
democrática, *f. democratic*
democrático, *m. democratic*
dentista, *m. dentist*
depositado, *deposited*
depositar, *to deposit*
depresión, *f. depression*
desaparecer, *to disappear*
desayuno, *m. breakfast*
describir, *to describe*
descripción, *f. description*
descriptiva, *f. descriptive*
descriptivo, *m. descriptive*
descubrir, *to discover*
despacho, *m. office*
despegar, *to take off*
despertaban *(imp.), they awakened, woke up*
después, *after, afterward*
destino, *m. fate, destiny*
destructiva, *f. destructive*
destructivo, *m. destructive*
destruido, *destroyed*
destruir, *to destroy*
di, *I gave; say, tell (familiar command)*
día, *m. day*
  todo el día, *all day long*
días, *m. days*
  buenos días, *good morning*
  unos días, *a few days*
  todos los días, *every day*
diccionario, *m. dictionary*
dice, *you, he, she says*
dicho, *said*
  bien dicho, *well said*
  un dicho, *a saying*
diciembre, *December*
dictar, *to dictate*
diecinueve, *nineteen*
dieciocho, *eighteen*
dieciséis, *sixteen*
diecisiete, *seventeen*
dientes, *m. pl. teeth*
diez, *ten*
diferencia, *f. difference*
diferente, *m. & f. different*
diga, *say, tell (command)*
  dígame, *tell me*
  dígale, *tell him, her*
dignidad, *f. dignity*
digo, *I say*
dije, *I said*

dijo, *you, he, she said*
dinamita, *f. dynamite*
dinero, *m. money*
diploma, *m. diploma*
diplomacia, *f. diplomacy*
diplomática, *f. diplomatic*
diplomático, *m. diplomatic*
dirección, *f. address, direction*
directa, *f. direct*
directamente, *directly*
directo, *m. direct*
director, *m. director*
disciplina, *f. discipline*
disco, *m. phonograph record*
discurso, *m. speech*
discusión, *f. argument, discussion*
discutir, *to argue*
diseño, *m. design*
distancia, *f. distance*
diste, *you gave (familiar)*
distracción, *f. distraction*
divertido, *m. amusing*
dividir, *to divide*
división, *f. division*
doce, *twelve*
docena, *f. dozen*
doctor, *m. doctor*
doctora, *f. doctor*
documento, *m. document*
dolor, *m. pain*
domingo, *m. Sunday*
¿dónde?, *where?*
dormí, *I slept*
dormir, *to sleep*
dormirse *(refl.), to go to sleep*
dos, *two*
doscientos, *two hundred*
drama, *m. drama*
dramática, *f. dramatic*
dramático, *m. dramatic*
dudar, *to doubt*
dudo, *I doubt*
duele, *hurts, aches*
  me duele, *it hurts me*
  me duele la cabeza, *my head aches*
  me duelen, *they hurt me*
duerma, *sleep (command)*
  duerma bien, *sleep well*
duermo, *I sleep*
dulces *(los), m. candy*
duplicación, *f. duplication*
dura, *f. hard*
  una vida dura, *a hard life*
durante, *during*
durmió, *slept*
  ¿cómo durmió?, *how did you sleep?*
duro, *m. hard*

E

economista, *m. economist*
edad, *f. age*
edición, *f. edition*
edificio, *m. building*
editorial, *editorial*
educación, *f. education*
educado, *m. educated*
educar, *to educate*
efectiva, *f. effective*
efectivo, *m. effective*
efecto, *m. effect*
ejercicio, *m. exercise*
el, *m. the*
él, *m. he, him*
  con él, *with him*
elástico, *m. elastic*
elección, *f. election*
eléctrica, *f. electric*
electricidad, *f. electricity*
eléctrico, *m. electric*
electrónico, *m. electronic*
elefante, *m. elephant*
elegancia, *f. elegance*
elegante, *m. & f. elegant*
elemental, *elemental*
elevador, *m. elevator*
ella, *f. she, her*
  con ella, *with her*
ellas, *f. pl. they, them*
  con ellas, *with them*
ellos, *m. they, them*
  con ellos, *with them*
el mundo, *m. the world*
emergencia, *f. emergency*
emoción, *f. emotion*
emocionado, *m. excited, thrilled*
en, *in, on*
enamorados, *m. & f. pl. in love*
enamorarse, *to fall in love (refl.)*
encantado, *m. enchanted, delighted*
  estaba encantado, *was enchanted by, loved*
encantar, *to enchant*
  le encantaban, *he, she was*

enchanted by, he loved
encontrar, *to find, meet, encounter*
energía, *f. energy*
enero, *January*
enferma, *f. sick*
enfermera, *f. nurse*
enfermero, *m. nurse*
enfermo, *m. sick; sick person*
enorme, *m. & f. enormous*
Enrique, *m. Henry*
ensalada, *f. salad*
entender, *to understand*
entrada, *f. entrance*
entrar, *to enter, to go in, to come in*
entre, *between, among*
entusiasmo, *m. enthusiasm*
envolver, *to wrap*
equipaje, *m. luggage*
era, *was, it was, were*
eres, *you are (familiar)*
error, *m. error*
es, *is, it is, it's*
es de, *he, she is from*
esa, *f. that*
esas, *f. pl. those*
escapar, *to escape*
escaparse, *to escape, get away*
escriba, *write (command)*
escríbame, *write to me*
escríbeme, *write to me (familiar command)*
escribir, *to write*
escribo, *I write*
escritorio, *m. desk*
escuela, *f. school*
ese, *m. that*
durante ese tiempo, *during that time*
eso, *neuter, that*
eso es bueno, *that is good*
esos, *m. pl. those*
espacio, *m. space*
español, *m. Spanish (language or person); m. Spaniard*
española, *f. Spaniard*
esparcir, *to spread out, to disperse*
espárragos, *m. asparagus*
espera, *f. waiting; wait (familiar command)*
sala de espera, *waiting room*
esperado, *expected, hoped for*
esperar, *to hope, wait, expect, wait for*
espere, *wait, wait for (command)*
espere a Juan, *wait for John*
espéreme, *wait for me*
espero, *I hope, I expect*
espiritual, *m. & f. spiritual*
esposa, *f. wife*
esposas, *f. pl. handcuffs*
esta, *f. this*
está, *you are; he, she, it is, are you?, is he, she, it?*
estaba, *you, he, she, it was*
estación, *f. station*
estacionar, *to park*
estado, *m. state*
Estados Unidos, *m. pl. United States*
estamos, *we are*
están, *you (pl.) are; they are*
estar, *to be*
estatua, *f. statue*
este, *m. (adj.) this*
esto, *m. pronoun, this*
esto es bueno, *this is good*
estoy, *I am*
estrella, *f. star*
estudiando, *studying*
estudiante, *m. & f. student*
estudiar, *to study*
estudio, *m. study; I study*
estudios, *m. pl. studies*
estuve, *I was*
eternidad, *f. eternity*
evadir, *to evade*
evidencia, *f. evidence*
evidente, *m. & f. evident*
exacta, *f. exact*
exactamente, *m. & f. exactly*
exacto, *m. exact*
examen, *m. test*
examinar, *to examine*
excelencia, *f. excellence*
excelente, *m. & f. excellent*
excepción, *f. exception*
exclusiva, *f. exclusive*
exclusivo, *m. exclusive*
existen, *they exist*
existir, *to exist*
expansión, *f. expansion*
experiencia, *f. experience*
experimentación, *f. experimentation*
experimental, *experimental*
experimentar, *to experiment*

exploración, *f. exploration*
explorar, *to explore*
explosión, *f. explosion*
explosiva, *f. explosive*
explosivo, *m. explosive*
exportación, *f. exportation*
exportar, *to export*
exposición, *f. exposition*
expresar, *to express*
expresión, *f. expression*
expresiva, *f. expressive*
expresivo, *m. expressive*
extender, *to extend*
extensión, *f. extension*
exterior, *exterior*
extraordinaria, *f. extraordinary*
extraordinario, *m. extraordinary*

F

fábrica, *f. factory*
fabulosa, *f. fabulous*
fabuloso, *m. fabulous*
factoría, *f. factory*
falda, *f. skirt*
familia, *f. family*
famosa, *f. famous*
famoso, *m. famous*
fantástica, *f. fantastic, "terrific"*
fantástico, *m. fantastic, "terrific"*
farmacia, *f. drugstore, pharmacy*
fascinante, *m. & f. fascinating*
fascinar, *to fascinate*
fascinarse *(refl.), to get fascinated*
favor, *m. favor*
  por favor, *please*
favorito, *m. favorite*
febrero, *February*
felices, *m. & f. pl. happy, very happy*
felicidad, *f. happiness*
feliz, *m. & f. happy; very, very happy, overjoyed*
  feliz cumpleaños, *happy birthday*
femenina, *f. feminine*
feo, *m. ugly*
feroz, *m. & f. fierce, ferocious*
festival, *m. festival*
fiebre, *f. fever*
fiesta, *f. party*
figura, *f. figure, shape*
¡figúrate!, *just imagine! (familiar)*
fin, *m. end*
  el fin de semana, *the weekend*
  por fin, *finally, at last*
final, *m. & f. final*
finalmente, *finally*
flexible, *m. & f. flexible*
flor, *flower*
florero, *m. vase*
flores, *f. pl. flowers*
florista, *m. & f. florist*
flotar, *to float*
fonógrafo, *m. phonograph*
formación, *f. formation*
formal, *m. & f. formal*
formalidad, *f. formality*
formar, *to form*
fortuna, *f. fortune*
  por fortuna, *fortunately*
fósforos, *m. pl. matches*
fotografía, *f. photograph*
francés, *m. French*
frasco, *m. jar*
  un frasco de mayonesa, *a jar of mayonnaise*
frase, *f. sentence, phrase*
frecuencia, *f. frequence*
  con frecuencia, *frequently*
frecuente, *m. & f. frequent*
frente, *f. forehead*
  en frente de, *in front of*
fresas, *f. pl. strawberries*
fresca, *f. fresh, cool*
frío, *m. cold*
  hace frío, *it's cold*
  tengo frío, *I'm cold*
frito, *m. fried*
frivolidad, *f. frivolity*
frustrar, *to frustrate*
fruta, *f. fruit*
fue, *you, he, she, it went; was*
fuera, *were*
  si fuera, *if I were*
fueron, *you (pl.) went; they went*
fui, *I went*
fuimos, *we went*
fuman, *you (pl.) smoke; they smoke*
fumar, *to smoke*
furiosa, *f. furious*
furioso, *m. furious*
fútbol, *m. soccer*

G

gabardina, *f. gabardine*
galletas, *f. pl. crackers, cookies*
galopar, *to gallop*
ganado, *m. cattle; won*
ganar, *to win, to earn, to gain*
garaje, *m. garage*
gasolina, *f. gasoline*
gatita, *f. kitten, little cat*
gatito, *m. kitten, little cat*
gato, *m. cat*
gelatina, *f. gelatine*
generación, *f. generation*
general, *m. general; (adj.) general, usual*
 en general, *in general*
generalmente, *generally*
generosa, *f. generous*
generoso, *m. generous*
genio, *m. & f. genius*
geranio, *m. geranium*
gimnasio, *m. gymnasium*
gobierno, *m. government*
golf, *m. golf*
gorda, *f. fat*
gordo, *m. fat*
gorila, *m. gorilla*
gozar, *to enjoy*
gracia, *f. grace*
gracias, *thank you*
gradual, *gradual*
grande, *m. & f. big, great*
grandes, *m. & f. pl. big*
 ojos grandes, *big eyes*
gris, *m. & f. gray*
grises, *m. & f. pl. gray*
gritar, *to scream, to shout*
grite, *scream, shout (command)*
 no grite tanto, *don't scream so much*
guantes, *m. pl. gloves*
guapo, *m. handsome*
guardia, *m. guard*
guiar, *to guide, to drive*
Guillermo, *m. William*
guitarra, *f. guitar*
guitarrista, *m. guitarist*
gusta, *sing. like*
 me gusta, *I like it, I like . . .*
 le gusta, you like, he, she, it likes . . .
 nos gusta, *we like*
gustan, *pl. like*
 me gustan, *I like (something pl.)*
gustar, *to like*
gustaría, *would like*
 me gustaría, *I would like*
gustaron, *pl. liked*
 me gustaron, *I liked them*
gusto, *m. pleasure*
 mucho gusto, *how do you do?*
 el gusto es mío, *the pleasure is mine*
gustó *(pret.), liked*
 me gustó, *I liked*

H

había *(imp.), had (aux.)*
 había comprado, *had bought*
 había, *there was, there were, was there?, were there?*
hablar, *to speak*
hablo, *I speak*
hace, *you do, make; he, she, it does, makes; ago*
 hace un mes, *a month ago*
 hace calor, *it's hot*
 hace frío, *it's cold*
 hace una hora, *an hour ago*
hacer, *to do, to make*
haces, *you make, do you make? (familiar); you do, do you do? (familiar)*
haga, *do, make (command)*
 haga café, *make coffee*
hago, *I do, I make*
hasta, *until*
 hasta que, *until*
 hasta mañana, *until tomorrow*
hay, *there is, there are, is there?, are there?*
 hay que, *one must*
he *(aux.), have*
 he comprado, *I have bought*
hecho, *m. made, done*
 hecho en México, *made in Mexico*
 dicho y hecho, *said and done*
helado, *m. ice cream*
hermana, *f. sister*
hermano, *m. brother*
hermanos, *m. & f. pl., brother & sister; brothers (& sisters)*

hice, *I did, I made*
hija, *f. daughter*
hijo, *m. son*
historia, *f. history*
hizo, *you, he, she, it did, made*
hoja, *f. leaf; sheet (of paper)*
hombre, *m. man*
honor, *m. honor*
hora, *f. hour*
    ¿a qué hora?, *at what time?*
horizontal, *horizontal*
horrible, *m. & f. horrible*
horror, *m. horror*
hospital, *m. hospital*
hospitalidad, *f. hospitality*
hotel, *m. hotel*
hoy, *today*
hubo, *there were (pret.)*
huellas, *f. pl. tracks, footprints*
huevo, *m. egg*

I

iba, *I, you, he, she, it used to go*
idea, *f. idea*
ideal, *m. & f. ideal*
idealista, *m. & f. idealist*
ido, *m. gone*
    he ido, *I have gone*
iglesia, *f. church*
ignorante, *m. & f. ignorant*
ilusión, *f. illusion*
ilustración, *f. illustration*
imitación, *f. imitation*
impaciencia, *f. impatience*
impaciente, *m. & f. impatient*
importancia, *f. importance*
importante, *m. & f. important*
importar, *to import*
imposible, *impossible*
impresión, *f. impression*
impulsivo, *m. impulsive*
incentivo, *incentive*
incidente, *m. incident*
incompetent, *m. & f. incompetent*
indiferencia, *f. indifference*
indirecta, *f. indirect*
indirecto, *m. indirect*
industrial, *m. & f. industrial*
inevitable, *m. & f. inevitable*
infección, *f. infection*
inferior, *m. & f. interior*
infinidad, *f. infinity*
influenciar, *to influence*
influenza, *f. flu, influenza*
información, *f. information*
informativo, *m. informative*
inglés, *m. English*
inmensa, *f. immense*
inmensamente, *immensely*
inmenso, *m. immense*
inocencia, *f. innocence*
inocente, *m. & f. innocent*
insecto, *m. insect*
insistir, *to insist*
insolencia, *f. insolence*
insolente, *m. & f. insolent*
inspiración, *f. inspiration*
inspirar, *to inspire*
instalado, *m. installed*
instalar, *to install*
instante, *m. instant*
instructivo, *m. instructive*
instructor, *m. instructor*
instrumental, *instrumental*
instrumento, *m. instrument*
insulto, *m. insult*
intelecto, *m. intellect*
inteligencia, *f. intelligence*
inteligente, *m. & f. intelligent*
intención, *f. intention*
intenso, *m. intense*
interesante, *m. & f. interesting*
interior, *m. & f. interior*
    ropa interior, *f. underwear*
interrogación, *f. questioning, question*
interrumpir, *to interrupt*
intolerante, *m. & f. intolerant*
inútil, *m. & f. useless*
inútiles, *m. & f. pl. useless*
invasión, *f. invasion*
invención, *f. invention*
inventado, *m. invented*
inventar, *to invent*
inventivo, *m. inventive*
inventor, *m. inventor*
investigación, *f. investigation*
invierno, *m. winter*
invisible, *m. & f. invisible*
invitación, *f. invitation*
invitar, *to invite*
invítela, *invite her (command)*
invítelo, *invite him (command)*

ir, *to go*
irresistible, *m. & f. irresistible*
irrigación, *f. irrigation*
isla, *f. island*
italiano, *m. Italian*
italianos, *m. Italians*

J

jabón, *soap*
jamón, *m. ham*
jardín, *m. garden*
jardines, *m. gardens*
jefe, *m. boss*
Jorge, *m. George*
José, *m. Joseph*
joven, *m. & f. young*
jóvenes, *m. & f. pl. youths, young men, young women*
joyas, *f. pl. jewels*
Juan, *John*
juego, *m. game*
jueves, *m. Thursday*
jugando, *playing*
jugar, *to play*
jugando, *playing (a game)*
jugo, *m. juice*
  jugo de naranja, *m. orange juice*
Julia, *f. Julia*
julio, *July*
junio, *June*
justicia, *f. justice*

L

la, *f. her, you, it; f. the*
laboratorio, *m. laboratory*
ladrón, *m. thief*
lago, *m. lake*
lámpara, *f. lamp*
lancha, *f. boat, launch*
  lancha de motor, *motorboat*
lápiz, *m. pencil*
largo, *m. long*
las, *f. pl. the; f. them*
latir, *to beat (heart)*
lavar, *to wash*
lavarse, *to wash (oneself)*
le, (object) *you, him; to you, him, her, it*
  ¿le gusta?, *do you like?*
lea, *read (command)*
lección, *f. lesson*
leche, *f. milk*
lechería, *f. dairy*
lechero, *m. milkman*
lechuga, *f. lettuce*
leer, *to read*
legal, *m. & f. legal*
leído, *m. read*
  ha leído, *has read*
lengua, *f. language, tongue*
león, *m. lion*
les, *m. & f. to them, to you (pl.)*
levantar, *to raise, to lift*
levantarse, *to get (oneself) up*
liberación, *f. liberation*
  liberación femenina, *feminine liberation*
libertad, *f. freedom, liberty*
librería, *f. bookstore*
libreta, *f. small notebook*
libro, *m. book*
licencia, *f. license*
limón, *m. lemon*
limonada, *f. lemonade*
limpiar, *to clean*
linda, *f. lovely. beautiful*
lindo, *m. lovely, beautiful*
lista, *f. list, menu; f. ready*
listo, *m. ready*
literaria, *f. literary*
literario, *m. literary*
lo, *m. him, you, it;·the*
  lo que, *what*
loca, *f. crazy*
local, *m. & f. local*
locas, *f. pl. crazy*
loco, *m. crazy, mad*
locura, *f. madness*
los, *m. pl. the; m. them*
lubricante, *m. lubricant*
lugar, *f. place*
Luis, *m. Louis*
Luisa, *f. Louise*
luna, *f. moon*
lunes, *m. Monday*
luz, *f. light*

LL

llamaba *(imp.), called, named*

se llamaba Juan, *his name was John, he was called John*
llamar, *to call*
llamarse *(refl.), to be called*
se llama Juan, *his name is John, he is called John*
llave, *f. key*
llega, *he, she, it arrives*
llegar, *to arrive, get here, get there*
llevar, *to take, to carry, to wear*
llevarla, *to take her, it*
llevarlo, *to take him, it*
llevaste, *you took (familiar)*
llévelas, *take them (f.) to (a place)*
llévelos, *take them (m). to (a place)*
lléveme, *take me (someplace)*
llévenos, *take us (someplace)*

M

macarrones, *m. pl. macaroni*
madre, *f. mother*
maestra, *f. teacher*
maestro, *m. teacher*
malo, *m. bad*
mamá, *f. mother*
mandado, *sent*
madar, *to send*
mande, *send (command)*
mándeme, *send me*
manera, *f. way, manner*
mano, *f. hand*
mansión, *f. mansion*
manual, *manual*
mañana, *f. morning; tomorrow*
manzana, *f. apple*
máquina, *f. machine*
máquina de escribir, *typewriter*
mar, *m. sea*
marchar, *to march*
Margarita, *f. Margaret*
margarita, *daisy*
margaritas, *daisies*
María, *Mary*
mariposa, *f. butterfly*
martes, *m. Tuesday*
marzo, *March*
Marta, *f. Martha*
más, *more; forms comparative and superlative;* grande, *big;* más grande, *bigger;* el más grande, *the biggest*
más tarde, *later*
mayo, *May*
mayonesa, *mayonnaise*
me, *m. & f. me, to me, myself*
me pesé, *I weighed myself*
mecánico, *m. mechanic*
media, *f. half*
media hora, *half an hour*
medias, *f. pl. stockings*
medicina, *f. medicine*
mejor, *m. & f. better*
melón, *m. melon, cantaloupe*
mención, *f. mention*
mencionado, *mentioned*
mencionar, *to mention*
menú, *m. menu*
mercado, *m. market*
mes, *m. month*
mesa, *f. table*
meses, *m. pl. months*
metal, *m. metal*
metropolitano, *m. metropolitan*
mexicano, *m. Mexican*
mi, *my*
mí, *m. & f. me*
para mí, *for me*
miedo, *m. fear*
miércoles, *m. Wednesday*
mil, *one thousand*
millones, *millions*
mina, *f. mine (noun)*
minuto, *m. minute*
mira, *look (familiar command)*
mirar, *to look, to look at*
mire, *look, look at (command)*
mire a Juan, *look at John*
míreme, *look at me*
mis, *m. & f. pl. my*
misión, *f. mission*
misma, *f. same*
mismo, *m. same*
misteriosa, *f. mysterious*
misterioso, *m. mysterious*
moderna, *f. modern*
moderno, *m. modern*
molestar, *to bother*
moleste, *bother (command)*
no se moleste, *don't trouble yourself*
no me moleste, *don't bother me*
momento, *m. moment*
montaña, *f. mountain*
montar, *to ride horseback*
moral, *moral*

morder, *to bite*
morir, *to die*
mosquito, *m. mosquito*
motivo, *m. motive*
motocicleta, *f. motorcycle*
motor, *m. motor*
  a todo motor, *full speed ahead*
mover, *to move*
mucha, *f. much, a lot*
muchacha, *f. girl*
muchacho, *m. boy*
muchas, *f. pl. many, a lot*
muchísimo, *m. very, very much*
mucho, *m. much, a lot*
muchos, *m. pl. many, a lot*
muebles, *m. pl. furniture*
mujer, *f. woman*
mujeres, *f. pl. women*
mundo, *m. world*
  todo el mundo, *everybody*
museo, *m. museum*
música, *f. music*
musical, *musical*
muy, *very*

N

nacer, *to be born*
nación, *f. nation*
nacional, *m. & f. national*
nacionalidad, *f. nationality*
nada, *nothing, anything*
  más que nada, *more than anything*
nadar, *to swim*
nado, *I swim*
naranja, *f. orange*
naranjada, *f. orangeade*
nativa, *f. native*
nativo, *m. native*
natural, *m. & f. natural*
naturalista, *m. & f. naturalist*
naturalmente, *naturally*
naval, *naval*
necesaria, *f. necessary*
necesario, *m. necessary*
necesidad, *f. necessity, need*
necesitar, *to need*
negativa, *f. negative*
negativo, *m. negative*
negra, *f. black*
negro, *m. black*
nena, *f. baby girl*
nene, *m. baby boy*
nervioso, *m. nervous*
nevando, *snowing*
  está nevando, *it's snowing*
nevar, *to snow*
ni, *neither, nor*
nietos, *m. & f. pl. grandchildren*
nieve, *f. snow*
niña, *f. girl*
niño, *m. child, boy*
niños, *m. pl. children*
no, *no, not*
¿no?, *isn't it?, aren't you?, don't you?, can't you?*
noble, *m. & f. noble*
noche, *f. night*
  esta noche, *tonight*
noches, *f. pl. nights*
  buenas noches, *good evening, good night*
nombre, *m. name*
nos, *m. & f. pl. us; ourselves*
nosotras, *f. we*
nosotros, *m. we*
notar, *to notice*
notas, *f. pl. notes*
novecientos, *nine hundred*
noventa, *ninety*
novia, *f. girl friend, sweetheart, bride*
noviembre, *November*
novio, *m. boyfriend, sweetheart, bridegroom*
nuestra, *f. our*
nuestro, *m. our*
nuestros, *m. pl. our*
nueve, *nine*
nuevo, *m. new*
número, *m. number*
nunca, *never*

O

o, *or*
obligación, *f. obligation*
obscuridad, *f. darkness, obscurity*
obstáculo, *m. obstacle*
obtener, *to obtain*
ocasión, *f. occasion*
océano, *m. ocean*
Océano Pacífico, *m. Pacific Ocean*
ochenta, *eighty*
ocho, *eight*

ochocientos, *eight hundred*
octubre, *October*
oculista, *m. & f. oculist*
ocupación, *f. occupation*
ocupada, *f. busy, occupied*
ocupado, *m. busy, occupied*
ofender, *to offend*
oficial, *m. & f. official*
oficina, *f. office*
ofrecer, *to offer*
ofrecido, *m. offered*
oído, *m. heard*
oiga, *listen, hear (command)*
oigo, *I hear*
oír, *to hear*
¡ojalá! *(oh Allah that), I certainly hope so! I certainly hope (that)*
ojos, *m. pl. eyes*
once, *eleven*
ópera, *f. opera*
operación, *f. operation*
opinión, *f. opinion*
opresión, *f. oppression*
optimista, *m. & f. optimist*
ordinaria, *f. ordinary*
ordinario, *m. ordinary*
organista, *m. & f. organist*
organización, *f. organization*
organizar, *to organize*
oriental, *oriental*
original, *original*
otoño, *m. autumn*
otra, *f. other, another*
otro, *m. other, another*
  el otro, *the other*
otros, *others*
oye, *listen (familiar command)*

P

Pablo, *m. Paul*
paciencia, *f. patience*
paciente, *m. patient*
Pacífico, *m. Pacific*
padre, *m. father*
padres, *m. pl. parents, fathers*
pagado, *paid*
pagar, *to pay*
página, *f. page*
país, *m. country (nation)*
pájaro, *m. bird*
palabra, *f. word*
paloma, *f. dove, pigeon*
pan, *m. bread*
panadería, *f. bakery*
panadero, *m. baker*
panorama, *m. panorama*
pantalones, *m. pl. trousers, pants*
pantuflas, *f. pl. bedroom slippers*
papá, *m. father, dad*
papas, *f. potatoes*
papel, *m. paper*
paquete, *m. package*
par, *m. pair*
  un par de zapatos, *a pair of shoes*
para, *for, in order to; he, she, it stops*
  para que, *so that*
paraguas, *m. umbrella*
parque, *m. park*
párrafo, *m. paragraph*
parrilla, *f. grill*
  a la parrilla, *grilled*
parte, *f. part*
pasada, *past*
  la semana pasada, *last week*
pasado, *past*
  el sábado pasado, *last Saturday*
pasaporte, *m. passport*
pasar, *to pass, to spend (time)*
  voy a pasar por, *I'm going to drop by*
pase, *come in, pass (command)*
  pase por aquí, *step this way*
pasó *(pret.), happened*
  ¿qué pasó?, *what happened?*
patente, *m. patent*
pececito, *little fish*
pedir, *to ask for, to order*
Pedro, *m. Peter*
peinarse, *to comb (oneself)*
  se peinó, *she combed her hair*
película, *f. film (movie, or for a camera)*
peligroso, *m. dangerous*
pelo, *m. hair*
penicilina, *f. penicillin*
pensamiento, *m. thought*
pensar, *to think*
pensión, *f. pension*
peor, *m. & f. worse*
pequeño, *m. small*
pera, *f. pear*
perder, *to lose*
perdido, *lost*

perdón, *pardon me, excuse me*
perdona, *pardon me (familiar command)*
perfección, *f. perfection*
perfecta, *f. perfect*
perfectamente, *perfectly*
perfectamente bien, *perfectly well*
perfecto, *m. perfect*
perfume, *m. perfume*
periódico, *m. newspaper*
periodista, *m. journalist*
perlas, *f. pl. pearls*
collar de perlas, *pearl necklace*
permanente, *m. & f. (adj.) permanent*
permanente, *m. & f. (noun) permanent*
permita, *allow, permit, let (command)*
permítame, *allow me (command)*
permitir, *to allow, to permit*
¿se permite fumar?, *is smoking allowed?*
pero, *but*
perro, *m. dog*
perseguir, *to pursue*
persistencia, *f. persistence*
persona, *f. person*
personal, *m. & f. personal*
personalidad, *f. personality*
personas, *persons, people*
persuadir, *to persuade*
persuasivo, *m. persuasive*
pesarse, *to weigh (oneself)*
pescado, *m. fish*
pescar, *to fish*
pesimista, *m. & f. pessimist*
petición, *f. petition*
pianista, *m. & f. pianist*
piano, *m. piano*
piense, *think (command)*
pienso, *I think*
pijama, *m. sing. pajamas*
píldora, *f. pill*
piloto, *m. pilot*
pimienta, *f. pepper (black)*
pintar, *to paint*
pintor, *m. painter*
pintura, *f. painting*
pipa, *f. pipe*
piscina, *f. swimming pool*
piso, *m. floor*
plancha, *f. iron*
planchar, *to iron*
planeta, *m. planet*
planta, *f. plant*
plantar, *to plant*
plástico, *m. plastic*
plato, *m. plate, dish*
playa, *f. beach*
pluma, *f. pen*
plural, *m. & f. plural*
pobre, *m. & f. poor*
poca, *f. a little bit*
pocas, *f. pl. few*
poco, *m. a little bit*
poco a poco, *little by little*
pocos, *m. pl. few*
poder, *to be able*
puedo, *I can*
podía, *you, he, she could*
policía, *f. police department; m. policeman*
pollo, *m. chicken*
pon, *put, set (familiar command)*
pone, *you put; he, she, it puts; sets (table)*
poner, *to put, to set (table)*
ponga, *put, set (command)*
ponga la mesa, *set the table*
pongo, *I put, I set (table)*
popular, *m. & f. popular*
populares, *m. & f. pl. popular*
por, *by*
por favor, *please*
¿por qué?, *why?*
por teléfono, *on the phone*
porque, *because*
portero, *m. doorman*
posibilidad, *f. possibility*
posible, *m. & f. possible*
posiblemente, *possibly*
posición, *f. position*
positivo, *m. positive*
postal, *postal*
postre, *m. dessert*
practicar, *to practice*
preciosa, *f. precious*
precioso, *m. precious, very beautiful*
preferencia, *f. preference*
pregunta, *f. question*
preguntar, *to ask*
preparación, *f. preparation*

preparado, *m. prepared*
preparar, *to prepare*
presentación, *f. presentation*
presentar, *to present*
presente, *m. & f. present*
presento, *I present, introduce*
  te presento, *allow me to introduce*
presidente, *m. president*
prevención, *f. prevention*
prima, *f. cousin*
primaria, *f. primary*
primario, *m. primary*
primavera, *f. spring*
primer, *m. first*
primera, *f. first*
primitiva, *f. primitive*
primitivo, *m. primitive*
primo, *m. cousin*
probable, *m. & f. probable*
probablemente, *probably*
problema, *m. problem*
productiva, *f. productive*
productivo, *m. productive*
producto, *m. product*
profesión, *f. profession*
profesor, *m. professor*
profesora, *f. professor*
programa, *m. program*
progresar, *to progress*
progresiva, *f. progressive*
progresivo, *m. progressive*
progreso, *I progress*
prométame, *promise me*
prometer, *to promise*
prominente, *m. & f. prominent*
pronto, *quickly, soon*
  de pronto, *suddenly*
prosperidad, *f. prosperity*
protector, *m. protector*
protestar, *to protest*
prudencia, *f. prudence*
prudente, *prudent*
publicación, *f. publication*
publicidad, *f. publicity*
público, *m. public*
pudiera,
  si pudiera, *if I only could*
puede, *you, he, she can*
  si puede, *if you can*
puedo, *I can*
  no puedo, *I can't*
puerta, *f. door*
Puerto Rico, *Puerto Rico*
puertorriqueño, *m. Puerto Rican*
pulmonía, *f. pneumonia*
pulso, *m. pulse*
pura, *f. pure*
puro, *m. pure*

Q

que, *that, than*
¡qué!, *how*
  ¡qué bueno!, *how good!, what a good thing!*
¿qué?, *what?*
  ¿a qué hora?, *at what time?*
quedarse, *to stay (refl.)*
quédese, *stay (command); stay here*
querer, *to want, to love*
quería, *wanted, loved*
queso, *m. cheese*
¿quién?, *who?*
¿quieres?, *do you want to? (familiar)*
  ¿quieres ir?, *do you want to go?*
quiero, *I want, I love*
  te quiero, *I love you*
quince, *fifteen*
quinientos, *five hundred*
quitarse, *to take off (oneself)*
  se quitó el suéter, *he took off his sweater*
quizá, *maybe*
quizás, *maybe*

R

radiación, *f. radiation*
radio, *m. & f. radio*
rama, *f. branch*
rancho, *m. ranch*
rápidamente, *rapidly*
raqueta, *f. racket (tennis)*
raro, *m. strange*
realidad, *f. reality*
recepción, *f. reception*
recepciones, *f. pl. receptions*
receptivo, *m. receptive*
recibido, *received*
recibir, *to receive, to meet*
  recibirla, *to meet her*
  recibirlo, *to meet him*
recibo, *I receive*
recomendación, *f. recommendation*

recomendar, *to recommend*
recordar, *to remember*
¿recuerda?, *do you remember?*
¡recuerde!, *remember! (command)*
recuerdo, *I remember*
  no recuerdo, *I don't remember*
reflector, *m. reflector*
refresco, *m. refreshment*
refrigerador, *m. refrigerator*
regalo, *m. present*
regla, *f. ruler*
regresar, *to return, to get back, to come back*
reírse *(refl.), to laugh*
religiosa, *f. religious*
religioso, *m. religious*
reorganizar, *to reorganize*
repetir, *to repeat*
representación, *f. representation*
representar, *to represent*
república, *f. republic*
repulsivo, *m. repulsive*
reputación, *f. reputation*
reservación, *f. reservation*
reservado, *reserved*
reservar, *to reserve*
resfriado, *m. (a) cold*
residencial, *residential*
resistir, *to resist*
respetar, *to respect*
respeto, *m. respect*
respirar, *to breathe*
responder, *to answer*
responsable, *m. & f. responsible*
respuesta, *f. answer*
restaurante, *m. restaurant*
resto, *m. (the) rest*
resultar, *to result, turn out*
revelación, *f. revelation*
revista, *magazine*
revolución, *f. revolution*
rey, *m. king*
Ricardo, *m. Richard*
rico, *m. rich*
ridícula, *f. ridiculous*
ridículo, *m. ridiculous*
río, *m. river*
risa, *f. laughter*
rival, *m. rival*
robar, *to steal, to rob*
  se robó, *stole*
  robarse, *to steal*
Roberto, *Robert*
robó,
  se lo robó, *stole it*
roca, *f. stone, crag, rock*
rodeaba *(imp.), used to surround, surrounded*
rodeado, *m. surrounded*
rodear, *to surround*
roja, *f. red*
rojo, *m. red*
romance, *m. romance*
romántica, *f. romantic*
romántico, *m. romantic*
romper, *to break, to tear*
ropa, *f. sing. clothes, clothing*
  ropa interior, *underwear*
rosa, *f. rose*
Rosa, *f. Rose (name)*
rosbif, *m. roast beef*
rosita, *f. little rose*
rubia, *f. blond*
rubio, *m. blond*
ruso, *m. Russian*
rusos, *m. Russians*
rumor, *m. rumor*
rural, *rural*

S

S.A., *f. Inc., incorporated* (sociedad anónima, *anonymous society)*
sábado, *m. Saturday*
sábados, *m. pl. Saturdays*
  los sábados, *On Saturdays*
sabe, *you know; he, she knows*
¿sabe?, *do you know?*
sabemos, *we know*
saber, *to know (facts)*
sacar, *to take out*
sal, *f. salt*
sala, *f. living room*
  sala de espera, *waiting room*
sale, *leaves (a place), goes out*
salga, *go out (command)*
  no salga, *don't go out*
salgo, *I go out, I leave (a place)*
salida, *f. exit*
salir, *to go out, to leave (a place)*
salmón, *m. salmon*
saltar, *to jump*
salude, *greet, say "hello" (command)*
  salude a Juan, *say "hello" to John*

salvación, *f. salvation*
salvar, *to save*
sándwich, *m. sandwich*
Sara, *f. Sarah*
sardina, *f. sardine*
satélite, *m. satellite*
satisfacción, *f. satisfaction*
se, *m. & f. sing. & pl. yourself, himself, herself, yourselves, themselves*
  se pesó, *he weighed himself, she weighed herself*
sé, *I know*
secar, *to dry*
secretaria, *f. secretary*
secretario, *m. secretary*
sedativo, *m. sedative*
seguir, *to go on, to continue*
segundo, *m. second*
seguramente, *surely*
seguro, *m. sure, surely; insurance*
seis, *six*
seiscientos, *six hundred*
semana, *f. week*
  el fin de semana, *the weekend*
señor, *m. mister, sir*
  el señor, *Mr.*
señora, *f. lady*
  la señora, *Mrs.*
señorita, *f. young lady*
  la señorita, *Miss*
sensación, *f. sensation*
sentarse, *to sit down (oneself)*
sentir, *to feel*
separación, *f. separation*
separar, *to separate*
septiembre, *September*
ser, *to be*
serenata, *f. serenade*
servilleta, *f. napkin*
sesenta, *sixty*
setecientos, *seven hundred*
setenta, *seventy*
si, *if*
sí, *yes*
siempre, *always*
siéntese, *sit down*
siento, *I feel*
  lo siento, *I'm sorry*
siete, *seven*
significante, *significant*
silla, *f. chair*
sillón, *m. armchair*
simpática, *f. charming*
simpático, *m. charming*
sinceridad, *f. sincerity*
social, *social*
socialista, *m. & f. socialist*
sociedad, *f. society*
sofá, *m. sofa*
sol, *m. sun*
sola, *f. alone*
solar, *m. & f. solar*
solas, *f. pl. alone*
solo, *m. alone, solo (music)*
sólo, *only*
solos, *m. pl., m. & f. pl. alone*
solitaria, *f. solitary*
solitario, *m. solitary*
solución, *f. solution*
sombrero, *m. hat*
son, *are (pl.)*
sonreír, *to smile*
sonreírse *(refl.), to smile*
sombrerito, *m. little hat*
sopa, *f. soup*
su, *your, his, her, their*
suave, *m. & f. soft*
suavemente, *softly*
subir, *to go up, to climb*
subscripción, *f. subscription*
suéter, *m. sweater*
suficiente, *m. & f. enough*
sufrido, *suffered*
sufrir, *to suffer*
superior, *superior*
supermercado, *supermarket*
supiera,
  ¡Si supiera!, *If you only knew!*
sus, *m. & f. pl. your, their, his, her*
  sus ideas, *his ideas*
Susana, *f. Susan*

T

tal,
  tal vez, *maybe*
  con tal que, *provided that*
también, *too, also*
tanto, *so much*
tarde, *f. afternoon; late*
más tarde, *later*
tardes, *f. pl. afternoons*
  buenas tardes, *good afternoon*

taxi, *m. taxi*
taza, *f. cup*
te, *you, to you (familiar)*
  te pesaste, *you weighed yourself*
té, *m. tea*
teatro, *m. theater*
teléfono, *m. telephone*
telegrama, *m. telegram*
televisión, *f. television*
temperatura, *f. temperature*
temprano, *early*
  más temprano, *earlier*
ten, *have this, take this (familiar command)*
tendencia, *f. tendency*
tenedor, *m. fork*
tenemos, *we have*
tener, *to have*
tenga, *have, take (command)*
tengo, *I have*
  tengo que . . . , *I have to . . .*
tenía *(imp.)*, *I, you, he, she, it had, used to have*
tenis, *m. tennis*
tenor, *m. tenor*
tensión, *f. tension*
terminado, *m. finished*
terminar, *to finish*
termo, *m. thermos*
termómetro, *m. thermometer*
terraza, *f. terrace*
terrible, *m. & f. terrible*
territorio, *m. territory*
terror, *m. terror*
tía, *f. aunt*
tiempo, *m. time*
  a tiempo, *on time*
tienda, *f. store*
tiene, *you have; he, she, it has*
tienen, *you (pl.) have, they have*
tierra, *f. earth*
tigre, *m. tiger*
tío, *m. uncle*
tíos, *m. pl. aunt and uncle, uncles*
típico, *m. typical*
tipo, *m. type, fellow*
título, *m. title*
toalla, *f. towel*
tocar, *to touch, to play (an instrument)*
tocino, *m. bacon*
toda, *f. all, every*
  toda la mañana, *all morning*
todas, *f. pl. every, all*
  todas las mañanas, *every morning*
todavía, *yet, still*
todo, *m. all, everything*
todos, *m. pl. every; everybody, all of us*
  todos ellos, *m. all of them*
tolerancia, *f. tolerance*
tolerante, *tolerant*
tomar, *to take, to have (food)*
tomate, *m. tomato*
tome, *take (command)*
tomo, *I take*
tónico, *m. tonic*
torero, *m. bullfighter*
toro, *m. bull*
tostada, *f. toasted, toast*
tostado, *m. toasted*
  pan tostado, *m. toast*
tostador, *m. toaster*
total, *total*
trabajar, *to work*
trabajo, *m. work (noun); I work*
tracción, *f. traction*
tractor, *m. tractor*
tradición, *f. tradition*
trae, *bring (familiar command)*
  tráeme, *bring me (familiar command)*
traer, *to bring*
tráfico, *m. traffic*
traiga, *bring (command)*
tráigala, *bring it (f.), bring her*
tráigale, *bring to him, her*
tráigalo, *bring it (m.), bring him*
tráigame, *bring me (command)*
traigo, *I bring*
traje, *I brought*
traje, *m. suit (man's or woman's)*
trajo, *you, he, she, it brought*
transparente, *m. & f. transparent*
tras, *behind, after*
  tras de él, *after him*
tratar, *to try, to treat*
  tratar de + *infinitive, to try to . . .*
  trató de ver, *he, she tried to see*
trece, *thirteen*
treinta, *thirty*
treinta y uno, *thirty-one*
tren, *m. train*
tres, *three*

trescientos, *three hundred*
triste, *m. & f. sad*
triunfo, *m. triumph*
tropical, *m. & f. tropical*
trotar, *to trot*
tu, *your (familiar)*
  tú, *m. & f. you (familiar)*
tulipán, *m. tulip*
turista, *m. & f. tourist*
tuve, *I had*

U

último, *m. last*
un, *m. a, an*
una, *f. a, an; one*
  a la una, *at one o'clock*
uniforme, *m. uniform*
universal, *universal*
universidad, *f. university*
uno, *one*
unos, *m. pl. some*
  unos años, *some years, a few years*
urgencia, *f. urgency*
urgente, *m. & f. urgent*
usar, *to use*
usted, *you (sing.)*
ustedes, *you (pl.)*
uvas, *f. pl. grapes*

V

va, *you go; he, she, it goes; you are going; he, she, it is going*
vacaciones, *f. pl. vacation, vacations*
valiente, *m. & f. brave*
valija, *f. suitcase*
valle, *m. valley*
vamos, *we go, we are going, let's go*
van, *you (pl.) go, they go, you (pl.) are going, they are going*
vapor, *m. vapor, steam*
variedad, *f. variety*
vas, *you go, are you going? (familiar)*
  vas a ver, *you'll see, are you going to see?*
vaselina, *f. vaseline*
vaso, *m. glass*
  un vaso de agua, *a glass of water*
vaya, *go (command)*
  váyase, *go away (command)*
veces, *f. pl. times*
  a veces, *at times*
veían, *they saw, they used to see*
veinte, *twenty*
veinticinco, *twenty-five*
veinticuatro, *twenty-four*
veintidós, *twenty-two*
veintiocho, *twenty-eight*
veintiséis, *twenty-six*
veintisiete, *twenty-seven*
veintinueve, *twenty-nine*
veintitrés, *twenty-three*
veintiuno, *twenty-one*
velocidad, *f. velocity, speed*
vemos, *we see*
  nos vemos, *I'll be seeing you (we'll be seeing one another)*
ven, *come (familiar command)*
  ven acá, *come here*
vender, *to sell*
vendido, *sold*
vendo, *I sell*
venga, *come (command)*
  venga acá, *come here*
vengo, *I come*
venía, *used to come, was coming*
venir, *to come*
ventana, *f. window*
ventilación, *f. ventilation*
veo, *I see*
ver, *to see*
verano, *m. summer*
veras,
  ¿de veras?, *really?*
verbo, *m. verb*
verdad, *f. truth, true*
  ¿verdad?, *true?, doesn't she?, isn't that so?*
verde, *m. & f. green*
verduras, *f. pl. vegetables*
verlo, *to see you (m.), him, it*
versión, *f. version*
verte, *to see you (familiar)*
vertical, *vertical*
vestido, *m. dress*
vestirse, *to dress (oneself)*
veterinario, *m. veterinary*
vez, *f. time*
  una vez, *once;* dos veces, *twice*
  esta vez, *this time*
vi, *I saw*
viajar, *to travel*

viaje, *m. trip*
viejo, *m. old*
viene, *you come, he, she, it comes, is coming*
¿viene?, *is he, she, it coming?*
viento, *m. wind*
  hace viento, *it's windy*
viernes, *m. Friday*
vigor, *m. vigor*
vine, *I came*
violencia, *f. violence*
violeta, *f. violet*
violín, *m. violin*
visible, *m. & f. visible*
visita, *f. visitor*
visitar, *to visit*
visitas, *f. visitors, company*
vistió, *dressed*
  se vistió, *got dressed*
visto, *seen*
  he visto, *I have seen*
vitalidad, *f. vitality*
vitamina, *f. vitamin*
¡viva!, *long live*
vive, *lives*
vivir, *to live*
vivo, *I live*
vocabulario, *m. vocabulary*
volar, *to fly*
vóleibol, *m. volleyball*
voluntaria, *f. voluntary*
voluntario, *m. voluntary*
volver, *to return*
votar, *to vote*
voy, *I go, I am going*
vuelo, *m. flight, I fly*
vuelva, *come back (command)*
  vuelva pronto, *come back soon*

Y

y, *and*
ya, *already*
yo, *I*

Z

zapatería, *f. shoe shop*
zapatero, *m. cobbler, shoe repairman*
zapatos, *m. pl. shoes*

INDEX